To

[handwritten signature]
18/8/10

FREE-FOR-ALL

THE POST-SOVIET TRANSITION OF RUSSIA

Dr. Gary K. Busch©

"Free For All: The Post-Soviet Transition of Russia," by Dr. Gary K. Busch. ISBN 978-1-60264-573-8 (softcover); 978-1-60264-574-5 (ebook).

Published 2010 by Virtualbookworm.com Publishing Inc., P.O. Box 9949, College Station, TX 77842, US. ©2010, Dr. Gary K. Busch. All rights reserved. No part of this publication may be reproduced, stored in a retrieval system, or transmitted in any form or by any means, electronic, mechanical, recording or otherwise, without the prior written permission of Dr. Gary K. Busch.

Manufactured in the United States of America.

PREFACE

There has been a long period of delay before I allowed myself to be persuaded to write this book. I have been busy elsewhere and many of those whom I knew as young, ambitious men starting their careers are now oligarchs and richer than even their own private dreams. They achieved their ambitions by hard work, sacrifice and choosing the right roof under which to shelter. With large fortunes they have achieved acclaim. As my grandmother used to tell me "With truth, justice, honour and ten cents you can make a phone call to anyone. However, if you don't have the ten cents you don't talk at all." I must thank them for allowing me to learn from their ascent and to use their dimes for calling.

I owe my education on Russia to too many people to name them all. However, some stand out. I am grateful to Niksa Lazaneo for travelling with me throughout Russia and explaining what I was seeing. Thanks, too, to Vassily Severinenko and Galina Gazina for introducing me to a uniquely Russian perspective on developments. I shall always be grateful to Edvard Gurvich who taught me Russian. There are many in the world of intelligence analysis and the military who have assisted me with my information gathering as well as many in the Russian mafia families and the Five Families in New York (along with the Westies) who have given me a unique view of the practicalities of the business-political nexus. They will have to remain nameless as will the prosecutors, lawyers and defence counsels with whom I have had conversations over the years and the journalists from all over the globe. This is not a business in which full disclosure is useful or relevant. The errors are mine; the misinterpretations are mine; alone.

I am particularly in debt to the wonderful people of Vanino Port who gave me a unique opportunity; Appolon Shengelia, Joseph Sandler, Valerie Savinov. Valentina Tsareva, Sascha Morozov, Irina Brokina and the many others. Alla Klepikova looked after us in Khabarovsk with great skill and patience. Hugo Barrett organised us all, even Victor Parness. I am also very grateful to David Reuben who opened the door for me to go to Russia and who took on the education of my son in the world of aluminium.

Mostly, however, I wrote this book in an effort to explain to my wife and children (Tristan, James and Caroline) what I was doing on my trips into the Russian maelstrom. They always had trouble explaining to teachers and dinner party guests exactly what it is I did. Maybe this will help. My twin sister, Gail, has been very helpful motivating me to complete the book and my wife, Carol, has been very patient and supportive indeed. I hope it is interesting as something more than a memoir. It truly interested me.

London 2010

TABLE OF CONTENTS

CHAPTER ONE

It was a bit disconcerting; indeed a bit frightening. We were at 32,000 feet over the wilds of Siberia, buried beneath us in a cover of dark clouds, when the fighting on board the aircraft began. Three men rose out of their seats holding their plastic trays in front of them. They stepped back along the passageway to a row opposite me but on the other side of the aisle and started attacking two passengers slunk down low in their seats. They beat them without mercy. Blood and teeth were on the floor and everyone was shouting and screaming in a language I could not really understand. Soon the stewardesses, one of whom was very large, succeeded in separating the combatants and shoved them back in their seats. Paper towels were brought and the captain made an announcement to the passengers. I had no idea of what he said.

My neighbour in the adjoining seat to me said something to me and I nodded, in pure ignorance but in an attempt to appear sociable. In a few minutes the plane descended and we taxied to a point where police were waiting. They took off the unruly passengers and their victims. A cleaner came on board with a bucket and threw water on the floor where the blood was just starting to congeal and clot. This was dried off with several newspapers. We taxied again out to the runway and we took off, continuing our long journey from Moscow to Vladivostok. Amazingly the plane was still full. Five new passengers had appeared and taken the seats of the combatants. No matter where one went, Russian planes were always full.

I really had no idea why all this had happened as there was no communication between the three aggressors and their victims; they just started yelling and smacking. I did notice that all three of the fighters had the same tattoo on their left hand. I later learned that this signified that they had all been guests at the same prison camp in the Gulag. As I later learned these three inmates had recognised the two men in the seats behind them as former guards at their prison camp and they wanted to express their unhappiness at their hospitality and care while there.

Like many others in the West I believed that the fall of the Soviet Union meant that the prison camps had been disbanded and that the prisoners had been set free. This wasn't the case. In the 1980s about ninety-nine percent of prisoners in the Soviet Union spent their sentences in the labour camps supervised by the Main Directorate for Corrective Labour Camps (Glavnoye upravleniye ispravitel'no-trudovykh lagerey--Gulag), which was administered by the MVD (Ministry of Internal Affairs). In post-Soviet times it was actually worse for the prisoners as rising crime and greatly diminished state resources meant that prisons were overcrowded and food and medicines rationed or miniscule. In 1995 Yeltsin's Human Rights Commission found that the prison conditions were appalling and made suggestions which it never carried out. It hasn't improved much today. The prisoners, better known as 'zeks' (from the abbreviation z/k 'zaklyuchennyi') were both criminals and political prisoners.[i]

The Commission found "In 1994 the total prison population was estimated at slightly more than 1 million people, of whom about 600,000 were held in labour camps. Of the latter number, about 21,600 were said to be women and about 19,000 to be adolescents. Among the entire prison population in 1994, about half were incarcerated for violent crimes, 60 percent were repeat offenders, and more than 15 percent were alcoholics or drug addicts".[ii]

This trip to Vladivostok was the beginning of my adventure into, for me, the new world of Russia. It was early 1992 and Russia had just thrown off the shackles of the Communist Party, had ostensibly embraced democracy, freedom and capitalism and had begun to open its doors to foreigners and foreign businessmen in particular. This was not something I would have naturally chosen as a path for my endeavours. I had been for many years deeply involved in Africa and African politics. As part of my African experiences I set up and ran transport and logistics companies; owning, chartering and operating marine vessels and trading in bulk commodities like cement, fertilisers and ores. I had imported cement into Africa; to New York and to the UK at Sheerness and Cardiff. I had done business with a fairly rum bunch of competitors like the Colombo and Genovese Families in New York; the European Cement Cartel in the UK and the Nigerian mafia for fifteen-odd years so I wasn't totally naive, even when there was a 'contract' on me.

My eldest son had just had the good fortune to be hired after his graduation from Edinburgh University by Trans World Metals. They were UK metals traders who were just beginning to expand into the new world of Russia in partnership with their new Russian business partners. Trans World concentrated primarily on aluminium trading as Russian aluminium was one of the major sources of world aluminium production.

Aluminium, much as copper, is really solidified energy. The manufacturing process of aluminium involves the electrolysis of several metallic compounds in giant electrical baths. Russia had two of the world's largest hydroelectric dams, at Bratsk and Krasnoyarsk in the Siberia, and it was there that the Russians had installed the two largest aluminium producing plants. There were others as well but these were the two biggest.

Russia had all the facilities to produce aluminium in their plants from domestic sources but they lacked the basic ingredient, alumina which is produced by the processing of bauxite with caustic soda. There were several alumina producing plants which were used, the largest was at Nikolayev in the Ukraine. The alumina plants imported bauxite from Africa, principally from Guinea, and sent the refined alumina the three thousand kilometres from the Ukraine to the smelters at Bratsk and Krasnoyarsk where it was turned into aluminium. It was then transported three or four thousand kilometres back to the ports of the Baltic or the Black Sea for sale overseas. The principal market was Japan; a voyage of many thousands of nautical miles. This, as one might guess, was not a very efficient system.

There was also a domestic alumina plant at Achinsk in Siberia which produced alumina through the nepheline process which produces a 'fluffy' as opposed to 'granular' alumina. It was close to the Siberian smelters but it suffered the same problems of lack of cash and disorganisation as that suffered by the aluminium smelters. It was clear that in order to make the Russian smelters work it would be necessary for their Western partner to supply all the inputs to the smelter and to market the product in the international metal markets. Also as important, it was necessary to find a way to import these raw materials through ports on the Russian Far East and to export the finished metals from the same Far East Russian ports to Japan and elsewhere in Asia. This would save millions in transport charges for the materials and the finished products. The Holy Grail was the quest for a Russian Far East Port which had the equipment and the rail links to serve as the hub of the aluminium export business.

This is why I was on the plane to Vladivostok. I had been visiting my son at his new place of work and had been engaged in conversation by David Reuben, the head of Trans World. David asked me what I did and I told him that my ships moved large quantities of cement and fertilisers around the world, and that our company also engaged in upgrading ports to handle bulk deliveries of these. He asked if cement was similar to alumina and I told him that cement and alumina are comprised of the same elements but in different proportions. He asked if we could move alumina and I assured him that this would be no problem.

A few days later I was invited back for a discussion. David explained his desire to open up the Russian Far East for this business. His partners in Russia, Lev and Mischa Chernoy, had suggested that they use the port of Vostochny, near Vladivostok, with which they had been in contact. David asked if I were game for an adventure. Would I like to travel to Vostochny, take a look at the port and assess its suitability as a hub for the business? There was no fee involved but Trans World would pay the expenses. I was intrigued. It was a whole new field of opportunity and David was so excited about the prospect of setting up the Russian business that his excitement was contagious. I agreed.

I eventually got my visa from the embassy and was given a ticket. I flew to Moscow. We descended from the plane in Moscow and there was a major scrum in the approach to the passport lines. Everyone was lined up and shoving to get to the front. I eventually got to the booth and the Russian woman there said something to me. I shoved my passport and visa towards her and she examined it carefully and scanned the passport under some light in a box in front of her. It was taking longer than I had anticipated and I tried to think if the Russians had some file on me from the past that was querying my status. It turned out that I had not checked the right box on the Russian landing form saying where I was going. She handed it back to me and indicated that I should fill it out. I did so and I could see she was looking at my pen with some interest. I offered her the pen, saying I had a couple with me. She said she couldn't possibly take it and put it in her purse. I was released into the melee fighting for our bags. After that I always tried to visit her kiosk when I arrived and I always brought a pen for her. One of the forms one had to produce was a currency form stating how much money you had with you. This was produced at customs. On my first trip I had been asked to bring US$25,000 in cash for the Trans World Moscow office and another $5,000 for expenses. I thought it would be foolish to declare this so I kept it in my bag and declared only what was in my wallet. This caused no problem and they let me through.

This became the precedent. I never travelled in Russia without at least $40,000 to $50,000 with me in cash. Once I had £120,000. No one ever asked me and I didn't volunteer. They knew that the money I was carrying was for Russians and that was good enough reason not to harass me.

I found a man with a sign with my name on it at Sheremyetyvo Airport and was taken to the Trans World office for a chat and a cup of tea. Later that same afternoon they drove me to a different airport, Domodedovo, and I was told to walk over to the boarding gate which they pointed out to me in the distance. It was a real surprise. There was no security at all. I walked across part of a runway and through a taxi stand for planes to find my boarding gate. I walked under two plane's wings and past several parked aircraft. No one cared. I arrived at the boarding gate and waited for the plane to Vladivostok. The journey was scheduled to last twelve and a half hours. Except for the emergency landing in Omsk to put off the participants in the brawl, the plane was on time. Fortunately for me I got on the right plane. There were other Westerners there who had travelled to the wrong destination earlier and were trying again for Vladivostok. The loudspeakers were broadcasting their news and announcements in a loud but unclear Russian and you had to listen carefully for the word Vladivostok.

I really didn't know what to expect to find in Russia. Like many in my generation we grew up in the throes of the Cold War. We had all learned in school about the fall of Eastern Europe under the Iron Curtain. I had watched the progress of the Korean War on our new black-and white television screen and I had sat for hours watching the broadcasts of the McCarthy Hearings. We all knew who our enemies were. Now, here I was on my own on the very heartland of the Evil Empire.

Our public schools in New York were flooded in 1946-1950 with the children of European refugees who were lucky to have escaped from post war Europe. They came to our classes, speaking barely a word of English, but eager to become assimilated. Within a short period of less than two months they were virtually fluent in English and eager to tell us of their recent experiences. Many of them, Czechs, Poles, Hungarians, Ukrainians and Armenians in particular, came with horror stories of the Red Army. We were sure that the 'Reds' had horns and long tails. For many of my schoolmates and their parents anything to do with Russia was bad, dangerous and unpatriotic.

For many of them this had been a sudden twist in the political road. The Russians had been despised in the late 1930's for their toadying to Hitler and their war against gallant Finland in the Winter War of 1939. Their efforts to carve up Europe with the Nazis after the Molotov-Ribbentrop

Pact alienated the West; especially the Socialists and Social-Democrats who were the first to be sent to the concentration camps and deprived of power in the new realities of Vichy France and Mussolini's Fascist Italy. In 1936-1938 the communists betrayed and destroyed the POUM in the battle against Spanish fascism. The communists of the West, including the US, French and Italian Communist parties supported the Hitler-Stalin alliance and betrayed, in the eyes of the Socialists at least, their countries and the Revolution. The Nazi decrees of Vichy France were disseminated to the French people in the Communist newspaper *"L'Humanite"*. It wasn't until mid-June 1941, when Hitler sent his troops against the Soviet Union, that the Communists shifted sides again and tried to forge a defensive alliance with the US, Britain and the Commonwealth.

After the Soviet Union was attacked by the Nazis the world press was filled by tales of the 'gallant Russians' fighting fascists; stories of "Uncle Joe" and his leadership. This lasted throughout the Second World War, but there were many of us who continued to despise the Russians even when they were still awaiting a 'Second Front'. I must confess to being a "Red Diaper Baby". My maternal grandfather was from Minsk in White Russia. After my father died, when I was nine, my grandfather and grandmother (from Kovna in Lithuania) came to live with us. He had been a major political figure in Minsk before he fled in 1905; he was the head of the Jewish Bund (a socialist and anarcho-syndicalist movement) and a chemist who hobby was making bombs for the revolution. When he escaped from Russia, with a price on his head, he came to America and took a job in the garment trades until he could learn enough English to pass his pharmacy board test. He was active in the newly forming labour movement and he, and my grandmother were founding members of the International Ladies Garment Workers' Union (ILGWU). I learned of this at his funeral when Dave Dubinsky, the head of the ILGWU, came to make a speech. He was the head of Minsker Progressive Branch Local 99 of the Workmen's Circle, a leading socialist and labour organisation in New York.

He would put me to bed at night, with my twin sister Gail, with bedtime stories of the Russian Revolution. I learned all about Lenin, Stalin, Trotsky, Martov, and the others in bedtime stories about what they did and how they did it. I didn't know they weren't fictional characters until I took my first Russian history course. My grandfather disliked the "Bolsheviki" and the "Communyaks" who had destroyed liberty in Russia and instilled a regime of fear and oppression; although he retained a soft spot for Trotsky. Most of all, he hated the

American Communist Party for its adherence to the Party Line determined by Moscow, in the face of "American exceptionalism". This came to a head over the Spanish Civil War where the American Socialists and Social-Democrats tried to send medicines and supplies to the POUM in Spain while the Communists prevented their arrival in Spain and took them for themselves; finally turning their own guns against the socialists and anarchists of the POUM. This was a betrayal that would never be forgotten or forgiven. My mother, who had been President of the Young People's Socialist League in New York, concurred. On the other hand, my father's family owned the dress factories in which my maternal grandparents toiled. It was a slightly schizophrenic wedding match. My paternal grandfather was a very successful entrepreneur. My family spanned the class struggle.

When I had returned from graduate school in the UK in 1963 I was lucky enough to become part of something I had always believed in. I was hired by the United Auto Workers' Union (UAW) as head of research for the International Affairs Department under Victor Reuther. Initially I was sent to Detroit in 1964 to work as an assistant to Walter Reuther in the preparations for the 1965 bargaining round. I worked in his office with Nat Weinberg, the Special Assistant. After bargaining was over I moved to Washington, D.C. for the UAW and finished my Ph.D. in International Relations; on Pan-African Trade Unions. My job was to keep track of what the multinational corporations were doing around the world and to devise a labour strategy to cope with these developments. I was in constant contact with labour unions across the world.

One of the most interesting of these assignments was working with the Czech unions during the Prague Spring of 1968. We maintained a close working relationship with the Czech metal unions and with Ota Sik, the economic guru of Dubchek's "communism with a human face" and Charter 77. I did the same to assist in the formation of the anti-communist unions in Rumania (the Rumanian Free Workers' Union–SLOMR), the independent unions in Yugoslavia, 'Solidarnosc' in Poland and the free unions forming in the Soviet Union after the breakdown in the system after the Novocherkassk rebellion with the rise of the Association of Free Trades Unions of Workers in the USSR and the SMOT (Free Interprofessional Association of Workers.. In these I had a direct, face-to-face confrontation with many of the communist authorities. That is one of the principal reasons why, despite numerous invitations, I had never visited Russia before.

When Walter Reuther died in the plane crash and Nixon took office as President I thought it was time to move out of Washington. Guy Nunn, a friend from the UAW, had moved to Hawaii and invited me out to teach at the University there. I went there and became head of the Center for Labor Management Education and taught African Politics as well in the Political Science Department. Within two years I was a tenured full professor and Chief Negotiator for the faculty union. Later, my wife finished her Masters' Degree and wanted to move back to Europe. I left academe and became Assistant General-Secretary of the International Chemical Workers' Unions in Geneva. I stayed there for a year and a half and then moved back to London where I began assisting the Nigerians who were in the process of changing to civilian rule. In the course of my political consulting I helped them start up their businesses. To do this I chartered ships and operated them; as well as supervised the trading of bulk commodities. I hadn't been trained in any of this but I learned by successive approximations. Soon I was doing very well and my Nigerian partners were happy. I had become a 'businessman' in addition to my politics. It was as a 'businessman' that I met David Reuben and agreed to start the Russian adventure. I am afraid I kept my prejudices even when I was making money.

So, when I finally arrived in Russia, new or otherwise, I carried the baggage of my background with me. I had a prejudice against the Russian political system which far transcended the Cold War leanings of many of my contemporaries. I disliked the Communists for what they had done to Russia and its citizens. It was very strange for me. I disliked the Russians for very different reasons than the businessmen from the West who were pouring in seeking their fortunes. To a large extent I shared the Russians' feelings about these capitalists and their greed and avarice. I couldn't bear listening to their plans for taking advantage of the weakness of post-Soviet Russia to rob the resources and further disadvantage the struggling Russian workers who were bearing the nightmare costs of the transition. It was wrong and no amount of profit would ever make it right.

Even though it was never made explicit I believe the reason I always got on well with Russians during my extended stays there is that they picked up on my ambivalence on simply acting out the capitalist script. I suspect I am an unreconstructed romantic, however flawed and hypocritical, but it makes me feel better about what I do.

So, when I landed in Vladivostok I was very curious about what I would find. I knew I would have no problem in assessing the port and the logistics but I was very apprehensive about the constraints on our plans by 'non-market' forces. I didn't have to worry. I was met at the Vladivostok Airport by a young Russian, from the Trans World office; Anatoly (better known as 'Tolya'). Tolya spoke reasonable English. My Russian was very poor. I had never studied the language and had only picked up a few words from my grandfather. He didn't speak Russian to my grandmother or to the family. So my Russian was, at best, sketchy. I needed an interpreter. Tolya took me to a very rundown and grotty hotel. I was a little surprised as I saw there were nice hotels in the city. We had a very simple meal and I went to spend my first night in Russia. It was awful. There were millions of mosquitoes flying around and the window didn't close. The shower was a hole in the floor above which was a faucet with a makeshift water rose. The bed was lumpy with a heavily stained mattress. During the night I kept seeing movement around the water drain on the shower. It was not very comfortable. I awoke early and found I was covered in bites. Tolya took us to the hotel's canteen where I had a piece of bread and a cup of tea. There was some form of 'kompott' of a dark red colour but Tolya lacked the word in English for translation and I wasn't feeling experimental.

Vostochny is quite far from Vladivostok. First one has to go through the port town of Nahodka and then around the bay to Vostochny. It was at least an hour and a half away. Tolya announced that he had worked out the public bus routes to Vostochny and thought he could get us there without a problem. At that I am afraid I became cross. I had no intention of taking a public bus to the port. If we were to make any impression as a serious Western investor who wanted to set up a multi-million dollar investment in the port we couldn't show up by public bus. I told Tolya I wanted to be driven there. He said he had to check with Moscow. This was not an easy thing. He had no phone and Moscow was seven time zones away. We'd miss a day just trying to phone. I told Tolya to just translate for me from then on and to make no decisions. I said he should get a cab. He did. I went to the cab driver and asked how much he would charge for a day's hire. Tolya didn't want to translate that but eventually I convinced him that I would guarantee that he got fired the moment I returned to Moscow if he didn't, or I could arrange to have him shot.

The cab driver said he would do it for $100 dollars. I told him that we all have the right to dream but that I would not pay that. We settled on $40 for the day. We got into the cab and set off for Vostochny. Tolya was to have arranged a meeting with the head of the port. He said he had but when I asked if he had confirmed the meeting he said he hadn't. When we arrived at the port the head was not there. In fact he was in Seattle and wouldn't be back for another day. He knew we were coming, his assistant said, but he was busy in Seattle so we should wait. I said that I would examine the port's facilities anyway so that I didn't waste my time. I was introduced to the Technical Director of the Port who spoke good English and we examined the port. The Technical Director expressed his embarrassment at the behaviour of the Head of the Port, Zebelev. He told me that everyone hated him. He had been the Director of the Port at Tallinn in Estonia and when Estonia became free they fired him. His mates had gotten him a job in Vostochny because the US company, Sea-Land, was planning on setting up a container operation there and they needed an English speaker.

Zebelev took the job and began displacing the locals and putting in his own people. The wages for the port workers were already three months in arrears. Access to the food in the canteen was restricted and prices were raised. He had joined up on every junket that would take him out of the port (recently to Seattle, Tokyo and Seoul) all in the name of promoting the port. He refused to delegate anything so the port virtually came to a halt when he left. He was not everyone's favourite.

However, as I spoke with the Technical Director and his staff I learned that the last laugh was on the Head of the Port. Zebelev had begun to build a large house on the hill next to the port; a house made of bricks. It was a lavish expense in a port which had, as yet, not attracted a large throughput of cargo. That was, they told me, where their wages were being spent. Every evening when he was away on his trips the workers would go up to his new house and tear away the bricks that had been laid for the new house. It had been under construction for over three months and only the foundations and part of the first floor were built. He fumed and fussed on his return but there wasn't much he could do to stop them. The port workers had their revenge. I visited the port again about seven months later and the first floor had been finished but nothing else.

They showed me the facilities at the port. It was very impressive. There was a large container-handling area which Sea-Land was planning on using; a well-constructed wood chip berth which was loading successive wood chip carriers for the Korean trade; and an ultra-modern coal handling facility. The facilities were very good. However, it had one big drawback; its location.

Vostochny fronted on a large deepwater bay so that was no problem. The quays were sound and in good repair. The problem lay with the rail connection. The port of Vostochny lies on a spur off the Trans-Siberian Railroad which heads towards the major seaport of Nahodka and then branches to Vostochny.

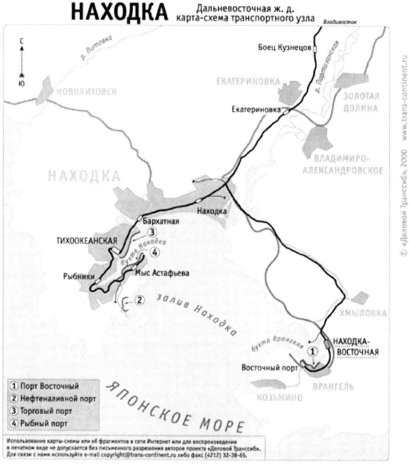

1= Vostochny 2.3.4 = Nahodka

That would mean that the Port of Vostochny would be below Vladivostok and Nahodka. It would have to compete for space on the rail line with these two ports, both of which were more developed. Nahodka was already virtually a Japanese port and its quays were full of freighters sailing to and from Japan. As trade volumes in both Vladivostok and Nahodka grew they would choke off development in Vostochny As we intended to ship more than a million ton of aluminium out of the port and import over 800,000 tons of alumina this was a recipe for disaster. The rail line couldn't accommodate us, no matter how much we paid. I could see from our trip to the port that this would not work out.

After my inspection I told Tolya that this would not work out because of the rail connection. He became a little upset and asked if our failure to make a deal with the port would not reflect badly on us. It soon became clear that this was his first trip to the Far East and he had had no experience travelling with a foreign businessman. That is why he chose the hotel and the bus to the port; because that is how Russians travelled. I told him that this was a different world. Success did not mean making deals. It meant making money. We could not make money at Vostochny so our trip was a success. I persuaded him to stay at a nice hotel in Nahodka (although he got the 'Russian Room' – different class of room than for foreign guests). I told the cab driver to pick us up the next day in Nahodka and we would repeat the adventure because we learned that the Head of the Port would be arriving there.

The next day we arrived back at the port. The Port Director told us to wait a bit since he had just come back from a trip and was very busy. He made no apology for the delay of a day. When he finally agreed to see us we were ushered into his room. I explained that we were going to take a major stake in the Russian aluminium business and that Vostochny, on the Trans-Siberian Railroad was one of the ports we were investigating. We estimated a throughput of about two million tons a year in and out and were inspecting the facilities to handle this volume. I explained that I had been taken to see the facilities by the Technical Director (who was doing the interpreting for us) and was very impressed with the facilities. He said that he was sure there would be no trouble in handling these volumes.

I replied that the problem I foresaw was not in the ability of the port to handle the volumes but rather the problem with obtaining sufficient rolling stock (railroad cars) to transport the goods to and from the port in competition for space by the other two ports. Zebelev became quite cross and asked if I wanted to make a deal or not. He was capable of arranging all the problems with the railroads through his connections in Moscow so I shouldn't worry. It would just cost us a bit more for 'commissions' in Moscow. I suggested that our connections in Moscow could arrange this for us but that this was a physical rather than a political problem. No matter how much we paid, the laws of physics still applied "two bodies cannot occupy the same space at the same time" (especially on a single-track rail line). He became further aroused and said "Don't you tell me what I can and cannot do. I want $10 a ton for me and I can arrange everything". I said that this was not why I had come to the port. I was not desperate to do a deal. I was only examining if it were worthwhile doing a deal. He was angry and said "Well, I knew I should have stayed in Seattle. This is a waste of my time". He rose out of his seat and said it was nice meeting us but he had serious work to do and would I excuse him. I said "Certainly, no problem." He turned at the door and said "I am sorry for wasting your time". I replied, "That's okay. I had had a good time with your friends removing bricks from your new house so it wasn't a total waste of time." I turned and left.

The Technical Director collapsed in laughter and went out to speak to his staff. They all burst out laughing and applauded. Tolya was very nervous. He asked me if I were not worried about the consequences of my rudeness to the Port Director. I explained that he was only the Port Director of a small port at the end of the earth and I couldn't care less. I owed him the respect he showed me. It was our money we were spending and it was up to us where we spent it. I suggested we return to Vladivostok airport and I would fly back to Moscow.

The lady assistant of the Technical Director told us that it would be difficult to get a ticket for Moscow on our own. She and two of her colleagues were travelling to Vladivostok to do some banking and would be pleased to give us a ride in their van and go to the airport to arrange a seat for me on behalf of the port. Her English was fairly good but her German was excellent. I thanked her and said I would be overjoyed to travel with them to Vladivostok and to accept their assistance.

I sent Tolya to find our driver and told him to go to the airport with the driver and to see if he could arrange the ticket. I would travel with the ladies and meet him there. He asked if I wasn't nervous travelling on my own and I assured him that I was very used to travelling on my own and that I was sure the ladies had nothing unpleasant planned for me. He agreed and left. Soon after I was seated in the port's van and we were off to Vladivostok.

We sat down in the Volkswagen bus and travelled in silence until we had passed out of the gates of the port. I could see their shoulders relax and smiles form on their faces as we passed through the gates. The German-speaking lady asked me where I was from. I said that I was from New York but was living in London. I mentioned that this was the first time I had set foot in Russia and was intrigued to be there. They told me that I was the first American they had ever had a chance to talk with and asked if I could answer some questions for them. Their first question was if the West and the US in particular harboured any ill intentions to Russia. Had our long enmity poisoned the relations between the two countries? I assured them that we respected the forces that had driven the communists from office and eagerly awaited the start of a new relationship. Of course many still disliked American communists because they weren't loyal to America in many people's eyes so that hadn't changed. I added that most of us hated the French even more than the Russians so they shouldn't take it personally. The ladies told me that they weren't too keen on domestic communists either but they had no opinion on the French.

The ladies told me that Russian communists were the elite of the country. You couldn't just join the Communist Party. Even if you were in the Young Pioneers and the Komsomol it was no guarantee that you would be allowed to join the Communist Party. You had to be chosen. Periodically in its history the Party was purged and offenders thrown out. However, once you were in all doors were open to you. There were many privileges and opportunities to Party members. None of the three was a Party member. I told them that to be a Communist Party member in the US involved choosing to be an outcast and certainly not eligible for any sort of privileges.

They were especially keen to tell me that the world should understand that there was a great deal of difference between the Russian people and the Russian Government. In my years in Russia I heard this sentiment very frequently. The best example of this was expressed by a scientist at Akademgorodok (in Novosibirsk). This was a Science City where many of the most productive and outstanding Russians worked together on scientific projects. A scientist there said to me, "There is a vast difference between the Russian people and their government. Here, at this very spot, Russian scientists built the first rocket ship to outer space. We put Sputnik into orbit and we changed the scientific face of the world. This was done by Russian scientists; by the Russian people. And do you know the first thing the Soviet Government could think to do with our splendid program? They decided to use it to starve a poor dog to death!" Poor Laika.

I explained that there was a change taking place in America as well. George Bush was being voted out of office and the Democrats, under Clinton and Gore, were taking over. Many looked forward to removing all traces of the economic disasters of the Republicans and trusted that the New Russia would participate as a partner in the economic boom. They soon tired of this kind of discussion and we moved on to the role of women and what they were wearing. I had to confess I had never had much contact with movie stars or rock singers and I was a fashion illiterate. I think I disappointed them with my ignorance of things that really mattered to them but we settled for a long discussion on food; a subject I knew better – perhaps too well they suggested politely.

We reached Vladivostok and they stopped at their bank to do what was needed. This took a little while but it was pleasant looking around downtown Vladivostok. The city had just opened for foreigners. As the main Russian naval base on the Pacific it had been a 'closed city'. That meant that no one could enter without a 'propusk'; a pass issued by a competent authority. It was closed to Russians as well as to the foreigners. First they lifted the restrictions on Russians and then the restriction on foreigners. I wasn't the first to set foot in the city but was one of the first Americans to do so. I attracted several long looks from passers-by but from most curiosity.

There were several cities and ports in which I was one of the first allowed to enter. Later on I had been issued a blanket visa which specified that I could go anywhere in Russia (the allowed parts). In Zarubina and Posyet I was the first. In Krasnoyarsk it was very funny. I had arrived in Krasnoyarsk and had been picked up by a group from the smelter and taken to the big hotel downtown. The woman behind the desk asked me for my papers. I handed over an American passport. She looked at my passport and turned pale. She shouted to me "Don't move!" She explained that Krasnoyarsk was a closed city. I was not allowed in. She didn't know how I got there but I was not to move an inch until she could call the local KGB who would deal with me. The man next to me smiled and said to her that Krasnoyarsk had become an open city three weeks earlier. He reached into his pocket and took out his little red folder and said "Don't bother to call the KGB. My name is Vladimir Cherbinin and I am the head of the KGB here and I brought him." This happened to me again in Tiksi in the North and at Anadyr. It took a while for it all to sink in.

The ladies came out from the bank and I offered to take them to a place where we could get cakes and coffee before we went to the airport. I was a little hungry and was afraid that there would be nothing to eat before I arrived in Moscow; and perhaps not then. One lady said she knew of a place nearby where they baked cakes and sweets but it was a bit expensive. I said I'd risk it. We walked down the street a bit and turned the corner. There was a very nice place which had seats inside. We all sat down and I told them they could have whatever they wanted. They looked and each chose a little cake and ordered tea. I ordered two and tea and soon polished them off. I suggested that they might want another but they said they were satisfied. I went to the counter and ordered a dozen more cakes for takeaway. The assistant packed them up and I gave them to the ladies saying that they needed sustenance for the return journey. It cost very little in roubles. The whole thing was eight dollars so I could afford to thank them for all their assistance. They said that anyone to talked to the Port Manager as I had, deserved their undying gratitude so we were even. They would dine out on that for years.

On a whim I asked them if they were interested in seeing the headquarters of the US Army which had occupied Eastern Russia and had had its headquarters in Vladivostok. They were amazed as the occupation of Russia by American, Japanese and Czech forces was not part of their history curriculum. I told them that most Americans did not know of the US role on the Russian Far East either.

After the Bolshevik Revolution and the displacement of the Menshevik Government in early 1918, and despite the peace treaty with Germany that ended the war in the West, the Russian Civil War continued across the rest of Russia. The Red Army fought the White Army throughout former imperial Russia. A large military force, the

Czech legion which had been brought in to fight the Red Army from the East was trapped by the Red Army successes and couldn't return home. The Japanese were exceptionally active and had stationed 72,000 troops in Siberia and were funding a wild bunch of Cossacks guerrilla under warlords like Semenov and Kalmikov. These were pathological murderers who tortured, raped, and decapitated innocent Siberians, according to US Army reports. They travelled up and down the Trans-Siberian Railroad is special "Death Trains", underwritten by the Japanese.

Even more importantly the Japanese were interfering with U.S. business. There were about 600,000 tons of U.S. supplies sitting in Vladivostok and the Japanese were threatening to take it or stop it being sold. As a gesture of neutrality, Woodrow Wilson ordered that an American Special Expeditionary Force be sent at once to Vladivostok under the leadership of Major General William S. Graves. He, and 5,000 troops, landed in Vladivostok on the first of September 1918. They were there, not to take sides in the civil war, but to try and rescue the Czech legions and the thousands of German and Austrian prisoners of war. They took up their duties patrolling the Trans-Siberian Railway and the Chinese Eastern Railway. They were attacked by all sides. The Red Army attacked them in battles along the Trans-Siberian Railroad; the Red Partisans attacked their encampments; and the Cossacks (pushed by the Japanese) fought the U.S. troops all over the Far East. The Japanese didn't fight but used their proxies to try and drive the U.S. out of their headquarters in Vladivostok and their regional headquarters in Khabarovsk.

Despite the kidnappings and executions of American soldiers by the Cossacks and the raids by the Partisans the Expeditionary Force tried to maintain its neutrality .In the winter of 1919-1920 the White Russian Army was defeated by the Red Army on the Volga Front and the Red Army succeeded in capturing Spassk in the Far East. The war was over and there was an outcry in the U.S. to bring the troops home. The last troops left on April Fool's Day 1920.[iii]

I saw the building in Vladivostok that looked exactly like the picture of the AEF Headquarters so I walked the ladies over and showed them. There was no sign or memorial plaque. The U.S. intervention was not considered 'neutral' by either side and has faded from history. It was a pity as over 320 American soldiers died there. It was not a success.

AEF Headquarters Vladivostok

We got back in the van and went to the airport. I met Tolya who said that he had been unable to get me a seat. He said he might have one the next day. The women said they could help. We went together to see the dispatcher, a crucial figure at any airport. They explained that they were trying to help me on behalf of the Port and would be happy if I could be given a seat. The dispatcher took me aside and asked to see my passport. I handed it to her with two $20 bills inside. She studied it carefully, removed the bills and said she had just found a seat free. She turned to the ladies from the port and said that their presence had convinced her to try harder and she had found me a seat. The ladies were very pleased. The plane was scheduled for departure in three hours. I thanked them profusely and took my ticket and boarding pass and left to find Tolya. The ladies left and I told Tolya I could make my way back so he was free. I saw him go to the bus queue for his long trip back to town. I begged him to call the Moscow office to pick me up and to arrange the transfer to Sheremyetyvo Airport for a flight back to London.

I managed to get on the flight and there was someone to meet me. I got back to London late in the evening and covered myself with calamine lotion to suppress the itching from all the mosquito bites. I called David the next day and he arranged a meeting with me that afternoon. My first trip to Russia was over. I loved it. I was hooked.

CHAPTER TWO

That afternoon I went over to the Trans World offices and was invited to speak with David Reuben. I told him that the Port of Vostochny was a good port in terms of its physical layout but, because of its position as a spur of the end of the Trans-Siberian Railroad, it would not provide the security of access to large and regular throughputs of aluminium or alumina. I said that there was a great willingness on the part of everyone I had met that this project be undertaken as soon as possible but that Vostochny was not the place to begin. David looked at the map I showed him and saw that I was correct.

He then asked me if there was somewhere else I could recommend. I said that I had no quick answer but that I would contact some of my colleagues in the shipping business and elsewhere and determine the best place. He requested that his intention of setting up such a massive business not be advertised and I promised my discretion. We arranged that I would take a week or so to do my investigations and would have a recommendation when he returned from his next trip to Moscow.

I left and began my investigations. I am a cautious person. I had been reading in the newspapers of the troubles Russia was having in making its adjustments to post-Soviet economic stability. I thought I had better check out more than the physical layout of the ports. I had done business with the Soviet Union before, as well as with Poland and Bulgaria. I knew a bit about how the Soviet system worked. Indeed one of the problems most Westerners had with dealing with the new Russia was that they had no idea how it worked before it became the New Russia.

There was nothing written in 'Pravda'. 'Isvestia' or 'Trud' which might have told them how the system actually functioned in reality. The USSR was not the place that was described in the Pioneer and Komsomol tracts; still less was it the place which appeared on television. A friend used to tell me that Russian television was the only place you could have fresh food delivered to your house. The system was fundamentally and irretrievably flawed.

Under the Soviet system most of Russia's trade was carried on through state-trading companies. These were specialist companies dealing with grain, wood, non-ferrous metals, etc. In each, or in charge of each, were representatives of the Organs. No negotiation could take place in the USSR or overseas in which the Organs were not represented. They controlled access to the internal transport system, they dealt with all exit permits for international travel, for space in the ports, and for the funding needed to buy or sell in hard currency. Their work was crucial to the business and supplemented the work of the ministries and the party organisation in each ministry. For those of us who traded with them, business was far from straightforward.

In the 1970s and 1980s we used to work closely with a number of Soviet state- trading company, buying cement and wood products from Russia, and handling the transhipment of products through Kotka and Hamina in Finland; and later we moved slop oil from the USSR to Finland. As one did business with these state trading companies it soon became clear that these were agencies, not only for trade, but as a source of hard currency for the Chekists. A 'Chekist' is a general, if pejorative, term for those who are or once were employed in the security operations of the Soviet state- KGB, GRU, MVD, FSB etc. (the 'Organs') Dzerzhinsky's original agency was the Cheka. In the trading side of their business the KGB maintained a large number of overseas accounts in Western Banks to handle their money. The one I used to deal with most frequently was the St. Dunstan's Branch of the Midland Bank in London. There the KGB had a special account for trade. So, when I had to make payments to the state trading companies, I made U.S. dollar payments to the KGB account in London. They would receive my dollars and then send the rouble equivalent home at whatever rate they thought was appropriate.

This was true for Poland and Bulgaria as well. We would contract to buy cement from the Polish state trading company, Minex, and they would tell us to which of their overseas subsidiaries (Interminex of Austria or Liminex of Germany) we should make payment. We put our ships into Gdynia or Gdansk and picked up cement and paid either Austria or Germany in dollars. How the zloty got back to Poland we never knew or asked. The same was true when we became the agent for the Bulgarian trading company Stroyimpex. There we paid our dollars to Austria. It was not a straightforward business.

Once our meeting with a Soviet energy minister was called off at the last minute. I was to fly to Helsinki for a meeting with him but they called me from Helsinki to say I shouldn't fly. The Minister had been arrested while leaving Leningrad; he was found with a handful of uncut diamonds in his toothpaste tube. We didn't know whom he had offended but, as a civil minister, he was as vulnerable to the Organs as anyone else. When we dealt with the state trading companies we dealt with ministry officials, party officials and the 'control' ministries. Occasionally we had to deal with the military (both the defence ministry and the GRU). There were at least three people for every important job in the USSR; one from the civil administration; one from the party organisation, and one from the control agencies. The power was not divided equally among them. This was even more complicated in the regions with local party and civil administrators participating and offering advice.

This was monumentally inefficient. No one had sufficient individual responsibility to run anything. There were phantom factories, phantom workers and phantom transport links. These were sufficiently well documented that they passed for reality and got their budget allocations and requisitions. In one year in the 1970s, the most efficient and productive facility in the USSR was a shoe factory near Lake Ladoga which had never been built. It did so well because there was no real factory and no real person was working, and they thus avoided the shortfalls and quota delivery problems which plagued existing companies.

The USSR economy was capable of producing the same quantities of aluminium, steel, coal, aircraft, oil, natural gas and even grain as Russia produces so profitably today. However, they didn't achieve anything like these levels of production. The system was skewed, corrupt and inefficient; primarily lacking in investment capital. The people who were running the USSR economy were incapable of making it fit the needs of the twentieth century. If it weren't for the Afghan War the USSR might well have crumbled six years earlier. It was a command economy with the inmates of the asylum in command. What did function was the military with its ability to annihilate the world. Russia was a Great Power but only militarily. It would have had a hard time competing economically with several Third World countries. Communism contained the seeds of its own destruction. Even if there were competent people in charge of key ministries or state trading companies, the fabric of the economy was threadbare. They had no resources or systems to make the needed changes. So they did their best to try to fit reality into an unreal system

This system functioned in Russia from about 1964 to 1988. Then there were three crises which occurred. The first was Gorbachev's order to disband Gosplan (the centralised state planning organisation); over

60,000 people lost their jobs. They didn't go quietly. They set about sabotaging the system so they would be needed to restore it to order. I was doing some business with Razno, one of the state trading companies, who told me that in the three weeks before their dismissal the workers at Gosplan ordered the wood for door frames from Krasnoyarsk, the wood for the actual doors from near Chelyabinsk, and had these sent to a factory in the Caspian Region near Rostov-on Don for assembly. The attendant cost and delays of shipping components thousands of kilometres were astronomic. This was mirrored across the Soviet economy; inefficiency was compounded by sabotage.

The next shock was the order to close up the state trading companies. This was an enormous wrench to the system, not only because people lost their jobs and control of industries, but because these state trading companies had joint ventures around the world which suddenly were also out of business. Who was able to market Soviet products on the world market when these trading companies disappeared? No one had a clue as how the goods should be priced as no one had an idea of the real costs (including transport, wages, etc.).

The other shock was the removal of the Communist Party from its place of monopoly in the political system. This had many political ramifications, but the economic effects were devastating. As the Party made up a third of the triumvirate of power in every factory or shop or agency, the vacuum was created into which no one dared enter.

When I was asked to look into the suitability of the ports I was well aware that there was much more involved than logistics even if this was not apparent to the businessmen. It was always a surprise to me how these talented, intelligent, successful traders had no interest in or patience in learning about the political dimensions of what they were doing. This was matched by the childlike, ideologically coloured view of the politicians and intelligence officials about how international trading companies actually functioned. They knew about each other, as my grandmother used to say "...as much as a pig knows about noodles." They knew when it was time to eat. It wasn't too hard to find out the needed information if one knew whom to ask.

I started my investigations by concentrating on finding the right sea port and rail line. I chatted with a number of ship owners at the Baltic Exchange at the weekly Monday assembly when cargoes were advertised and traded. None really had any extensive knowledge of the Russian trade or ports. I avoided Russian owners as I expected they would be competitors. I then went to the journals and the reports on Russian business without much success. I decided that I should go to the horse's mouth. I asked myself who would know about Russian ports and railroads? There was one obvious answer, the U.S. Department of Defence; especially Naval Intelligence. Surely they knew all about Soviet sea defences and the layout of the railroad systems. I was lucky in that I had had some prior contacts with the Defence Intelligence Agency (DIA) and went to Washington where I had a meeting set up with them and some friends from the CIA. There were three specialists on Soviet port and transport operations. I was advised to go to the U.S. Department of Commerce to buy copies of the Operational Navigation Charts (ONC) and the Tactical Pilotage Charts (TPC) for the parts of Russia in which I had an interest. These were detailed maps produced by US satellites which showed road and rail links, the contours of the land and the radar sites and their frequencies.

I had to laugh. In 1979 when I was visiting Geneva during the talks on Zimbabwe independence (e.g. Rhodesia) I had been working on a plan for ZANU to join the rail line in Tete Province in Mozambique to the newly-built Canadian rail line in Malawi terminating at Nacala, This would take an independent Zimbabwe's trade away from the reach of South Africa. As part of my outline which I presented to them on this I displayed the ONC and TPCs for the region. Jo Tongongara, the commander of the ZANU forces looked at the maps and shouted, "Where the hell did you get these maps? We have been looking for them for four years. The Rhodies took them away with them and we couldn't steal them from them or South Africa. How did you get them?" I said that I had bought them at Stanford's Map Store in London, near Covent Garden. He said "Bought them; bought them? My God that is the only thing we didn't think of doing!".

The three specialists told me that I should not believe any Russian map. The Russians lied as a matter of course on their maps in public circulation and deliberately changed the information. When a Russian plane flew, as I saw myself later, the passengers went on board first and took their seats. Then the pilot, co-pilot and navigator boarded the plane. Then the security people boarded the plane and secured the real flight map and plan under a piece of Plexiglas and left the plane. On arrival the security men boarded the plane and retrieved the map. Then the pilots and crew left and then the passengers. The Soviets were paranoid about maps and controlled their circulation.

They did say that they might be able to help me later by showing me some maps of the underwater approaches to several ports or at least telling me of the depths of the ports which they might have measured. This would be premature until I had made a decision. Both agencies were interested in the plans to set up a shipping hub on the Far East and I promised I would keep them apprised of any developments.

These maps and their advice were very helpful. I could now look at proper maps and get an idea of where to start. What was missing was some Russian input. I needed to know whether the Russians looked favourably on this plan for importing and exporting aluminium. It would have been very foolish to jump into this blind. Fortunately I had some contacts among officers of Soviet Military Intelligence (GRU) whom I had met in Africa when Vassily Solodovnikov ran Soviet operations from the embassy in Zambia. One was employed at the UN Headquarters New York and I managed to have a chat with him about the New Russia. He told me many things of value and I promised to keep in touch to let him know what was going on. He gave me the name of someone I should contact in Moscow and a contact in Khabarovsk who worked at the Mongokta Airbase nearby (the one that shot down the Korean airliner). I had now done most of the groundwork for my business.

The only thing missing was a chat with some people in New York who could tell me about the Russian Mafia in Little Odessa in Brooklyn and the role of 'Yaponchik' in reorganising the Russian Mob in the US. I had dinner at Ratners with some contacts from the NY families and the Westies who told me that the Russian Mob were monsters; they were terribly violent and were very vindictive. They were going through a mini-war between Marat Balagula and Evsei Agron, so Yaponchik had been sent to end it because the NY police and the FBI were looking too closely at them. This had nothing to do with my business but it was interesting to know. I went back to London with my research and began to put the pieces in place.

I found in my research that after almost seventy years of sporadic development, there had been a major shift in the infrastructural requirements of the former Soviet Union. The break-up of the USSR into constituent republics within and without the C.I.S. made regular access to seaports more problematical and seriously called into question the reliability of adequate and timely internal transport of goods on the rail system. The Russian Republic found itself deprived of unrestricted access to what were traditionally reliable Baltic ports and in a potentially conflicted situation with the Ukraine over free access to the Black Sea/Crimean ports. The resurgence of the "nationalities question" brought to the fore the problem of who owned and controlled the rolling stock on the railroads and created the potential for delays and disruption whenever trains crossed what were formerly internal borders but which now marked the borders between nations claiming various degrees of sovereignty

Yet this same problem also represented an opportunity for Russia. The major growth in the patterns of world trade was in the Pacific Rim. The growth of intra-Pacific trade and commerce had grown much faster than trade in any other area. The Pacific Rim nations, with the exception of Australia and the U.S.A. are largely resource poor but wealthy. They are potentially the best customers for Russian raw materials, semi-finished and refined goods. Russia is fortunate to have several good ports in Russian Asia; including the deep-water natural bay port of Nahodka which is capable of all-year navigation, close to all the major Pacific Rim trade routes and at the end of the main Trans-Siberian rail line; Vostochny, which lies below Nahodka and constitutes a bay (Wrangel Bay) which is part of the Nahodka complex; Vladivostok, which lies north of Nahodka on the Trans-Siberian rail line; Vanino which lies further north on the Eastern Coast near Sovetskaya Gavan, a sheltered deep-water all-year port lying at the terminus of the Baikal-Amur rail line; and several newly-accessible former fishing ports like Posyets and Zarubina in the south by the Chinese-Korean border near Kraskino. These all provide, with varying degrees of advantage, sea-rail links to a window onto the Pacific Rim for the export of Russian goods and for the import of products required for Russian industrial expansion.

There was an acute crisis of Russian ports and Russian rail lines. The dismemberment of the former USSR into its several constituent parts left the warm-water ports of the Baltic largely in the hands of the newly independent states of Estonia, Latvia and Lithuania. The Black Sea ports were largely incorporated into the new Ukraine, Georgia and Azerbaijan. The capacity of the remaining Russian ports after the breakup of the Soviet Union was about 187 million tons per year or a reduction of about 58% of the USSR's former capacity. This reduction in its port facilities meant that, even at current volumes of trade,

Russian ports could handle only 54% of this trade. The balance of Russian trade (46%) had to travel to and through other countries. These shipments via foreign ports cost Russia dearly as this trade took place in hard currency; at 1992 rates these transfer payments amounted to about $2.3 billion per year and, in terms of a rapidly declining rouble, made up a geometrically-escalating cost for Russian commerce.

The loss of access to Russia of its former ports was qualitative as well as quantitative. The loss of the Baltic ports meant that Russia lost modern transhipment complexes it had built for potassium salt (8.8 million tons per year); petroleum products (39 million tons per year); chemical wet cargoes and compressed gas (1.3 million tons per year); grains and pulses (5 million tons per year); perishable goods (0.5 million tons per year); as well as a key train ferry reloading facility for Germany (5.3 million tons per year). The main grain port and grain silo area in Novo Tallinn, only operational in 1986, with over 370,000 ton grain storage space was lost. The major Soviet oil export terminal at Ventspils was lost as was the modern container port at Riga. In the south, Russia lost port facilities for handling black oil and light petroleum products (1.7 million tons per year); chemical wet cargoes and condensed gas (3.6 million tons per year); urea (1.5 million tons per year; grains (9 million tons per year) as well as six major grain elevators in the port, especially at Odessa, the major grain port. Special port handling complexes for ore and coal reloading were lost (10 million tons per year) and a train ferry for handling cargo to Bulgaria (4.8 million tons per year). The last loss was compounded by the fact that its loss denied Russia direct access to the newly-opened international trade channel of the Rhine-Main-Danube Canal.

Western Russia has only shallow depth, highly congested ports with little capital infrastructure to handle the bulk of its trade. Russia now had only one port grain elevator and one import complex for raw sugar; at Novorossisk. The sugar facility had a capacity of 0.8 million tons a year although Russia urgently required an import of sugar of about 4 million tons a year at current levels of consumption. On the Azov Sea there is only the shallow water port of Taganrog; and on the Caspian Sea only Makhachkala with a maximum of 7.0 million tons per year capacity. Over 60% of Russian ports are shallow depth ports incapable of handling modern vessels. Northern ports are frozen for large periods of the year and are kept open only by expensive nuclear-powered ice-breakers. Western insurance companies couldn't agree to approve regular trade to these ports like Archangelsk or Murmansk. Also, in many ports like Makhachkala, Poti, Baku and others, there were civil wars and ethnic strife where rail lines had to pass through such troublesome areas as Chechnya, 'Free Georgia', etc. where the security of goods in transit could not be guaranteed.

The only safe, reasonably well-equipped and reliable ports lay in the Far East. The whole question of the ports, however, could not be understood in isolation from an understanding of the Russian rail system.

For a long period of its history, Russia lagged behind many of the other nations in Europe in the building of an efficient rail network. The first major Russian rail line was begun in 1837, when Peter built a rail link between the new capital at St. Petersburg as far as Tsarskoye Selo, fourteen miles away. In 1851 this link was extended to Moscow. Although there was talk at this time of building a rail link across Siberia there was nothing done about it until the end of the century.

The political climate of Russia and the extraordinarily harsh climate of Siberia were the primary causes of the lack of initiative in building railroads. Russia was blessed with an extensive network of navigable rivers, including the Don, Dnieper and the Volga in the West. In Siberia the Ob, Yenisei, Lena and Amur Rivers offered opportunities for travel and cargo transport. The normal form of land communication in Siberia was performed by the "Trakt", the Great Siberian Postroad. This was, in effect, the "Wells Fargo-" of Siberia, where post riders and post wagons/sleighs travelled between small post houses located every 10-20 miles between Moscow and Irkutsk. There horses could be changed, wagons repaired and cargo and passengers picked up and delivered. These post roads were frozen in winter requiring the use of sleighs and bogged down in mud in the spring where vast tracts of marshland had to be crossed on makeshift bridges.

Siberia can be described as naturally divided into three distinct climatic zones; the tundra, the taiga and the steppe. In the far North is the tundra. This is an area above the timberline with a climate which is one of the harshest on Earth. It is a vast expanse of frozen marshes, whose only vegetation is lichens, mosses, dwarf trees, shrubs and coarse grasses. The ground is permanently frozen ('permafrost') which makes any working of the soil impossible. In the short summer's slight thaw, the melting snow and ice create giant swamps where huge and voracious insects breed in vast numbers. In the winter this freezes again and is covered by a thick blanket of crusted snow.

To the south of the tundra can be found the area of the taiga. This zone of taiga comprises about 4.6 million square miles of Siberia and extends about 4,600 miles from east to west and between 600 to 1,200 miles north and south. This area is covered primarily by enormous tracts of virgin timber interspersed with huge swamps. In the transitional zone between the tundra and the taiga the land is mostly frozen all year long and is covered by widely-spaced trees. In the north these trees are primarily pine, larch, cedar, birch and cherry while in the southern reaches of the taiga the trees are mostly elm, aspen, poplar and maple. In the winter the taiga is frozen solid and covered with a thick blanket of snow. In the late spring and summer it is a vast swampy marshland in which scores of insects breed. Temperatures in the taiga, although generally less cold than in the tundra, often reach -50° F and have been known to reach an all time low of -90°. Travel is only possible in the winter when the ground is frozen.

The most southern area of Siberia is the steppe. There the northern ranges of the steppe, vast rolling grasslands, are interspersed with heavy stands of timber which disappear as one goes further south. Although a very cold winter dominates the steppe for six or seven months it is comparatively free of snow. The weather of Siberia is essentially cold and dry. Because of the mountain ranges in the south (Sayan and Yablonevy Ranges), the warmer southern air never reaches Siberia and the north-south pattern of mountain ranges in the north (Verkhoyansk and Chersky Ranges) channel cold Arctic air down into Siberia. The Urals of the West and the range of mountains which border the Pacific virtually enclose Siberia in a ring of mountains. Enclosed in this wilderness of taiga is the largest freshwater lake in the world, Lake Baikal. covering over 12,000 square miles of water, stretching some 395 miles north to south and about 18 to 50 miles in width.

Siberia first came into the hands of the Muscovy tsars after the defeat of the khan, Kuchum, in 1582 by the Cossack, Yermak. Despite the incursions of Russian explorers like Beketon who founded the city of Yakutsk in 1632; Moskvitin, who travelled to the Sea of Okhostk in 1639 to found the first Russian city on the Pacific in 1640, there was little actual settlement of Siberia. Gradually forts were built across Siberia and fort towns like Tomsk and Tyumen became major trading cities. In the late 1600's a great walled trading town, Mangazeya, was established in the Arctic Sea to which England and Holland regularly sent merchant vessels to trade in the summer months when the water was free of ice. This arrival of foreign merchants soon frightened the Tsar who closed the port and the town and trade died. This town also traded with China through smaller vessels which plied the river route of the Yenisei; trade with Moscow was by ship from Archangelsk and the Kara Sea.

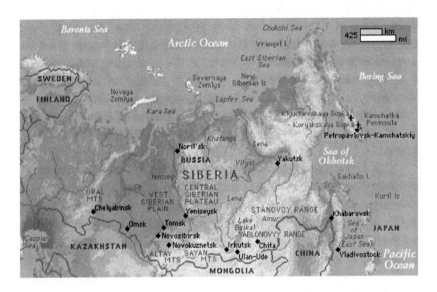

Under Ivan IV (1533-1584) a thirst for scientific exploration led the tsars to encourage travellers to Siberia to write up tales of their travels and by 1629 there were detailed sea maps prepared. In 1643 Vassily Poyarkov crossed Siberia overland from the west, reaching the Pacific via the Amur River. In 1648 Semyen Dezchev sailed from the west through the Bering Straits proving that there was a sea route direct to the warm water ports of the Pacific, Eight years later, Vitus Bering sailed to make detailed charts of this region, The next year, the intrepid Yerofei Khabarov led an expedition down the Amur to where the city of Khabarovsk is now located. Under Peter the Great (1682-1725) more expeditions were sent and the settlement of Siberia was encouraged. The large bulk of those who settled Siberia were convicts and political prisoners who were sent out to establish villages in

Siberia. These were joined by escaped serfs and the occasional Cossack seeking free land in the East. In 1861, with the freeing of the serfs by Alexander II, settlement of Siberia was accelerated by the offer of free crown land to all settlers.

A mass resettlement of serfs in Siberia began in 1862. Then large migrations from the Ukraine and from central Russia trekked across Siberia, attracted to this 'Green Land' by three benefits; exemption from the poll-taxes, exemption from billeting of soldiers and exemption from recruitment for military service for ten years. Soon the Russian State offered free travel to settlers, Arriving by sea each year from Odessa were 2,000 families setting up home in new cities like Vladivostok, Blagovochensk and Khabarovsk. In addition, settlements on Sakhalin Island and the Kamchatka Peninsula were established using criminals and political prisoners. These settlers began to carve out farmlands from the steppe. They were joined by fur trappers in the taiga whose depredations virtually wiped out most of the fur-bearing animals of the region. The discovery of gold in the North led to a Gold Rush in Siberia and the introduction of steam and packet boat traffic on the major rivers and on Lake Baikal.

This burgeoning population and the discovery of the vast mineral resources of Siberia demanded a link between these remote mining centres and settlements with the consumers in the West. At the turn of the century Russia embarked on the massive project of building a rail link through Siberia to its military outpost at Vladivostok. The appearance of British railroad contractors engaged by the Emperor of China to build massive rail links across China gave added impetus for this line. The Tsar appointed a Trans-Siberian Committee. Under the supervision of the Finance Minister, Serge Witte, the Committee divided the work into three separate subtasks. The work would commence on each section simultaneously supervised by the local committees. The West-Siberian section stretched from the Urals at Chelyabinsk to the Ob River at Novosibirsk; the Mid-Siberian from Novosibirsk to Irkutsk at the southernmost tip of Lake Baikal at the banks of the Angara River; the Trans-Baikal eastwards to Sretensk; the Amur which leads to Khabarovsk; and the Ussuri Line which runs north-south from Khabarovsk to Vladivostok. Work commenced simultaneously on these lines in 1892-1893. The most difficult area of a number of difficult areas was the Trans-Baikal section. Lake Baikal is ringed by giant granite cliffs on all sides, rising to 5,000 feet and periodic huge winds whipping up fifty foot waves across the lake. The first solution was to build three packet steamers to sail across the lake. The first built was the 'Baikal' which was built in Britain and transported in pieces to the lake where the pieces were reassembled into a vessel. It was late 1899 when the 'Baikal' was assembled and put into service. The following year a slightly smaller ship, 'Angara', was put into service. However, the ice-breaking capabilities of the 'Baikal' were overrated and during midwinter the railroad company laid rails on the ice across the lake, occasionally with disastrous effects.

By 1904 the need for good Trans-Siberian communication was urgent as the war between Russia and Japan had begun. A crash program to build a Circum-Baikal Line was begun and over 33 bridges and 200-plus tunnels were constructed to connect the rail lines across the southern tip of Lake Baikal. This cost, in those days, was a staggering 250,000 roubles per mile to build, but it was completed within seven months of the Japanese attack. Workmanship was poor and the first train was derailed ten times. In 1950 Russian engineers built a new dam on the Angara River. This had the unplanned effect of drowning a major section of the Circum-Baikal Railroad. A new, 84-mile section built to replace the submerged sections of the railroad was completed in 1956, connecting Irkutsk to Port Baikal.

Work was also progressing in the East. However, the Japanese had attacked China in 1894 and seized control of Port Arthur and Tallenwan. In addition Japan demanded heavy indemnities from China. Under pressure from Russia, Austria, Prussia and England, Japan agreed to give back the ports in exchange for further indemnities. China was unable to pay these indemnities and concluded a secret treaty with the Tsar in which Russia would give China the money to pay Japan in exchange for the right to build a railway across Manchuria, linking Baikal with Ussuriysk (a few miles from Vladivostok) This had to be done in secret under the fiction that this was a purely Chinese railroad. It was called the Chinese Eastern Railway Company. Construction of this 600-mile rail link began in 1897 and, in order to help defray the enormous cost of this construction, China signed a secret treaty with Russia in 1898 to cede Port Arthur to the Russians on a long-term lease. This was the final incident which sparked the xenophobic Boxer Rebellion of 1898 in China. In the violence of this rebellion much of the lines already built on this railway were destroyed. After the Great Powers restored order in China this line was completed and opened to service in 1903. This is why many Russians consider that the Great Chinese Eastern Railway is a Russian rail line, albeit of a different gauge than the wider Russian rail lines.

In 1904 the Japanese struck against Russia. The vulnerability of the Great Chinese Eastern Railway to attacks from the Japanese in China revived the plans to complete the Amur section of the Trans-Siberian Railway and construction began in 1908. The 1,200 mile long section was completed only with great difficulty as the climate only allowed about four months of the year as possible work periods. In those four months of the year when the earth was soft enough to work, the workmen were plagued by swarms of hungry insects which bred in the permafrost pools. Many of those who survived the ravages and disease spread by the insects suffered from malnutrition. About 75% of the workmen suffered from scurvy and other dietary diseases. The work was completed in 1913 with the completion of the 22-span bridge over the Amur River near Khabarovsk. In that year it was finally possible to take a train from Moscow to Vladivostok.

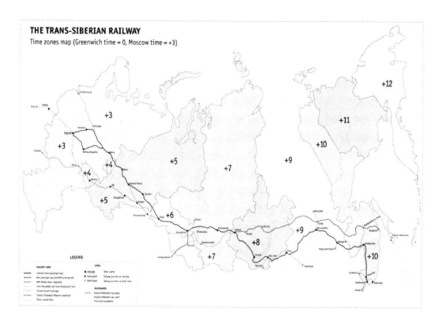

THE TRANS-SIBERIAN RAILWAY
Time zones map (Greenwich time = 0, Moscow time = +3)

The Civil War which followed the revolution in 1917 had a major impact on the Russian Far East. The Great Powers, the U.S. and Japan became embroiled in the Civil War and sent troops to Russia. The US and Japan were active in the Far East which was a key theatre of conflict. During the period 1918 to 1922 the Japanese and the Americans controlled Vladivostok, Khabarovsk and Northern Sakhalin Island. When I was in Vladivostok I took the opportunity to show the ladies the offices of General Groves, the US general who led the occupation of the region. It was not until the Bolshevik victories at Volochaevka and Spassk which led to the withdrawal of the occupying forces and the imposition of a 'Cordon Sanitaire' that the Russian Far East returned to control by Moscow. The new government considered the Far East an area ripe for development and sent many of its best educated and most talented citizens to these areas to construct new towns and factories. These new settlers were not often given the choice of where they were to go as they came primarily as political prisoners sentenced to nation-building the hard way. Occasionally, as in 1932, the government persuaded a group of idealistic young people to volunteer to found a new city. One such town is Komsomolsk-on-Amur where the Komsomol youth movement furnished the volunteers to build a new city on the banks of the Amur above Khabarovsk. The desperate famines in 1932-34 which starved almost half the population of Kazakhstan and the Ukraine, led to a further waves of immigration to Siberia.

The Russian railroads were the primary focus of the First Five-Year Plan (1928-1933) as the key to industrialisation of the new nation. In the course of the Second Five-Year Plan it was decided to build the needed supplementary rail line which runs north of Lake Baikal. This Baikal-Amur Railway (or as it is now known as the 'BAM') was started in 1933. About 112 miles of the BAM were built, linking the BAM station on the Amur through a line running northwards to the town of Tynda. However, events overtook this endeavour. When the Germans threatened the Soviet State at Stalingrad in 1942 the government ordered the dismantling of the BAM. Its steel rails were transported westwards where they were melted down into armaments for the war effort in the West.

Construction of the BAM was recommenced in 1974 and fully completed ten years later. It runs at a distance of about 250 to 400 miles north of the Trans-Siberian Railroad and extends from the Sea of Okhotsk town of Sovetskaya Gavan and its seaport Vanino 2,700 miles westward to its terminus at Taishei in Eastern Siberia. It links with the Trans-Siberian Railroad at several points with north-south links. The

BAM was built in atrocious conditions. Almost 40% of the BAM runs across permafrost whose frozen grip on the earth reaches down some 20 metres. In winter the temperatures dropped to -50° to -60° C. The workers were harassed by blood-sucking insects and malnutrition. The builders had to construct over 3,000 earthworks in this snow-covered frozen stretch of permafrost. Virtually all of the work done on this railroad was completed by prisoners and convicts, although some young volunteers were also a part of the building programme. No one knows how many people died in the construction of this line but there are reliable estimates that the human cost of constructing the Siberian railroads claimed the lives of about sixty-five people for every mile of track laid. Even more died during the prisoner transport through the Russian Far East to Magadan and Sakhalin and north to Vorkuta and Norilsk. In the forced settlement and construction of the Siberian region there were well over one and one-half million deaths since 1932, and countless dead before.

One of the most difficult aspects of developing the Siberian region is the skewed pattern of distribution developed over the last seventy years of Moscow rule. The Soviet system was one in which planning played a very important part. This had both positive as well as negative effects. On the positive side, the Soviet system sourced and delivered regular supplies of food, clothing, fuel, hot water and heat to remote areas of the nation. The ability of the Soviet system to keep up the supply of food stuffs, hot water and fuel to even its most remote areas was a remarkable achievement. This achievement enabled factories to continue producing goods for the larger Soviet market and delivered raw materials for this productive base from incredible distances

This was coupled with a policy of deterring internal mobility through the use of internal passports and closing off whole regions and cities to even internal immigration. The vast military-industrial complex of Russia was largely buried in the centre of Siberia; from Tomsk to Khabarovosk and concentrated in major industrial towns like Krasnoyarsk, Bratsk, Novosibirsk, Bernaul and Omsk.

Another aspect of this distribution system was the use of massive state trading companies to make the purchase and sale of goods to and from Russia. A giant trading company like Razno (Raznoimport and Raznoexport) handled the purchase of the total requirements of whole industries; e.g. the aluminium industry and the sale of the products produced by this industry. So, Razno would arrange the import of bauxite from Africa, petroleum coke and other carbon products from Europe; soda ash from the Middle East, etc. and would arrange the sale of the finished aluminium to internal Russian customers as well as overseas. This type of mass buying and selling by giant state enterprises was the rule throughout the whole of the Soviet economy. This was facilitated by the use of a central bank clearance system in which internal accounts were calculated in rouble credit and debits across an industry, a ministry, or a state trading organisation. The accounts were all paid into and out of the "centre". There they were allocated by the "Gosplan" planning committees as part of a "plan" for the needs of the industries and matched by establishing quotas for production. External payments in hard currencies and hard currency sales were conducted by the central banking system without regard or reward to the importer, exporter or producer. As long as the "centre" existed and functioned this planning model creaked on.

It was a typical Soviet model in which there was duplication of virtually every function, from planning to distribution. It suffered from having to operate under political restraints which impeded the Soviet planners in their search for improving efficiency. In order to maintain dependency amongst the several regions and republics of the USSR the planners built industries far from the sources of raw materials; built processing plants far from the consumers of these plants; and kept a static population by way of "closed cities" and "closed regions". To use the aluminium industry again as an example, bauxite was imported from Africa to Nikolayev in the Ukraine. It was turned into alumina there and at Pavlodar in Kazakhstan and then shipped about 2,000 miles to Bratsk and Krasnoyarsk in Siberia to be turned into aluminium. Much of the aluminium was used in the military factories of Siberia, but the rest was then shipped thousands of miles back into Western Russia for use and or sale. The system stressed mutual dependency as much as it stressed efficiency.

This system broke down in an effort to establish "perestroika". The first people to lose their jobs were the planners at "Gosplan". The Yeltsin victory and the introduction of Gaidar's and later Chernomyrdin's reforms sought to decentralise the control of the CIS and later the Russian economy. This was a positive step towards establishing a market economy but a dreadful wrench for the existing manufacturing sector. Because all purchases and sales were made through the "centre" there was no aggregation of capital which belonged to any factory or ministry or trading company. There had been no "profits" so there were no accrued earnings. Productive enterprises owed goods to the system and requisitioned materials from the system. There were no real cash transactions among the enterprises nor was there an accounting system which measured who owed whom, for how long or why it owed it. The introduction of reforms made life terribly difficult for state enterprises and trading companies.

For example, in the aluminium industry the aluminium smelters were obliged to produce and deliver finished aluminium; but had no means of paying for alumina, coke, cryolite or any of the other materials needed to make aluminium. They had not "sold" aluminium previously but merely delivered it as the state determined. They could not "buy" alumina from the alumina producers because they had no money to do so. In any event no one knew what the price for alumina should be. The alumina producers could not sell the smelters alumina anyway as they had no money to buy bauxite from Africa, neither in roubles or in dollars, to make the alumina. Equally as problematic was arranging the internal transport of these goods within Russia. If there was no means of exchange how would these companies pay the railroads for handling their goods? What price should they pay? To whom should they pay it? Should it be paid to the Ministry of Transport, the Ministry of Rail; the Trans-Siberian Railroad; the railroad's own agency company "RITM", or to some other body? Reform, in short, however small, brought chaos.

In the intervening years this system has changed, largely through the efforts of outsiders; Western businessmen were willing to pre-finance sales and willing to enter into "tolling" operations in which the raw materials were purchased by the Western company and imported into Russia for processing. The Western company pays a "tolling charge" for this processing and then takes the finished product itself for sales outside Russia. This initially solved many of the production problems and the cash accounting. However, this hasn't solved the distribution or the political consequences of these problems.

The distribution problems arise out of three essential factors. The first is that it has been a tradition in Russia that many of the needs of the workforce for consumer goods, foodstuffs and services (police, fire, education, health, etc.) have been provided by the enterprise itself as part of the compensation package offered its workers. Workers were able to get food parcels, clothing, etc. from the place of work. This stopped them having to leave work to join the endless queues, and offered an 'on the spot' system of distribution. The state arranged a minimum standard of living for all and was responsible for delivering sufficient food, clothing and services to even the most remote areas to permit a difficult but not impossible life. One of the immediate consequences of reform is that the production planning function has been divorced from the distribution function. It has proved very difficult for the new state and regional bodies, as well as the enterprises themselves, to purchase and take delivery of the quantity and quality of these consumer items and services formerly provided by the State. Largely because of this there has been a massive depopulation of rural areas, particularly in Siberia, where a newly mobile population has left the challenging life on the edge of the tundra for a more secure, if impoverished, life nearer the big cities. In the vast areas of rural Russia, as in between Bratsk and Komsomolsk-on-Amur on the Baikal-Amur Railway line, population dropped in eighteen months by almost thirty percent, Towns and factories stand deserted; houses lie empty alongside roads with no traffic; industries just closed their doors. The state proved unable to provide food and supplies sufficient to maintain the population levels so the areas shrunk in size to serve a diminishing population.

A second factor complicating the distribution system was that the railroads themselves were not able to generate the income that they need to upgrade and repair the tracks and rolling stock to make their operations congruent with the needs of industry and the civilian population. The railroads generated decreasing revenue in real terms. Additionally there were very sharp divisions which developed between the Ministry of Transport and the railroads themselves as to which has the power to control and shape railroad policy. Even more difficult is the regionalisation of the railroads into Far Eastern, Western, Southern, etc. administrations which seek to raise and control their own revenues. In the Far East, for example, the Far Eastern section of the Trans-Siberian Railroad, controlled from Khabarovsk and the Eastern section of the Baikal-Amur Railway, controlled from Komsomolsk-on-Amur, refuse to recognise the RITM (the agency set up under Moscow Ministry control to act as an agent for relations between the railroads and non-Russian clients). These Eastern sections rejected the notion of paying the lion's share of the earnings generated in hard currency to an office in Moscow when they feel that it was they and their railroad which actually did the work. This regionalism was increasing and centralised control of the railroads was largely disappearing. Regional centres, like Khabarovsk, Komsomolsk-on-Amur. Mineralnaya Vody, Tynda, Chita, etc. shaped railroad policy to the dismay of the several ministries.

The third area of difficulty with the distribution system was that there had been virtually no provision, for warehousing and storage. The major operator of storage and warehouse facilities outside of the ports was the Soviet military. Various ministries and regional administrations operated small depots but on a project by project basis as opposed to any notions of a commercial enterprise. In the wake of reform the internal storage and distribution systems have proved inadequate to the changing needs of free and open competition. Ironically, Russia is particularly well set up for a modern and efficient distribution system. On the outskirts of virtually every town and city across Russia and the former republics, the railroads have sidings with warehouse and storage space. These are in various states of repair. Some, as around the Krasnodar Region, were well developed and operational. Others, as in the North in the Komi Republic, or near Murmansk were in a state of disrepair. In mid-Siberia and the East they could easily be rebuilt or modernised. In many cases the Russian military had large depots, cold stores, etc. which cou;d be made commercially available if a proper organisation took place. This warehousing off the rail spurs was a largely neglected area.

The ports of the Russian Far East have been closed to free commercial traffic for long periods of their existence. It was not until 1990-1991 that these ports were effectively opened to foreign vessels. The military considerations overweighed the commercial and the main Soviet naval presence at Vladivostok took precedence. With the opening of these ports the world was surprised to learn of the size of a port like Nahodka handling several thousand vessels each year. The nearby port of Vostochny in Wrangel Bay has grown into a large port which specialises in container traffic, as it lies at the terminus of the Trans-Siberian Railway. The problem with these ports is twofold. The first is that the Trans-Siberian Railroad cannot handle anything like the volumes of cargos that wish access to and from the Pacific. The narrow and inadequate rail bridge at Khabarovsk is a bottleneck as are the vulnerable rail lines south of Vladivostok which are subject to flooding, subsidence and washouts of bridges. More importantly, as Vladivostok, Nahodka and Vostochny grow, the port furthest north will choke off those below it with its rail traffic. If Nahodka gets bigger it will choke off Vostochny; as Vladivostok grows in volume it will choke off both Nahodka and Vostochny. A further consideration is that this rail line is a strategic route for moving troops, equipment and supplies to the Far East, especially to the Ussuri border. This puts a limit to how congested freight cargo can be allowed to become, although further military hostilities with China seemed unlikely.

A minor but not insignificant problem is that for certain months of the year vessels which call at these ports are banned from North America as a result of Gypsy Moth larval infestation. A vessel which has called at these ports is prohibited from U.S. and Canadian waters if there are Gypsy Moth larvae on board. They invariably have this infestation during three or four month period. Further south, the port of Zarubina is now emerging from its isolation. Although it is hampered by its rail links via the Ussuri section of the railroad, it is ideally placed to service the province of Heilongjiang (Harbin in China) and North Korea. It can serve as a major entrepot for the imports and export from a region long troubled by its transport isolation. The port of Posyets, nearby, is not ice-free all year.

The conclusion to my research was that the port most favoured for growth into a major world-class seaport was Vanino. It lies at the terminus of the Baikal-Amur Railway and has direct access to the most mineral-rich areas of Siberia. Its railroad tracks are quite new and, at least as far as Khabarovsk, are an efficient double-line railroad. The rail bridge at Komsomolsk-on-Amur is much better than its counterpart further south on the Trans-Siberian rail line. The distance between Vanino and the western regions is between 600 and 1,500 kilometres shorter than the Trans-Siberian link. That translates to about a week's savings on transport and much better turnaround time between the Russian West and the port for scarce rolling stock.

Vanino was not a major city so there was wide scope for development and the undeveloped coastal territory was available for the growth of industries as well as port facilities. There was a regional organisation of more than 60 firms and enterprises which had joined together to promote the advantages of the Vanino Port complex, including ferrous and non-ferrous metal, fertiliser and other industrial giants of Siberia and Kazakhstan. Vanino had a treasure trove of mineral wealth ready to flow through its ports to the world's markets; including coal, mineral fertilisers, apatite, petroleum products, wood, aluminium, copper, steel and manufactured goods. These could come in bulk in hopper cars, on flatbed railcars, in closed carriages and in containers.

I checked with everyone and they agreed that I should investigate Vanino further. However, they pointed out that the Russians listed the draught (the depth of water alongside the quay) as only seven meters. That would mean we could only use shallow and smaller vessels. I checked with Naval Intelligence in Washington and their official comment was "Horseshit! The depth is fourteen to seventeen meters. The Russians are lying. Ignore them." That is why I called David Reuben and told him that Vanino was likely to be the place for us to start.

He asked why no others had come up with that port if it was so great and I told him that was because the Russians were lying about the draught. He said he wasn't sure and would ask his partners. I begged him not to. If they checked and found the truth we would be in competition with others. This way we had an open door. He agreed not to say anything until I had returned. I made ready to go to Vanino.

CHAPTER THREE

I started to get my things together for my trip to the Russian Far East. I mentioned that I was going to the Russian Far East to my Russian teacher, Edvard Gurvich. I had decided that it was a good idea for me to learn Russian as quickly as possible if I were to understand what was happening around me. Edvard was recommended to me as an excellent teacher, with a good sense of humour, so we arranged that he would come twice a week to teach me Russian. He did very well and I was able to make some quick progress in understanding the language. I had always picked up languages fairly quickly and Russian, once I adapted to the Cyrillic alphabet, was relatively easy. It felt comfortable to speak the Russian sounds and I realised that I had a reasonable passive vocabulary from my grandfather and from Bulgarian.

I speak or read most of the European languages and now I could add the Slavic root languages to the list. When I was working in Bulgaria I soon grew able to understand Bulgarian to the point that they didn't need to translate for me, although I couldn't speak the language with any degree of intelligibility. The changeover from Bulgarian to Russian was not difficult. Now that I was using the language it became easier. I had studied Arabic and Japanese earlier but when I hadn't used them for a while my ability to speak had dropped dramatically, but Russian came back.

Edvard told me he knew of Vanino. Indeed most of Russia knew all about Vanino; not, I must add, as a port but rather as the last stop on the prisoner trains to the Kolyma Gulag. Prisoners were gathered from all over Russia and sent down the rail line to Vanino where they were removed from the trains and herded into slave ships for the week-long journey to the Port of Magadan. At Magadan the survivors were led off to the Gulag camps in Kolyma. As explained by Robert Conquest in his "Gulag History"[iv]:

"The prisoners were then transported in packed and unsanitary cattle trucks for journeys often of weeks, with minimal rations, with not even water given regularly, with hardly room to stand in almost total darkness. In the case of the Kolyma camps in Northeast Siberia, 'the pole of cold and cruelty' of the system, as Solzhenitsyn put it, prisoners then had to face a week or more packed into the holds of the slave ships, even more filthy and crowded."

After this interlude, they faced a deadly environment. There were often executions in the camps. Ten thousand were specifically ordered by Moscow in 1937. Others were carried out for local offenses such as failing three times to work, or simply as a means of removing those showing any other sign of independence, or uttering any "anti-Soviet" words. Some were done locally, others in special camps serving a whole area such as the Serpantinka in Kolyma. There were even small execution camps outside of any particular group that handled a few hundred brought in at a time, two or three batches a week.

A further horror of the Gulag was that, in most camps, there were a proportion of members of the old Russian criminal caste, the _urkas,_ who had been given privileges in the camps as they helped keep order among the prisoners. These were favoured by the authorities, and, together with the camp officials, they terrorized the noncriminal prisoners in an alliance productive of both physical abuse and starvation.

The sheer horror of that existence was captured by the Ukrainian artist, Nikolai Getman, in his series of paintings "I Remember Vanino" which showed the world of hunger and deprivation and oppression with extraordinary clarity and vision. It portrayed a system, in the words of Yeltsin's Report, in which "death was caused by unbearable toil, by cold and starvation, by unheard of degradation and humiliation, by a life that could not have been endured by any other animal." There was a famous ballad which was a reminder of this, "I Remember Vanino".[v]

In learning of this I was a bit apprehensive of what I might find. I need not have worried as the people I met there were the friendliest and most accommodating people I had ever encountered. However, they, too, had not forgotten the story of Vanino's history. In the middle of Vanino, just north of the port is a very large (about three acre) field which lies fallow, covered with grass. In my ignorance I asked why such a piece of prime real estate in the middle of a town should have been left empty. It wasn't even a park. Nobody even walked there. I was told it was empty out of respect. The trains that brought the huddled, shivering prisoners across the wilds of Siberia to Vanino on their journey to the Kolyma Gulag often brought prisoners who were dead on arrival; dead from exposure; dead from starvation; dead from disease or dead from attacks by fellow zeks. In late August and early September of each year the authorities in Vanino would dig three deep trenches before the ground froze. When the trains discharged their dead they were dumped into these trenches. When the ground defrosted they were covered up with fresh earth. The man who told me the story said there were at least five thousand people buried there.

Sometimes, he said, the prisoners would rebel and resist being pushed into the slave ships for Magadan. The authorities would respond by turning the hoses on the prisoners. They froze to death as they stood. They were laid out, like cordwood, and transported to Magadan. It made no difference if they got there alive or dead, as long as their arrival was accounted for. They weren't expected to live very long at Kolyma anyway. Their meagre rations were stolen by the criminal gangs and the medicines were unavailable for prisoners. Aleksandr Solzhenitsyn quotes the Kolyma camp commander as establishing the new law of the Archipelago: "We have to squeeze everything out of a prisoner in the first three months — after that we don't need him anymore." [vi]The system of hard labour and minimal or no food reduced most prisoners to helpless "goners" ('dokhodagya', in Russian) who wandered about waiting to die. The numbers of people who died in or on their way to the Gulag is estimated at over three million. It wasn't until the publication of Aleksandr Solzhenitsyn's "Gulag Archipelago" in 1973-1978 that these facts emerged, even inside Russia. I looked forward to meeting those still there.

I checked in at the Trans World office in London and was told that everything was ready. This time I would be travelling with a new companion, a Croatian by the name of Niksa Lazaneo who worked at the Moscow Office. Niksa spoke excellent English and Russian and had been in touch with the port. They were awaiting our arrival. This time I would fly to Moscow and meet Niksa. Together we would fly to Khabarovsk and then take a smaller plane from Khabarovsk to Sovetskaya Gavan. From there we'd drive the five miles to Vanino. I got my visa and my ticket.

I thought it important to discuss with David what he'd like to see from the trip. He said that he would like to find a port that could start handling the export of finished primary aluminium from Bratsk and Krasnoyarsk as soon as possible. He was willing to pay around $10 a metric ton to the port for handling but would like that figure lower if possible. He reckoned we should begin with a monthly delivery to the port of 5,000 tons to start with.

David was very clever. He had done his homework well. He said that no matter what I agreed with the port it would not work because they couldn't fulfil their side of the bargain because they had no money to do so. If we ordered 5,000 tons of space they would have to deal with the railroads, hire the stevedores and assume a range of costs which they likely couldn't afford. David said that the only way we could make this work was if we paid them in advance. I should take with me enough money to pay for the first month's deliveries in cash. Then the port could fill its responsibilities with the funds we had supplied.

Secondly, it was very important for me to assess if it were possible to build a facility there to import alumina from Australia. I needed to ascertain if it were possible and to suggest a method that would fit in with the port's ideas. I listened and agreed to try to achieve these goals. I called Niksa and we arranged a schedule.

My next port of call was the South African butchery in Richmond. This South African butchery produced a wide range of _biltong_ (an air-dried piece of wildebeest, kudu or ostrich), _droewors_ (a dried sausage) and _stokkies_ (pencil-sized biltong) which I could take on my trip so that I would always have food if I needed it. My trip to Vostochny taught me that I had to be independent of the Russian food supply. This was not because it wasn't good; it was because it was so erratic. I loaded up on _biltong_, _droewors_ and _stokkies_ for the _trek_. I was ready. I had already picked up the cash I would need.

I packed a small carry-on bag with some clothes. I had learned travelling around Africa that it was the height of folly to check in a bag on an airline. If you were lucky enough to see it again you would have been delayed at least a half an hour waiting for it to arrive at the baggage area. Then you would have to negotiate with customs to get your bag released. When we had to carry bags and check them in we always packed a carton of Marlboros on top of the clothing. The customs would take the cigarettes and you could bring in almost anything. It was a sort of ritual. I did this in Africa and throughout Latin America. I was sure Russia was the same.

This was no different than on ships. I had to take one of our vessels through the Suez Canal coming from Jurong Port on the way to Greece to load cement. The vessel, about 34,000 deadweight tons, had special piece of loading equipment, a Siwertell screw, in the midships section which was very tall so we had to carry 5,000 tons of cement in the hold as ballast to give it stability. In passing the Canal, vessels are charged at a different rate if they are empty (in ballast) as opposed to laden with cargo. My vessel was empty except for the 5,000 tons of cement used for ballast. The captain rang me approaching Aseb to say that they were charging the ship as a 'laden vessel' because of the cement ballast. I called our Canal agent, Leth, and explained that the cement was used as ballast and that I didn't want to miss the second convoy through the Canal. I told the captain to give the pilots two cases of scotch and four cartons of cigarettes from the bond on board. That worked. It saved me $60,000. The customs of customs are universal.

I boarded the plane to Moscow. On arrival I went as quickly as possible to my lady at the passport booth. I produced my pen and I passed through without incident. I had no problem with customs as I had declared $2,000 with me which I showed them. The other $75,000 stayed in my bag. I moved out to the general area where I was greeted by Niksa who was waiting for me. I was very impressed by Niksa. He was bright, articulate and had a good sense of humour. This was wonderful as we spent most of our years in Russia laughing. Niksa had worked for the Yugoslav firm "Iskra" in Moscow for a number of years. There were many Croatians involved in Russian trading in the 1980s and 1990s. In fact our agents in many of the Russian ports were Croatians working for a Croatian port agency company based in Vienna, There was another Croatian, Goran, working in Trans World Moscow's office as well. He was a Croatian of Serbian extraction.

I was amused that they had worked for "Iskra". The word 'iskra' in Russian means "the spark". That was the revolutionary Russian emigrant newspaper from the turn of the century edited, initially by Vladimir Ilyich Ulyanov (better known as 'Lenin'). The other staff members included Iliya Cederbaum (better known as Julius Martov), Georgi Plekhanov and Lev Davidovich Bronstein (better known as 'Trotsky). The paper was taken over by the Mensheviks and run in opposition to the Bolsheviks until 1905. My grandfather had told me tales of the in-fighting as part of my bedtime stories. Taking over 'Iskra' was one of their success stories.

Niksa took me to the Trans World office. We entered the office past a couple of armed guards. I was introduced to Goran Stanojevich and some of the others. We had time for a small tea and biscuits. I delivered the $25,000 from the London office to Goran. It was very difficult to arrange bank transfers at that time as there was very little foreign currency available. I was always welcomed in Moscow very cordially as I brought the cash to them. They had credit cards but not many people accepted them. Niksa and Goran briefed me on as much as they knew about Vanino. They asked me if I was sure about the draught. I assured them there was plenty of water at the quay. I didn't tell them how I knew.

Soon it was time to go to Domodedovo Airport. Niksa and I got in his Volvo and drove to a churchyard near to where he lived. The church was renting out parking spaces to make some extra cash. I was amused to see that Niksa removed his hub caps and his windshield wipers from his car when he parked. This was common in Moscow. There was a booming business in second hand hub caps and windshield wipers so everyone removed his when they parked. It was not unusual to see businessmen walking to their offices clutching windshield wipers. The Trans World driver who had followed us then took us to the airport.

We arrived in Domodedovo Airport and Niksa went over to see if we had our seats on the airplane. We were told that all was in order and that we should walk over to the boarding gate to check in and get our seats. Once again we walked under the wings of aircraft parked along our way with no thoughts of security. We arrived at the boarding gate and Niksa took care of everything. This was a much better way to travel; Niksa even understood the announcements that were being made over the loudspeakers. I can barely understand them in English; Russian was a bridge too far.

Our shuttle took us out to the aircraft and we boarded. I believe it was an IL-82 with 320 seats (3-3-3). There was only one class on the aircraft which I guess was appropriate for the classless society. There were no internal partitions; just rows of seats. There was limited overhead storage space but we were on the side row of three seats so we had a place to put our bags. The plane was full. I kept a watch to see if I saw a group of people with tattoos on their hands but there weren't that many. There were a number of soldiers scattered around. Our plane took off without incident and on time. In fact most Russian planes took off on time. They may have been three or four days late owing to scheduling, but they were on time the day they finally departed. It was to be a journey of about nine and one-half hours to Khabarovsk.

We flew for several hours when the stewardesses passed through the cabin with small plastic tea cups. They had hot water as well and we made our tea or coffee. They picked up the cups. About a half an hour later they brought us each a tray for dinner. It consisted of a hard roll and a plate with a portion of boiled chicken, looking pale and wan. There was some sort of salad made from shaved vegetables. For dessert there was a cookie with what looked like congealed diesel in the middle. I was assured it was 'kompott'. I thought I was lucky that I had brought my biltong with me. I asked Niksa if he wanted my chicken and he assured me he was having enough trouble get his own past his lips. I offered it to my neighbour who gratefully devoured it in a few bites and gave me back the bones. I took down some biltong and some droewors and started to eat. All my neighbours were interested. They took out goodies from the plastic bags they had brought with them on the plane, including sweets and several bottles of vodka. They began to pass these around. I was obliged to take a knife and share my biltong with them. Everyone was getting quite jolly. Unfortunately, they loved biltong and I had to take out another piece to share.

I disappointed many when I refused the vodka. I don't drink alcohol. It is not that I have some moral qualms about alcohol; nor am I a Muslim. I just don't like the taste. It tastes like medicine. Ever since I was a child I had avoided alcohol. Sometimes at dinner parties I have to take a sip of wine to be polite, or drink part of a can of beer at a football match, but I don't like it very much so just sip at it. It was a stumbling block in Russia where drinking is a part of the culture and occasionally part of the lack of culture. I thought I'd better start as I wanted to finish. If I never took a drink people would get used to it and not think I was being aloof or impolite. I constantly had to apologise for my lack of drinking but, as my colleagues saw that I didn't drink anywhere, it was soon overlooked as a weird condition that I suffered. There is a lovely Russian word, 'pasashok' which signifies the end of drinking. I used to long to hear it finally called out to the group.

It was a fairly uneventful flight to Khabarovsk where we were met by a very nice Russian lady, Alla Klepikova who worked at the firm 'Vedi' which provided tourist services. Niksa and Goran had arranged this. There were a couple of hours before the flight onward to Sovetskaya Govan so we went off to a restaurant for a meal. I was interested to see

Khabarovsk. It was a fairly nondescript town, clearly a bit down on its luck, and in need of some repair. There were a number of unfinished construction projects. One feature stood out as we drove into town. There was a water reservoir made of concrete, about forty feet off the ground, which was designed in a pure Tuscan style. It looked just like the one on the road north of San Gimignano. That was always my landmark when navigating Khabarovsk. I always wondered about the origins of that design as it was unique. The main building in town was the Governor's residence, formerly the Communist Party headquarters, in which most government business took place.

We went to this restaurant in the middle of town near to the Intourist Hotel. It wasn't far from the Amur River which ran nearby. We walked down to see it. It was a very large river, but one could see the opposite shore. That is the problem with tourism and Siberian rivers. A number of people I knew had signed up for a cruise on the Lena River. I asked them how they enjoyed it and they told me it was awful. The boat was fine; the food was good and the entertainment very interesting. The problem was that the Lena was so wide they couldn't see either shore so they could have been anywhere. The Ob and the Yenisei were not that much different.

The Russians are highly skilled technicians but they are very poor planners. When I visited Krasnoyarsk I was taken to see the mighty dam on the Yenisei which produced masses of hydroelectric power for the aluminium plant and the national grid; the second largest dam in the world. The only thing they forgot when building it was that the Yenisei is a navigable river. The dam blocked the river. The Russians then built a floating dry-dock on the dam which lifted boats 97 meters in the air and deposited them on the other side of the dam so that the river was navigable again. This was an engineering practice that I noticed all over Russia. When a planning error interfered with the success of a project brute force was brought to bear and the problem solved, however expensively. There was a serendipitous effect of the Krasnoyarsk moving dry-dock, however. On a hill on the south side of the dam newly married couples would come to celebrate their nuptials by watching the boats moving up and down the dam. I am not sure of the symbolism but it was very popular.

We returned to the airport and moved to the local terminal. They were building a new airport building but the construction had been stopped for three years. It was just starting up again. Khabarovsk airport was unique in Russia. It had connections to Nagoya in Japan and to Anchorage in Alaska; therefore it was an international airport. That meant that the airport clocks in Khabarovsk were set to local time and the schedule of flights were stated in local time. Everywhere else in Russia (which spans twelve times zones) all flights were given in Moscow time. One had to calculate back to Moscow time to know what the schedules meant. Khabarovsk was different; its schedules were stated in local time. This was important to remember.

Russia was for many years unique in terms of its measurement of longitude and latitude as well. The Russians calculated their positions with reference to the Pulkovo meridian, not the Greenwich meridian. This represented a line passing from the north to the south of St. Petersburg through the telescope of the Central Pulkovo Observatory Building. It deviated 30 degrees and 19.6 minutes from the prime Greenwich meridian. The Pulkovo meridian had long been a zero point for calculations of geography for Russia. It was abandoned only after the international Meridian Conference in 1884, albeit slowly. The French didn't give up using the Paris meridian until 1911.

Well now that we were sure of where we were and what time it was we were escorted out to the apron of the airport, past the gold statue of Lenin with his arms akimbo as if warning us of the transitory nature of fame. We put our bags in the forward hold of the small aircraft, in the front of the plane, and then boarded the steps inside. I noticed that the undercarriage of the plane was slightly bowlegged, as if it had made too many heavy landings. I mentioned this to Niksa but a man behind me told me not worry as the undercarriage was bent equally on both sides so there would be no problem. Having been thus comforted we sat down in the sling seats. When we were fully seated, the captain and the navigator entered the plane and passed forward to the cockpit. They were followed by a security man with the map. The security man left and the door was closed. We took off and flew the short hour and twenty minute flight without incident. The reverse of the procedure took place on landing. The security man came on board to take the map. The captain and the navigator left the cockpit and, to some applause, left the airplane. Then we were free to go out, get to the front of the plane to regain our luggage, and to leave via the wooden terminal building.

We exited the terminal building and were greeted by a young lady and a very interesting gentleman from the port. He was Valery

Vladomirovich Savinov. Savinov spoke good English and, as I later found out, very good Japanese as well. He stood out because he didn't look like all the Russians I had seen so far; he was a Buryat. That meant he was a member of the largest ethnic minority in Siberia who were the northernmost Mongols. His features were very distinct because of his Asiatic origins. He was a well-educated and urbane host. He greeted us and we climbed into a four-wheel drive car for the short journey from the airport to the Vanino Port.

The ride was interesting as well as we passed through several small villages along the road. These were nestled in beautiful scenery of trees, whose leaves were just starting to change their colour for the fall season, and rivers and lakes surrounded by hills covered with forests. The air smelled clean and fresh. I noticed that the trees, though abundant, were very thin in diameter. I asked if this was the result of growing in such a cold climate. I was told that around most Russian towns and cities, particularly in Siberia, the trees were cut down during the Second World War (or as the Russians know it, the Great Patriotic War) for firewood for heating. These new trees had grown up since 1950 which is why they weren't that large. There was always a Russian twist to the answers to my questions and I learned early that whatever seemed obvious wasn't always the whole truth. There was always a Russian reason. This has always been a staple of Russian humour. I told them that this reminded me of the Russian story about a village that was troubled by an infestation of mice. They weren't successful in driving them away so they asked for advice. A visitor to the town said "Why don't you put up a sign saying 'Collective Farm'. That should do it. Half the mice will die of hunger and the other half will run away."

I got some funny looks at my story, although Niksa laughed a little nervously. Savinov grinned. I said I hoped I hadn't offended anyone. He smiled as said that kind of story wouldn't offend anyone in Siberia. None of the people I would be meeting were there of their own volition; they weren't volunteers. They were sent there or their parents were sent there. It was less politically correct than I might have imagined. They were grateful for the changes and the new freedoms. They were less happy that things were improving so slowly. I remember on my fourth trip to the port the Technical Director asked me, "I was sentenced here for fifteen years. What the hell are you doing here?"

We arrived in Vanino. I was impressed to see the size of the port and the clearly defined sections, including the ferries to Sakhalin Island. I noticed some Finnish portal cranes (the cranes used to lift and stack containers). There weren't any containers but they were fully equipped. There were many heavy Takraf cranes along the quays (East German cranes which could safely lift about 45 tons). It was impressive. The port had handled over ten million tons in its peak year but was down to around six and one-half million tons when I arrived. Clearly there was scope for handling our tonnages.

I also noticed that each quay had three rail lines. The smallest was for the cranes to move along, but there were two rail lines parallel to the quayside. In all my travels around Russian ports I never saw a turning area on the rail line. That meant that a locomotive had to push or pull a set of rail cars along the quay to the berth. Only a few rail cars could reach the berth as the other rail cars could not be advanced. The locomotive pulling or pushing the rail cars travelled blind most of the time as the lines did not allow any repositioning of the locomotives. That meant that the cranes had to move along the berth to reach the rail cars and the vessel had to be warped frequently to catch up to the cranes. This was ok for discharging but it made loading bulk materials from a fixed point, like a hopper, dependent on a constant locomotive presence. It was very inefficient.

I asked why there was no turning circle for a train to maintain a constant flow of rail cars past a fixed point and was told that this was not in the Russian design manual. This became a point of interaction later. It was like the unspoken rule that in Siberia no step on a stairway should ever be the same height or depth as the step above or below it. If you didn't walk up or down a stairway with your eyes fixed on your feet you were guaranteed to trip.

However, these were not insuperable obstacles. I was very interested to meet the port authorities and to ascertain their interest in our project and their suggestions as to how we might get started. Niksa and I were escorted into the office of the Port Director, Apollon Mikailovich Shengelia. He was joined by his number two, the Technical Director, Joseph Sandler and the resident director of the Vanino Economic and Transport Association, Vladimir A. Pogodin. We were introduced and Niksa translated for me. I explained that we were there to explore the possibility of contracting with the Port to handle the export of about 250,000 metric tons of finished primary aluminium from the port to nearby Far Eastern ports and the import through the port of about 800,000 to 1,000,000 metric tons of alumina from Australia. I explained that the Trans World Group (which included Trans-CIS Commodities and others) were engaged in acquiring aluminium from the Bratsk and Krasnoyarsk smelters on the BAM and it made sense for us to use the terminus of the BAM at Vanino to export this aluminium.

I further explained that in order for the Russian smelters to maintain their production the Trans World Group would have to supply many of the raw materials for the manufacture of aluminium to the smelters. We wished to use the port as the point of entry for these raw materials. This would mean installing the equipment for handling these imports in the port and the use of a dedicated berth to handle these deliveries.

First, I needed to know the draught of the berths which we might be able to use as we intended to use around 25,000 deadweight ton vessels for the delivery of the alumina from Australia. This would mean that we would require a minimum of 10 meters draught alongside the quay. I was told that there was at least 12 meters mean draught so that there should be no problem. I then asked about ice and the free access to the port. I was told that the pack ice didn't reach Vanino; its lowest reach was about forty miles north nearer to Sakhalin There was some ice in the winter but the port undertook to keep the access clear with its ice breakers. However it would be useful to use at least Ice Class III vessels for the carriage to get full insurance protection.

An Ice Class vessel is constructed somewhat differently than normal ships. The ribs (the 'scantlings') of the vessel which extend from the keel (the bottom midline of the ship) to the gunwales (the handrails around the ship) have to be closer together to resist the pressure of the ice on the hull. The bolts ('pintles') which attach the rudder to its mounting plate have to be stronger, and the thickness of the steel of the hull has to be more than in non-ice class vessels. Even if there are ice breakers which clear a path into the port the period of immobility of the vessel at the berth during loading or discharging allows ice to form around the waterline of the vessel. This cannot be cleared by an icebreaker so an ability to move through ice is required in berths which freeze. I needed to know whether Ice Class III would suffice. I was assured that an Ice Class III would have no problem.

I knew there were enough Russian ice-class ships available, owned by Sakhalin Shipping (SASCO) of Kholmsk and Far Eastern Shipping (FESCO) of Vladivostok that we should have no problem chartering (renting) vessels for our needs. That covered many of my shipping questions. I then needed to know if the port had sufficient forklift trucks to discharge the railcars delivering primary aluminium to the port.

The aluminium would come from the smelters in several forms. Some were ingots, some were billets, some were sows and a large number were delivered as T-bars for the Japanese re-rolling mills. I needed to know if the port was equipped to handle these. If not I was perfectly happy to deliver the needed forklifts or portable cranes but the port assured me this was unnecessary as they had everything we needed. They assured me they could also handle the small "chushkis" and wire rod in coil. They had experience with them all. This was marvellous. There seemed to be no impediment to our starting immediately.

I said that this was wonderful and that, perhaps, we could agree to start the export of the aluminium as quickly as possible. I would then come and present my ideas about the bulk delivery of alumina once I had studied the contours and dimensions of the berth we were to be allocated. We could study them together and work out a suitable plan.

It was their turn to speak. They gave me a short history of the port and its desire to regain the volumes it had achieved previously and to develop new products for its cargo mix. The Vanino Economic and Transport Association ('VETA') had been formed for this and was anxious to attract as much appropriate business to the port as it could. They listed the many advantages of the port; in fact the list was almost the same as my list which I had shown to David Reuben.

They wanted to know a little more about our company and who was behind it. They needed to know that the company was financially stable and that they could count on it to perform its tasks and duties. Niksa spoke to explain a little about the Moscow operation and the Russian partners. I spoke about the organisation in London and Monaco. They were very interested and asked several questions. Valery Savinov asked if we had any brochures of our company; perhaps a calendar or pens or souvenirs. I apologised for not having anything like that with me. They then asked if I had any pictures of our operation or top management. I looked in my attaché case for anything and found a small 3 x 5 sepia print. I had picked up a number of the sepia prints for my son James for a project he was working on in school about American Indians (or Native Americans to be correct) One of the prints was still in my case. I thought, "What the hell, why not?" I took out the sepia print of Red Cloud, principal chief of the Oglala Sioux and said "Here's our chief".

The Russians looked at the print. They turned and looked at each other and then burst out laughing. They called in some people from the adjoining room and told them that this was the chief who was coming to Vanino to bring them aluminium. Niksa was howling as well but looking a bit nervous. Shengelia came over around the table, shook my hand, and said this was a negotiation he would never forget. No one had ever made such a joke in the serious business of arranging things at the port. He asked if he could keep the picture and I said "Of course". It was posted on the main bulletin board of the port's office with a note in Russian "David Reuben, Chief of Trans World". It may still be there. I did not include this in my report to David on my return.

They said that they were willing to go along with this idea but would have to check with the authorities and the Russian rail operators in Komsomolsk-na-Amur where the BAM offices could be found. However, they could agree in principle. They suggested we write up a Protocol of our meeting. They asked if we were pressing for exclusivity for our aluminium. I said that this hadn't been discussed. I asked if everyone asked for exclusivity. They told me that many visitors had asked for exclusivity in their Protocol. I asked if they often granted this exclusivity. They told me they were happy to. I pointed out that competing exclusivities would effectively be an oxymoron but I was assured that the Russians were sure that at least 90% of their visitors would never be back to the port anyway so it did no harm. I warned them that I would be coming back on a regular basis and that we were very serious.

The port had indicated that if we were bringing through the type of tonnages we said we were we could work out a rate which would include the unloading of the rail cars, the storage in the port and the loading of the vessel for 339 roubles per metric ton, plus 23 roubles for ice dues, 25 roubles for forwarding services and 1,500 roubles for each marshalling and removing of trucks. These, and some other charges, were the standard charges in every Russian Port. In addition we would pay an additional US $5.00 per ton to the port for their assistance in setting this up and administering the project. That meant, at the current rate of the rouble a net figure of around US $8.00 per metric ton all in. I said that we would ship, initially 5,000 metric tons per month of aluminium. They agreed to put all this into a protocol which they would send us and we would sign.

They then asked when we thought we would start. I said we were happy to start immediately with a test month's shipment of 5,000 metric tons. We would pay for 5,000 metric tons a month even if we shipped less than 5,000 metric tons unless the problems which impeded us were caused by events at the port (_force majeure_). We agreed that while all the paperwork was being prepared we would start shipping aluminium to show that the system worked. Niksa and I would return to sign the papers and we would put the export transport side in motion. Later we would discuss the import of alumina.

I then took out US $40,000 in cash and put it on the table in front of Mr. Shengelia. I told him that this was the $8.00 a ton for the first 5,000 tons that month. We would pay the port each month in advance. This would serve to show our good faith in the port and to assist them in mobilising quickly. There was a sharp intake of breath and a straightening of shoulders. They knew we were serious and that we were committed to the business. I explained that developing the export-import port in the Russian Far East was critical to Russia's economic advance and that we were ready to do our part. I explained that this was a ham and egg kind of business. In this type of interaction the chicken is 'involved' but the pig is 'committed'. We paid our money up front; we were committed.

I think this might have lost something in the translation but they knew we wanted to get things moving as soon as we both could. We then broke off the meeting and had a drink of tea. We chatted a bit and we explained that we would need to use a local agent at the port and would have to hire staff there. We would be happy to be guided in this by the Mr. Shengelia. As it happened he had a number of people whom he thought would be appropriate and Mr. Savinov had a part interest in a local port agency. This agency was in partnership with a firm of Croatians based in Vienna who were friends and contacts of Niksa who operated in ports throughout Russia. It was very good news indeed.

We were taken on a small tour of the administration building and introduced to some of the port staff, including the key transport person of the port and the port agents, Valentina Tsareva. Valentina would be a great asset to us over the years and worked very hard to make the various parts of our business mesh with the interests of the port.

I then told Niksa that it would be good to have a private discussion with Mr, Shengelia about our future co-operation. We moved together to his office and we explained that we were really serious about this business and valued his continued goodwill and supervision of the business as we could not be there all the time. If everything worked out we would start up a new, private, company Trans-Vanino Corporation in which he would have a direct stake as its Chairman. He could see we were serious and we were also serious about Trans-Vanino. Niksa then left the room and I explained that the chairmanship of Trans-Vanino would not be a charity and that we expected to reward our friends with a profit share of the business. I handed over US$10,000 as a down payment on the profit shares we would be dividing and promised the equivalent each month. He seemed satisfied. My initial work with the port was done.

We thanked the port officials for meeting with us and said we would be in immediate touch about the Protocol and the date for the first delivery of the first aluminium. In the meantime I would also prepare an outline of how I would suggest we created a facility for the import of alumina. We were driven back to the airport and took the last flight back to Khabarovsk where we stayed overnight at the

Intourist Hotel there, right on the Amur River. We were very pleased with our negotiation.

Niksa called his office and made arrangements for our flight back to Moscow the following morning and a connection for me from Moscow to London. We flew back to Moscow and went to the office. I met some more of the staff and waited for the London office to open. I was able to speak with David Reuben. I explained that the port was perfect. It had everything we would need and was ready to handle the aluminium exports. I told him that we had agreed US $8.00 all in, including the usual Russian charges. He asked when he could begin to ship. I told him he could ship "Today". Everything was ready. I had prepaid for 5,000 tons and they were ready to receive the aluminium. They would draw up the final protocol for Niksa to sign soon but the first 5,000 tons were all arranged. I explained about the parallel arrangement with Shengelia and this was approved. David was happy with this as it locked him into the system.

I said I was returning to London that day and would drop in the next day at the Trans World offices to answer any questions. If there was anything else he wanted me to do; like prepare the import facility drawings and suggestions, I should be happy to discuss this with him. He said I should come in.

I thought I had performed my task there and prepared the groundwork for a longer relationship between Trans World and Vanino. I had had a good relationship with Niksa; we worked well together. At that point I was not working for Trans World; I was not paid for my work but had agreed to go out the see what could be done. It remained to be seen if I would continue. My company, International Bulk Trade ('IBT'), continued to operate ships into Africa and I thought that I might be able to add Russia to our area of expertise using the Trans World connection. Trans World was essentially a 'screen trader' at that time. It had been in the London Metal Exchange ring earlier, as 'Landal' but were now engaged in the buying and selling of metals on the LME. They used the international storage and metal depot company Steinweg to do most of their shipping for them but had a specialist in the office to monitor the dealings with Steinweg and to deal with the bills of lading. I thought that with our expertise in shipping and handling we could assist Trans World to be a company which would become a 'physical trader'. That is a company which owned physical metal and could deliver it to the buyers with an entirely 'in-house' operation. This is what I had in mind when I went to see David at the Trans World office the next day.

I had no intention of working for Trans World as an employee. I have a character fault, I am told, which prevents me from being a good employee. I don't like taking instructions or orders. I like to make my own decisions on the basis of my experience. I had run my own business since 1975 relatively successfully and was not really prepared to join up in anyone else's business. However, this was a very good business with which I could associate myself. It had a broad horizon of opportunity.

When I went to the Trans World office and met with David I shared with him my experiences in Vanino and discussed the opportunities which this connection opened for delivering metals from the Russian Far East. David asked if I would be willing to continue to assist the company in expanding its transport and logistics operations in Russia. I said it would be an honour. We agreed that Trans World would pay a regular retainer to IBT for our services and that I would spend a lot of my time in promoting the Trans World business.

If we were able to build a proper import facility in Vanino IBT would take a small percentage of the ownership of the facility. As for the shipping, IBT would assist Trans World in the shipping. IBT would not take a fee for the shipping from Trans World but would seek the lowest price in the market. IBT would take a commission from the ship owners of 1.5% of the charter hire as its 'address commission'. Normally a ship owner allocates a maximum of 5% of the hire of the vessel as an 'address commission' for the brokers and charterers to share. In most cases the broker takes 1.5% and the others, if any, take a 1.5% share. This is not paid by Trans World; it is paid by the owners. We were providing a shipping service to Trans World at cost to them. It seemed to me that if Trans World were shipping millions of tons this would be a profitable business for IBT to undertake I explained this and David agreed. From then on I spent most of my time in promoting Trans World business.

CHAPTER FOUR

It is not really possible to understand the many and profound changes taking place in Russia after the fall of the Soviet Union from the perspective of the changes in one industry, however important. There were major political, economic and social changes taking place at breathtaking speed and the political structures and organisations of the Soviet Union were incapable of dealing with them effectively. The new system had to be invented or adapted by a political class which had never had to deal with these problems in such a direct way before. The Soviet leaders were never too sure of whom their friends were, but they were pretty certain about their enemies.

These enemies did not suddenly have a change of heart and welcome the Russians into the embrace of comradeship with open arms and packages of assistance. The U.S. and the Western European countries maintained a cautious distance, waiting to see how the new political structures would develop. Russia's most immediate neighbours, those who had been part of the Warsaw Pact, were nervously testing their degrees of freedom from the Soviet embrace. The invasions by Soviet tanks of the East Germans in 1953, the Hungarians in 1956, the Czechs in 1968 and the long history of Polish – Soviet conflict were too recent for these countries to forget. As a Russian colonel described it to me later "It wasn't just the Europeans who were getting uppity. Even the 'black asses' of the Caucasus thought they could throw us out without our getting even."

The third largest army in the world, the East German, was out of business. Massive quantities of East German (e.g. ex-Russian) military supplies were being offered at cut prices to the world as the re-unifying German state moved to change over to NATO equipment. One of the Soviet Union's major industries, the arms industry, had the bottom fall out of its market. This was coupled with the enforced withdrawal of Soviet forces stationed in bases across Eastern and Central Europe. The Warsaw Pact disappeared; the COMECON disappeared and there was not enough money in the reserves to keep paying, unilaterally, the costs of keeping Russian troops outside of Russia.

The soldiers were never paid much to begin with but the fall of the Soviet Union meant that they had very little indeed. These soldiers sold, with the connivance of their commanding officers, anything that wasn't nailed down. They sold it for food and they sold it for trophies that they would carry home as they were demobilised. Most importantly there was no place in the physical Russian military establishment where these troops could be stationed. There were not enough bases inside Russia where the returning troops could be housed. There were no jobs for thousands of trained officers and NCOs. The offset costs for the Soviet Occupation paid by their former 'satellites' were no longer forthcoming. There were too many mouths to feed and too few bases in which they could be sheltered. No one was sure what to do but everyone recognised the danger of a disgruntled army full of people with grievances and with nothing to do.

The Soviet Union's power was its armed forces and its ability to destroy substantial parts of the world with its nuclear weapons. It was a powerful military presence and, within the constraints of the Cold War, able to exert its influence across the globe. As an industrial power, however, it was a dwarf. It could barely feed itself as harvest after harvest failed. It was a major importer of grain. Its heavy industries produced copious quantities of capital goods but very few commercially successful consumer goods. There was no realistic way in which Russian products could compete with the factories of Czechoslovakia or East Germany, let alone West Germany, France or Great Britain for a place in the world market. The years of pretence of communist self-sufficiency were exposed to a real market place.

It was explained to me by the Stalin story. Stalin was visiting a collective farm and saw a peasant sitting on a tractor. Stalin asked "Tell me comrade, how big was the potato harvest this year?" The peasant hesitated and said "Well Comrade Stalin if you placed one potato on top of the other they would reach to the feet of God." Stalin frowned and said "But comrade, you know there is no God." And the peasant replied "And you know there were no potatoes."

The Russian authorities had now to admit what the Soviet authorities had swept under the rug, there were shortages and inefficiencies. Equally as important the Soviet planners had deliberately decentralised the integration of the productive processes. Raw materials and semi-finished goods had to be transported vast distances to the place where they would finally be assembled into finished goods. Some of this was for strategic reasons (protecting against foreign attacks); some for political reasons (spreading the jobs around the several republics); and some because of sheer ineptitude.

Whatever the reason, to modernise the economy of a nation the size of Russia required massive capital inputs; inputs the Russians didn't have.

The political system was the very opposite of the economic system. It was highly centralised and dominated by the Communist Party. The ascension of Gorbachev to become the General Secretary of the Party in March 1985 marked a turning-point in Soviet history. He later became head of state in 1990 and lasted in that position until 1991. He introduced the concepts of glasnost ("openness"), perestroika ("restructuring"), demokratizatsiya ("democratization"), and uskoreniye ("acceleration" of economic development) at the 27th Congress of the CPSU in February 1986. These were most successful in the public relations field and had less effect in actually promoting change. People were disappointed that changes were so slow in coming. The best popular distinction was the question "What is the difference between "demokrasiya" (democracy) and "demokratizatsiya (democratization)?" The same as between "kanal" (sewer) and "kanalizatsiya" (the stuff that flows down a sewer)".

Gorbachev ultimately failed and was forced to hold an election. This pitted Gorbachev's candidate, Nikolai Ryzhkov, against Boris Nikolayevich Yeltsin who was elected president of Russia with 57% of the vote on 12 June 1991. On 18 August 1991, an attempted coup was made against Gorbachev by the leadership of the KGB and other hardliners who feared perestroika and liberalisation. The coup makers held Gorbachev in the Crimea while Yeltsin raced to the White House to defy the coup. There Yeltsin, standing atop a tank, made a speech which rallied the people against a return to the Communist orthodoxies. He was aided by the steadfastness of Gen. Yevgeny Shaposhnikov, the Minister of Defence who refused to participate in the coup.

Gorbachev returned to his post as General Secretary of the Communist Party but gradually lost power, bit by bit, to the forces of change represented by Yeltsin. On 6 November 1991, Yeltsin issued a decree banning the Communist Party throughout Russia. Gorbachev was out of a job and the responsibility of turning Russia into a modern state was taken on by Yeltsin and his associates. The modernisation of Russia, although prompted by Gorbachev, was largely achieved on Yeltsin's watch.

The challenge of developing this new Russia can be seen from several different vantage points, all of which contributed to the change.

The most important part of this process was the political change which led from Gorbachev to Yeltsin and then to Putin and the continuing role of the KGB and the Chekists in this development. A second, and related, aspect was the creation and rise of the new Russian businessmen; the oligarchs to facilitate this process. The third important aspect was the rise of successful, and tolerated, organised criminal gangs which operated key aspects of the change. Finally, there were the related but often frustrated efforts to control these processes under the continuous investigations and aborted prosecutions of Russian and international law enforcement officers seeking to enforce the rule of law.

I was very lucky to have had the opportunity to be an observer of these developments from a close vantage point at several levels. By chance I had several advantages to understanding what was going on. When I was working for the UAW International Affairs Department in Washington D.C. in the mid-1960s our office was directly across 16th Street from the Russian Embassy. My boss, Victor Reuther, was engaged in an extended dialogue with the Russians, especially its Labour Attaché and Harry Gevournian, the U.S. correspondent for Trud (the labour newspaper). Victor Reuther and his brother Walter had been sent by Ford Motors to help set up the new auto plant in Gorky (Nizhny Novgorod) in the early 1930s. They both worked there and learned a great deal about Russia and the Russians. Despite their strong anti-communism (Walter threw the Communists out of the CIO in 1949) they maintained their interest in Russia. They were particularly interested the development of the Russian labour movement. Victor had been the CIO representative in Paris after the war when the split in the World Federation of Trades unions (WFTU) took place. The fight for dominance between the free trades unions of the newly formed International Confederation of Free Trades Unions (ICFTU) and the communist unions of the WFTU was a major battlefield in the Cold War. It was through the international labour movement that I first became acquainted with the Soviets.

Most people have no idea about the importance of the international labour movements in the history of the Cold War. One of the most important of the international non-governmental voluntary organisations has been the international trades union movement. Except for the transnational corporation there has been no international organisation which has been more active or played such an important role in international relations than the international labour movement. This has not been solely a result of the vitality of the union organisations or their broad international perspectives. Rather it is because throughout the history of this movement, governments and political parties have used the international labour movement as one of the principal vehicles for their covert interactions with political parties and governments in foreign nations. The international trades union movement has been, and continues to be, a vital tool of governments in the shaping of the political destinies of foreign political parties and states and is an important part of most nations' foreign policy system.

The principal reason behind the importance of the trades union movement in the political process has been the weakness of political parties. In most nations except for the communist parties of Eastern Europe political parties were not strong. They frequently lacked funds, manpower and organisation. They were capable of generating interest and support from their constituencies during the electoral campaigns but soon after, their continuity and direction was left in the hands of their parliamentary parties. The maintenance of their continued interaction with their membership was most often left to the activities of the voluntary organisations with whom they are associated. These voluntary organisations (trades unions, corporate groups, civic associations or religious groups) maintain the continuity of contact at national level between the members and the parties between elections.

Because of this close relationship between the political parties and the trades union movement, the work of the national unions has been almost exclusively political. Trades union leadership at the national level has been deeply involved in sustained interaction with the processes and offices of government. There has been a flow of trades union leaders away from-the unions into high political posts, especially when their party has assumed the responsibility of office. It is precisely because the trades unionism practised by the unions is so intimately involved with the political forces of the state that there has been such an interest in the growth of international trades unionism. The strategic role of the trades union movement within the political and economic life of the nation has proved to be a tempting target for outside interests seeking to intervene in or influence the party and state with whom the national union interacts. There are few nations which have not sought to influence the policies of their neighbours through the labour movement and still fewer which have not feared the effects of such intervention in their own affairs.

In addition to the political links which exist between trades unions and parties, there are other compelling reasons for a nation to use the vehicle of trades union intervention as a method of extending its outreach. In most nations of the world there are trades unionists active, outside their trades union role, in the conduct of private and public business as workers or employees. There is probably no better source of commercial intelligence than the workers employed in the plants and offices of the company. The trades unions have legitimate 'need to know' vital information such as sales, markets, suppliers, types of products, production processes and similar matters often regarded as confidential by management. With the growth of increased participation by the representatives of the workforce in the management of commercial enterprises, this problem has become more acute. Access to this fund of critical knowledge by external powers can often be crucial in economic, political and military planning.

Access to trades unionists at shop floor level, in industry and in governmental agencies, can often provide a form of insurance for those seeking to alter the system in which these unionists operate. Throughout the industries and government departments of the world there exist 'sleepers'; agents waiting to carry out vital tasks in the event of conflict. These sleepers and their contacts stand ready to disrupt war supplies, halt energy production, cut transport and communication links and generally assist in disrupting the defence apparatus.

It is hardly surprising then that the subject of international trades union activity has been a matter of active concern for the intelligence and security arms of national governments. There is probably no area of concern, outside of military intelligence, which is more vital to the security of a nation than the activities within and through the international trades union movements. Importantly, the very obscurity in which this international union interchange takes place makes it more attractive to governments. For a very long time, and most vitally since 1948, the international trades union movement has been the arena of the most open Cold War struggles. First in Europe and later in the Third World, this competition and conflict between the Cold War protagonists has not diminished despite moves towards 'detente' in other spheres. The conduct of national foreign policy through the medium of the international trades union movement has written many chapters in modern political history. It is hard to think of a major change of government, especially in the Third World, in recent years in which the activities of the trades union movement in those nations and internationally did not play a significant role.[vii]

It was in my role as a trades unionist that I became acquainted with several Russians engaged in the same business. I met them at international meetings and on the ground in several countries in Latin America and Africa. The UAW was opposed to the use of the AFL-CIO as an agency of the U.S. government dispensing government money around the world in the name of U.S. workers. We fought against their policies; and especially the virulent anti-communist rantings of Jay Lovestone, formerly Secretary-General of the U.S. Communist Party and then head of Foreign Relations for the AFL-CO. This was one of the key reasons for the UAW disaffiliation from the AFL-CIO in 1968. The Reuthers were sure that working in partnership with anti-labour multinational employers in Latin America was the not the proper role for the US labour movement.

I was speaking at a conference in Boulder, Colorado and flew back to Washington on the same plane as two Soviet representatives. We had a nice chat on the flight back. The next week I was asked if I'd like to go to lunch and I agreed to meet them at a restaurant nearby. I met with the attaché I had flown with and a new man whom I had never seen. It was strange. The new man asked if I wouldn't mind conducting our lunch discussion in German as his German was better than his English. I asked the attaché, Isakov, if he spoke German but he said that he didn't. The other man, Popov, said never mind we'd talk in German and he would translate in Russian for Isakov. After some pleasantries Popov suggested that I might want to brief him periodically on the political developments in the U.S. labour movements. He then asked what I was doing in Czechoslovakia with the Czech metalworkers. I had a great deal of trouble remembering what I was doing with the Czechs so I couldn't answer his question. We walked back together to the Embassy and I crossed the street to our office. Popov said he would invite me to lunch again soon as we could discuss this further

By chance I was having lunch a few days later with some friends from the CIA at the Cosmos Club and I mentioned the fairly crude attempt to recruit me. They told me not to be concerned because the

FBI was getting ready to PNG Popov from the U.S. for recruiting some sergeant in Virginia. A few days later he was put on a plane and was gone. I joked about this with Harry from Trud and he said these things happen. I had some better relations with some more adept Russians at the UN where I was consulting with the UN Special Committee on Apartheid. In this we had some shared objectives. Oliver Tambo was in New York for the Banks Campaign and he introduced me to some UN Russians with whom I kept in contact. I met some of these Russians again in Lusaka a few years later when I was visiting to deliver a Varitype machine and some printing equipment to ZAPU. Dumiso Dabengwa introduced me to some of the Russians operating out of the embassy and was surprised to find that I knew two of them already. They were intelligent and knowledgeable observers.

Over the years I occasionally kept in touch with them to share information that was of interest. They sometimes told me what I wanted to know and I sometimes told them. It was not critical information but interesting to us both. In the arena of political intelligence there are two major and often unrelated lines of activity, overt and covert. The first represents a much more academic approach, dealing with primarily open source materials. The second relates to information received from humans "humint" in your employ or from whom you have stolen the information or electronic intercepts "elint" which relates to intercepting messages on the phone, telex, fax, email or satellites. The covert side is a very different business which involves spies, counterspies and a variety of spooky equipment. I have never had any contact with the covert business. If you ever have the opportunity to have lunch at the CIA headquarters in Langley you will find a wall in the cafeteria dividing overt from covert employees. The division of labour is taken seriously. In the "Aquarium" (the GRU headquarters) outside Moscow near the ring road by the airport I am told they have separate dining areas for regular Army, overt and covert employees.

My job at the UAW consisted primarily of reading large quantities of newspaper, magazines, labour publications and economic analyses and briefing Victor Reuther on what I found. In the campaign to unionise Foster Wheeler, Victor had one of his eyes blown out by a shotgun in an assassination attempt and he could read only with difficulty. I was his 'reader'. I had access to all sorts of publications, in many languages, and I read and absorbed them so that I could brief

Victor when he needed information. It was a graduate student's dream job. I have very poor handwriting skills. In fact I can't read my own handwriting very well at all. That meant that throughout my life I have had to memorise everything. This was a habit I brought to my job. I had vast amounts of current information from all over the world and had been trained in my graduate studies in international politics to be able to analyse this information and to see, however imperfectly, how the isolated bits of information fit into a pattern.

This has been very useful to me over the years. Because of my collection of information I have been useful to those who have some use for the information. None of this information I have is derived from any 'operations' by any government or agency. I have no contact with any operational work nor am I bound by any oaths of secrecy to anyone, except for friends. I do know a lot of people in the public and private intelligence fields because they often speak to me asking me for information. I sometimes write up reports on various subjects or people and bill them for my information. Most of the time I am happy to tell them what they want to know in exchange for information about something they know and I don't. I am very curious and enjoy learning things. Sometimes I am told lies but that is often as interesting as the truth. I make an effort to always tell the truth, or as close to the truth as I can without imperilling those who told me the information.

So, when I joined up with Trans World to help create the physical trading system in aluminium in Russia I already knew several of the people engaged in the different levels of the political process. They knew they could ask me about what was happening and I knew I could be informed, however indirectly, about how they wished the outcomes would be achieved. It was interesting, illuminating and much safer than trying to operate on my own in such an unusual period of political flux. I was fortunate in my endeavours as I had no ideology to promote or defend; I had no major stake in the financial success of the ventures as I was not trading in any of the products; and I was foolishly romantic enough to believe that I might be of help in making a better life for the poor, suffering, people of Russia.

Because of my connections I was able to communicate with Russians in the government, the Organs, among the oligarchs, with the several 'Mafias' and with the prosecutors in addition to my logistical

FREE FOR ALL

and transport work with the international companies like Trans World. In short, I was a 'participant observer' in the system.

It is probably best to describe, in general, what was happening in the political and business environment. When I first went to Russia I found that the communist system had collapsed; the whole command economy had disappeared virtually overnight. Factories existed but they had no idea how to get raw materials or to sell or transport their production or how to pay their workers. They had no bank accounts, no savings and no markets. The railroads had no idea how to buy coal or electricity nor was there anyone to buy from. No one knew how to pay a wage or provide food and medical assistance to the population. The notion of price or supply and demand, which is the root of the capitalist system, was missing from the equation.

Everything was tried; barter, stealing and borrowing were the main systems. There was no law. There was no 'proper way'. There were no rules

The remnants of the 'old order', the KGB, the GRU and the military realised that something drastic had to be done and done quickly. The First Chief Directorate of the KGB and the Sixth Directorate had been concerned about the potential political and economic collapse of the USSR for a long time. Long before the August 1991 attempted coup against Gorbachev the handwriting was on the wall. The massive state trading corporations were dissolved. The planners at Gosplan were fired, en masse, from their positions. The First Directorate (INU - Innostrannoye Upravleniey, First Chief Directorate - Foreign) which was responsible for foreign intelligence collection, analysis, offensive counterintelligence, and active measures had been assembling a large cache of hard currency in banks outside Russia. They, and the Sixth Department (which dealt with international economic programs) knew that the chaos which was about to overwhelm Russia in the wake of the political crises would leave Russia without an economic structure which could perform the tasks needed by the Russian State.

From 1988, the KGB intelligence service focused primarily on following domestic developments in the Soviet Union rather than foreign espionage. Also, it was "preparing" for future market reforms in the country. The number one priority of any KGB officer was to work on establishing new businesses or penetrating existing businesses, including the banks.

69

When Boris Yeltsin abolished the Communist Party's monopoly of power, the KGB rushed in to fill the political void as well. Prior to the 1990 elections for the Congresses of People's Deputies in Russia and the other Soviet republics, the KGB set up a special task force to organize and manipulate the coming electoral processes. It held political organization training courses for favoured candidates, arming them with privileged information about their constituents' problems, needs and desires. Admitted KGB officers, some 2,758 in all, ran in races for local, regional and federal legislatures across the USSR; 86% won in the first round, according to an internal KGB newsletter.

The trends were similar in Russia's business community. It was the KGB and the Komsomol that established the first stock and commodities exchanges, "private" banks, and trading houses through which the Soviets' strategic stockpiles of minerals, metals, fuel and other wealth could be sold. The West would not allow the Soviets to dump these stockpiles of raw materials and finished goods on the open market for fear of depressing world prices, so the KGB took the alternative route of selling these through organized criminal channels, to get the hard currency Moscow desperately needed.

These networks were facilitated by the strategic placement of support personnel abroad. KGB Chairman Vladimir Kryuchkov's son, as station chief in Switzerland, was implicated by a parliamentary commission in a scam to bank fortunes in hard currency for the KGB and Communist Party leaders and their families. The son of former Soviet Prime Minister Valentin Pavlov, who worked in a Luxembourg bank, was implicated in the same scandal. Even as the Russian government went through the motions of tracking down such monies, foreign intelligence chief Yevgeny Primakov blocked all parliamentary investigations from looking further, and the matter was forgotten.

By 1990 Russia stood in a very precarious position. It had vast wealth in terms of resources but no way to trade them; a mighty army but an army that was retreating from Eastern Europe without a shot being fired; a banking system with no liquidity as all funds were held in Moscow and there were no regional banks. There was a gold rouble trading at $1.20 to the U.S. dollar and a free rouble trading at $0.66. Behind all of this was a nervous and hostile West, especially the glavni vrag, the "main enemy" the U.S., who would certainly prevent Russia from dumping its products on the world market and who was refusing realistic credits to Russia. In addition, the break-up of the USSR into

Russia and the CIS left many of Russia's ports in the hands of local nationalists in Lithuania, Estonia and Latvia which restricted Russian access to the markets.

There were several major crises with which the Russians had to deal all at once. The first was food. There was little food in Russia at the best of times, exacerbated by the problems of logistics and supply. Under the Soviet system the factory or place of work in rural Russia often offered most of the social services provided by the State, including food. With the end of the Soviet system these factories or places of work had no ability to fulfil these tasks using their own resources. Because their factories operated under the strictures of the command economy there were no profits, no accumulated savings or other funds upon which they could draw. They couldn't buy raw materials; they couldn't pay for utilities or services; and they had no reachable market for their goods. In the giant aluminium plants there was no way to pay for the alumina (which was derived from bauxite imports from Guinea); no way to pay for electricity; and no way to pay wages and no way to get the finished aluminium to market.

Equally there was no way to price these internal transactions as there never was anything other than notional prices for transport, notional prices for raw materials and notional prices for finished products. There was no money in the system; only a notional internal clearing mechanisms.

The leaders of the First, Fifth and Sixth Directorates of the KGB developed a two pronged plan. The first part of the plan included inviting in foreign capitalists to prepay the expenses of the factories to get production moving. These capitalists would pay for raw materials, pay for transport and earn the right to sell the completed goods on the world market. They would pay, in addition, a fee or 'toll' to the factory for producing the goods. This system of tolling would only work if there were an internal currency which could be used to start the payment system and establish prices. There was no state mechanism capable of handling this. So, the planners decided on an ambitious, if risky, system. They would make an alliance with the small and disorganised criminal groups in Russia to develop a parallel system to the government's official currency business. They opened up the floodgates on a massive haemorrhage of roubles onto the world markets to get hard currency and to prime the rouble pump inside Russia.

In early 1990 trainloads and truckloads of roubles left Russia, escorted by KGB police guards, for Western Europe. In Italy the Mafia, the Camorra and the 'Nhdragheta purchased millions of dollars worth of roubles from their illicit profits. Russia became the greatest laundry for money that was ever known. Bankers in the West were offered letters of credit in roubles with a Russian guarantee that these could be brought back into Russia. Santo Pasquale Morabito, a notorious Italian drug dealer and launderer for Pablo Escobar of Colombia swapped US$4.6 billion for 70 billion roubles (or less than half the official rate). The main Sicilian outlets were Ciccio Madonia's family in Palermo and Nitto Santapaola's in Catania. Everyone got into the act. A Sicilian Castellamarese capo called Tommy Marsala bought half a billion roubles for the Lebanese Druse leader Walid Jumblatt, who used them to buy small arms and rockets from Russia.

The money continued to flow out of Russia. Ordinary roubles became 'gold roubles' when they passed the border. These were gold roubles- because they were backed by gold held in the Russian Treasury. Between 1990 and 1992 the Russian gold reserves had mysteriously disappeared. When Gregori Yavlinsky, the reformer, went to the September 1992 G-7 meeting in Bangkok he reported that of the 2,000 tons of gold in the Russian reserve only 240 tons were left. In November even these were gone. In a little over a year over US$22 billion in gold left Russia at a heavy discount to cover the massive rouble river costs. Europe was full of stories of this group or that offering to place $140 million with one bank or the other. What did happen is that most of this money, in roubles, returned to Moscow; albeit at a discounted rate.

When this money returned to Moscow it had to be used and directed for the urgent projects decided upon by the leaders. The KGB and its allies, under Silayev, Kryuchkov, Kasbulatov and Soskavets set up a system in which loyal and trusted members of the Komsomol system and friendly businessmen could form their own banks - Russian banks. Men like Khodorkovsky, Aven, Fridman and others were chosen from the ranks of the Komsomol and set up in the money business. They used the banks to channel the returning Mafia money into long-term businesses. With few exceptions, those chosen for this were all Jews. When Western pioneers like Marc Rich, David Reuben, Gerry Lennard or Alan Cligman agreed to work within this system by creating the 'tolling' business, they were given a kick start of roubles to help pay for the initial costs of the tolling system, They, too, were mainly Jews, albeit foreign Jews.

Between these two groups there was another layer of 'facilitators'; people who knew the parallel system. They set up the deals. They traded the hard earned cash from commodities like aluminium into cigarettes and vodka which could be brought back into Russia and sold for cash, providing liquidity to the system. These facilitators were among the first private businessmen in Russia. They had ties to the organised criminal private sector which had access to the raw materials and the internal organizations which could deliver on the agreements made; the Izmailova (the late Anton Malevksy), Soltsnevo, Lyubarsky, Long Pond groups to name but a few. The facilitators included the Chernoy brothers (Mischa and Lev), Sam Kislin, and the 'institutionals' (those set up with institutional government support) Gregory Luchansky, Semyon Mogilevich or Vadim Rabinovich in the Ukraine. Most of these, too, were Jews. Without these men the Russification of Russia couldn't have taken place. They provided the only working capitalist system in Russia. Even in the far reaches of Siberia or the outposts of the Far East one could always find someone from that fraternity "bratsky krug" who could provide what was needed

As this worked and metals or oil were produced and sold, these companies retained a part of the hard currency earnings the foundations of Russian capitalism were laid. As these banks and investment trusts prospered, Russia became less and less dependent on the Mafia for its business. They also became less and less dependent on Western capitalists to introduce them to commodity trading. They brought the roubles home and, in the various stages of privatization, they invested these in Russian businesses. Quite often this privatization was a sham but that wasn't the point. The point was to bring the money home and take over the shares and the businesses.

One might well ask on what basis these 'oligarchs' were chosen. The main reason, in addition to their competence, is that they were mainly Jews or outsiders (Potanin's father was a trade official and he lived outside Russia for years). As Jews they were without a political base. No Russian member of the Duma would dare stand up to protect a rich Jew. These oligarchs were dependent on their KGB bosses for their security. Many of the cleverest Jews had already left. A familiar story was "How does a clever Russian Jew communicate with a stupid Russian Jew? By telephone, from New York".

A second aspect of this was that in virtually every major Soviet enterprise, at least in the metals sector, the second-in command in the enterprise was a Jew. The Russian Red General in charge of the plant was backed up by a Jewish number two who did the operational work. So, when it came to contacts with foreign businessmen, it was a Jewish plant number two talking to a foreign Jewish entrepreneur and handling the business operations with a Jewish 'deltsy' and with financial matters handled by a Jewish oligarch in the making. I can recall several meetings, involving Russians, Australians, Americans and Europeans in which the only common language was Yiddish.

The most successful element of change was the creation of banking organisations which could handle the new Russian international business. Menatep (Khodorkovsky's bank) was the vehicle through which almost all the transfers of serious money in and out of Russia took place from 1992 to 1998. When we started 'tolling' aluminium and others started tolling copper and nickel we did not send the proceeds of our sales back to Russia. On the advice of Russian Prime Minister Silayev, Deputy Prime Minister Oleg Soskovets, presidential aide Aleksandr Korzhakov and Speaker Ruslan Kasbulatov we were told to make all our payments to Menatep Bank. Sometimes it might be Menatep Cyprus, sometimes Menatep Gibraltar, Menatep Finance Geneva, Menatep Inc. New York, etc. When we sold the metals we had tolled a small fee was paid to the smelters. A payment was sent to them through their designated bank, often Citibank in NY. However, the bulk of the money was sent to Menatep marked "for onward transfer to "-.Company" or "- Account" at "-- Bank". We did not know the recipient at the end of the chain. It wasn't our business. We paid what we had agreed and that was all. Only Menatep know exactly to whom these payments were going after we deposited the funds. These were not trivial sums; our payments for aluminium alone often amounted to US$60 million a month. Menatep monitored the cash flow and directed the funds to the accounts of the highest powers in the land (the Presidency, the Government and the Chekists) that staffed the parallel infrastructure. Menatep had been set up by these people and Khodorkovsky was chosen to be at its head; not the other way round.

There was virtually no aspect of what Menatep was doing which wasn't controlled by, monitored by and directed by these same leaders. This included providing government-sanctioned services to organised crime. From its early days the young men at Menatep provided financial services to the Solntsevo, Lyubarsky, Uralmash and Izmailova families. Through his connections with Semyon Mogilevich, Menatep began moving currencies and investments to and through Hungary and then to the U.S. Menatep handled the foreign exchange business of Grigory Luchansky of Nordex and moved large sums into the U.S.

In addition to its foreign currency and money laundering business Menatep also provided investment services. In the submissions before a U.S. judge in the "Avisma Case" Menatep was said to be the perpetrator of a gigantic con in which tens of millions of dollars were diverted from the company. Khodorkovsky and fugitive banker Alexander Konenyikin started the Antigua-registered European Union Bank which was described in a House Banking and Financial Services Committee as a "KGB money-laundering operation with stolen funds that were passed through Khodorkovsky of Menatep Bank as a KGB-controlled front firm" According to the investigators the entire operation was coordinated at SVR headquarters and was personally supervised by Yeltsin confidante, Aleksandr Korzakov. Through Korzakhov and his friendships with Mikhail Stepashin and Yuri Primakov, Khodorkovsky was given access to the Bulgarian and the Hungarian services to replicate his work for them. The main person in charge of security operations in Khodorkovsky's companies was Mikhail Yosifovich Shestopalov former head of the Division for Combatting Thefts of Socialist Property and Speculation of the Ministry of Internal Affairs. The head of Menatep's and Yuko's information and analysis section was Karabinov, former head of the KGB Centre for Public Relations (the man who ran the "Miss KGB" contest).

The point of this is to make clear that virtually everything Khodorkovsky did was directed, supervised and monitored by the very people who ultimately attacked him. There were Chekists at every level of Menatep and Yukos. There were no mysteries. The politruks and the pakhans supervised everything. Everyone knew what was happening. It was quite public. Because of Menatep the international tolling companies had no direct ties with the invisible government, except when we had to provide credit cards to top key individuals. One might reflect that Vladimir Putin's first job when he left the KGB was to supervise metals sales for Sobchak in St. Petersburg. Our first contract to ship metals through St. Petersburg is signed on the bottom by Vladimir Putin.

The development of Menatep is a good example of how the Chekists ran the Russian transition. Khordokovsky was born into a relatively well-off Moscow Jewish family, He went to university in Moscow and stayed on to do an advanced degree in chemistry. He was very politically active since university days and was the Deputy Komsomolsk secretary for the Frunze District of Moscow. He got his start in business when Communist Party Deputy General Secretary Yegor Ligachev decided to encourage youth activists to enter business. A technology business centre was attached to each district in Moscow. In 1987, Khodorkovsky, was named the head of the centre in his home Frunze district. ("Menatep" is the acronym for Frunze's"Inter-Branch Centre for Scientific and Technological Programs" the local chapter). The Menatep Group evolved from these business activities, especially through the resale of computers, where profits were made capitalizing on the difference in price between domestic and foreign markets as well as the differential rates of exchange. The young men running Menatep formed allegiances with many of the fringe operating groups in Moscow then entering into the business of "trading" and provided the foreign currency exchange function to their businesses. In addition he was selected as the KGB conduit for external money placements. Soon they had enough working capital from these groups to start a bank. The bank was officially registered in 1988. Its patron in 1990-91 was former Russian Prime Minister Silayev. The bank's public offering in 1991 was the first since Bolshevik Revolution. The bank grew quickly after 1991 on currency speculation. This speculation put them in close relationships with many Russian entrepreneurs and politicians.

Menatep had ties to a wide range of Russian leaders, including Anatoly Chubais and Viktor Chernomyrdin, though the links appeared much stronger to the conservatives. The most important of these links was with former Deputy Prime Minister Oleg Soskovets, former presidential bodyguard Aleksandr Korzhakov, former Oil and Gas Minister Yuri Shafranik and former Supreme Soviet Speaker Ruslan Khasbulatov. Through these men the new metal magnates, oil magnates and gas magnates drifted towards Menatep as their bank. By 1995 Menatep had grown into the holding company, Rosprom, and acquired the majority assets of the second largest oil and gas company in Russia. Yukos.

This development of a system for moving goods and cash was very important for Trans World. TWG was very closely tied to the activities and ambitions of several Russian government officials, especially Oleg Soskovets and Sports Minister Shamil Tarpishchev (a close friend and schoolmate of Mischa Chernoy). Together these two guided the activities of TWG and assisted in providing access to metals and to the support of the Government. The assistant to Soskovets, Vladimir Lisin (now an oligarch in his own right as head of Novolipetsk Steel) went to work as assistant to Lev Chernoy. The assistant to Michael Cherny was Iskander Makhmudov (now the oligarch in charge of UGMK copper) and a valued business supporter of Nazarbayev of Kazahkstan. Lev and Mischa used to travel with Tewfik and Ruslan, two of Nazarbayev's bodyguards. Both Lev and Mischa were very much involved in the political scene in Russia.

Oleg Nikolaievich Soskovets has been First Deputy Chairman of the Council of Ministers; Chairman of the Executive Commission under the Council of Ministers; Chairman of the Export Control Commission of the Russian Federation; Chairman of the Interdepartmental Commission on military cooperation with foreign states; Co-chairman of the Staffing policy council under the Russian President. Soskovets' duties in the cabinet included overseeing the dividing up and selling off of Russia's huge aluminium industry. According to Itogi, (TV) Soskovets and former sports and tourism minister Shamil Tarpischev provided patronage to a western-based company named TransCIS Commodities.

The key role of Soskovets has been his chairmanship of Rosvooruzhenie (now Rosboronexport), the military-industrial complex. It was Rosvooruzhenie, which sold arms and equipment all over the world. During the period in which the KGB took an active role in setting up the banking structures and moving money out of the country using banks like Menatep, Soskovets acted for the GRU (the military intelligence) in supervising the 'privatisation' of the chain of companies (aluminium, steel, aircraft frames, alloys, copper, etc.) which comprised the supply system to the USSR war machine. He was an important ally.

It was Soskovets who found TWG rather than the other way round. He found them through Trans-Cis Commodities. The Chernoys (Mischa, Lev and David) and Anton Malefsky of the Izamailovo Gang were the original partners in Trans-CIS Commodities. This company specialised in iron and steel trading and some trading in wood products. It was close to the Izmailovo Mafia family and was an important link in bringing 'Yaponchik', Vyacheslav Ivankov to the U.S.

In 1990, David Reuben had virtually retired from business and spent most of his time playing golf. A family member, Alan Bekhor, had moved in as managing director of TWG, after the family had contributed some money to help bail out Trans World from its debts incurred during the collapse of the tin market and the downward spiral of the London property market. Simon Reuben had nothing to do with the metal trading business at all, except to borrow money to help prop up the failing property business.

At that point David met with some friends from Razno, and was introduced to Lev Chernoy. Lev told David that the Russians were privatising their metals business but had a serious problem. They had no access to the London Metal Exchange (LME) and no one would buy Russian metal FOB because they didn't believe that the goods would arrive. Also no one would issue documentary credits to the Russian exporters without performance guarantees which the Russians could not afford. David had been mentioned as someone who was a friend of Russia, who had (at that time through Landal) a seat on the LME. David knew that Marc Rich had also been approached to do something similar with oil and metals. David agreed to meet further with Lev and soon they agreed to work together. David went to Moscow a few times and met with Lev and his colleagues. He also met with Mischa and the others at Trans-Cis. David was told that he and Lev would do the aluminium business and Mischa would concentrate, with Sam Kislin, on the iron and steel business. For about eight months the two companies were kept separate. In late 1991-early 1992 the Chernoys became unofficial partners of TWG, e.g. no shares were ever transferred, and a banking system was set up in Monaco to supervise the transactions. The introductions, support and planning involved Soskovets and his friends.

Until mid-1992, when TWG agreed a joint business arrangement with my company, International Bulk Trade (IBT), the trading of aluminium by TWG was essentially screen trading. The aluminium was provided by the smelters under the tolling arrangements and the shipping was subcontracted to the LME warehouse operator, Steinweg in Holland. As soon as the aluminium reached the warehouse in Holland it was either put on LME warrant (the A7E quality) and thus marketable instantly or delivered into the warehouse for sale (A6, A5 alloys) where Western companies could buy them already in the West.

With the agreement with IBT it became possible to enter the physical trading of the metals. IBT arranged the chartering and operation of the ships; it arranged rail transport to and from the smelters, it opened ports in the Russian East for export to supply the Japanese market without the long distances from Europe. And it built an import facility in the East for Australian and Indian alumina. Until this point there was full co-operation between David and Lev. Mischa was always disgruntled and unhappy. By 1994 Lev and David bought Mischa out to keep him out of the business. By then they were investing in banks, stocks, warrants, etc. which Mischa neither understood nor was interested in. Mischa returned to Kislin and Trans-Cis.

Lev had always been operating in Russian politics. He had created a working relationship with Boris Berezovsky who was close to Tatiana, Yeltsin's daughter and with Voloshin, a prime figure in the presidential power establishment. Lev was involved in the acquisition of shares in the smelters. David concentrated on the aluminium trading business. It should be remembered that David spoke no Russian and only understood what was going on when someone translated and explained to him what was happening. As David has little patience or concentration he never let people finish their explanations so only ever got a sketchy idea of what was being said. His role in politics was marginal at best. David was happy to make money and to leave the rest to Lev.

There is a story told to me by Goran who was the interpreter at the meeting, from TWG which illustrates David's situational ethics and lack of interest in knowing why things happened. On a visit to Krasnoyarsk smelter in mid-1992 Lev, David, Tewfik and Ruslan met with Turaschev, the general director of the plant. Turaschev told them that Krasnoyarsk already had an exclusive arrangement with AIOC to do tolling and market their aluminium. On returning to the guest house Lev turned to Tewfik and Ruslan and told them to go to Turaschev's house and set fire to it. Then they would meet him again the next day. David asked what was going on. Lev explained and David said that this was not the right way to do things. Lev explained that this was customary in Russian business and not to worry. David thought about this and said, "Well, don't do it while I'm in the country".

This characterised many of the subsequent business crises in Russia. David did not want to know and was convinced that Mischa was, indeed, a bad guy but that Lev was not in the same kind of business as his brother and partners. By early 1994 it became clear to most of the people in the aluminium business that the Russians had acquired a lot of expertise in metals trading; had agglomerated large sums of cash; and that they were eager to dispose of their erstwhile Western partners and return the industry to Russian control. The wave of privatisation was in full flow and Western partners interfered with the politics of Russian political and economic horse trading. Moves were made to replicate the Russian experience in Kazakhstan and the Ukraine but they were short-lived and costly. Soon the Berezovskys, the Abramovichs and their ilk took over. They paid TWG for the business but they soon found they were left out in the cold and expendable. Only Mischa, who was able to put his own people (Deripaska, Makhmudov, etc.) in as oligarchs was able to keep a stake in the business.

That was the start; the background to the business.

CHAPTER FIVE

Soon after my return to London Trans-World signed an agreement with Bratsk Aluminium to start shipping primary aluminium to the port of Vanino for export. These shipments began but they were much slower to reach the port than expected. I went out to Vanino again to see about the delay and to supervise the loading of our first vessel carrying 5,200 tons of aluminium to Japan. The vessel loaded very efficiently and sailed the two-day trip to Japan. The export system was working well once the metal reached the port. I then investigated why the metal wasn't moving quickly down the BAM to Vanino.

I spent some time with the lady who ran the railroad terminus and discovered that there was a problem we hadn't reckoned with. As the metals were loaded into rail cars at Bratsk they were put onto a siding at the plant and attached to an assemblage of rail cars destined for the port. As each railcar carried as much as 45 to 50 tons of metal there were often only three or four cars completed each day. It took about four hours to process the paperwork for each car, delineating the amount, quality and batch numbers for the metals.

Each train had to be announced and accepted by the port. Sometimes the train was made up of railcars full of metals, mixed in with railcars full of wood products, coal and other goods. The port had to have space in the docks for each of these materials. As there was a lot of wood being transported from this region, this often caused delays as the port had no extra space for the wood. The train had to wait for the wood in the port to be cleared first. The composition of goods carried on the train had a marked effect on the delay in getting to the port. It was clear that to improve the speed of delivery of the metals to the port we would have to control the composition of what the Russians called the "mashroot", or 'set' of railcars.

Under the Soviet system this was not a problem. There was no penalty for waiting the extra few days in getting to the port. Under the capitalist system that was different. If we were talking about a train carrying say four hundred tons of metal taking an extra five days to reach the port that would mean we were paying the carrying cost of four hundred tons of metal at around US$1,400 per ton (e.g. $560,000) for the extra five days (interest on the money we had invested in the metal). The carrying cost of the delay amounted to around $180 per each day of delay; that was wasted money. We were paying for the metals ex-factory in Bratsk and we couldn't get paid ourselves until we produced a bill of lading at the port showing the title to the goods had passed to the person to whom we sold the metal. Every day cost us money. Time was a factor in our profitability.

It was clear that we had to speed things up. The Soviet system had provided for general sidings in the marshalling yards at which the rail cars were assembled, awaiting a through locomotive. We needed special sidings for the aluminium. I travelled for a week along the BAM, from Bratsk to Vanino getting out and walking along the line until I could find a suitable unused siding; often at a factory or military site on the rail line. I chose four and made an agreement to rent them from the BAM Administration. They were largely unused anyway so it was very inexpensive. I then hired a man to work with us at each siding. Whenever he saw a railcar with our aluminium coming along he would segregate it onto our siding. When he had put together a 'mashroot' of fifteen or so cars he would put all fifteen into the larger train, most often also made up of aluminium from our other sidings and these would go directly to the port without delay. There was always room for aluminium in the port. Within two months I had shaved off four days from the delivery time for the train from the smelter to the port. This saved us a lot of money and was much safer as the metal was moving, not stuck in the boondocks waiting for permissions. I also could keep tabs on where our metals were along the route.

Initially the Russians didn't understand why I was agitated about the delays on the railroad. It was arriving at the speed they usually received trains. They had never had to figure out the cost of money needed to finance the transit of the products before but they soon understood very well. The BAM Administration, led by Mr. Leonov, developed a sliding rate for speeding up deliveries on a whole range of goods which he offered to his clients on his railroad. This was matched by the port which charged a slight premium for accepting goods more quickly. I had opened the channels of commerce and they needed no guidance from me as to how to turn it to their advantage. Efficiency bloomed.

My primary task, however, was the creation of a facility to import alumina safely and efficiently into the port from Australia. I made three trips to Vanino to meet with their technical people and introduced them to my plan for doing this. The system was very simple. We would use a floating alumina silo equipped with gear to discharge incoming ships and with gear to load railcars on the quay alongside the vessel. I had already done this before, using the 'Abu Loujaine' vessel in New York and the larger 'Al-Jabalaine' in the UK.

This type of floating alumina silo consists of a converted ordinary bulk carrier. On its deck is a piece of equipment, manufactured by Siwertell in Sweden, which is a rotating screw which reaches into the hold of an incoming ship and discharges the alumina from that ship into its own holds. All of this is done with closed hatches. On the land side of the vessels are three screws which take the alumina from the holds of the silo vessel and discharges the alumina into railcars or trucks alongside.

When we used them for cement we also had a facility for bagging but this was unnecessary for alumina so we would use three bulk dischargers instead.

This system is very efficient. The Siwertell on the deck can discharge incoming vessels at 450 metric tons per hours. The incoming bulk carrier can then just leave. The alumina in the holds can be discharged into rail cars alongside, dust free at a rate of 200 metric tons an hour for each discharger. It will fill up three 50 ton rail cars simultaneously in fifteen minutes. That is faster than they could position the rail cars. The most important aspect is that it is unnecessary to open the hatches to discharge so there are no delays for rain, snow or winds. There is nothing that needs to be built on the quay as the rail cars run along the quay. I explained this in great detail to the technicians in the port.

The bottoms of the holds are 'fluidised'. That is they agitate the alumina so that it flows unaided down a trough to the mechanical screw in the hold which takes it up to the discharger. The most efficient method for achieving this can be found in the description contained in my patent covering this process[viii] for the bulk handling of powdered or granular products. There is no need for human intervention other than pushing a start and a stop button. There is a sensor in the discharger which stops the railcar from overfilling. The only labour required is opening the hatch on the top of the railcar to allow the discharger to begin its discharging and to close it up when it finishes.

I have always used mechanical systems rather than pneumatic systems. They are equally as efficient as pneumatic systems but there is a lot less dust. To make a pneumatic system function requires adding air under pressure. That means that somehow this air has to be taken out again at the other end and that often involves dust. In the case of alumina, this 'dust' is very expensive. If a pneumatic system breaks down for any reason it will leave undischarged product in the conveying line. This means that when the system starts up again the newly conveyed product will come in contact with the inert product already in the conveying pipe so will require extra pressure to move this 'head'. Pneumatics are always more difficult than mechanical systems.

I explained this to the port and showed them pictures of my use of these floating silos in New York and London. I assured them that if it met the environmental standards of the port authorities in London and New York it might also match the environmental standards of Vanino. To that end, on my third visit, I invited the local environmental activists of the region to come to my briefing to hear of my plans for the project. I explained the care we were taking to reduce any environmental degradation of the port and gave them kits of materials for them to study. They were happy as were the technicians from the port.

I reported that we had several options for getting this started. The easiest way would be to contact Arabian Bulk Trade of Al-Khobar in Saudi Arabia from whom I had chartered both the Abu Loujaine and the Al Jabalaine. They had another floating silo which was not then in use. It was less efficient than would be ideal as it was older (its bearings were less resistant to the abrasive alumina so would have to be run more slowly). However, we could bring it to Australia within four weeks, load a full cargo of 32,000 metric tons and arrive about twenty-five days later in Vanino. As it was working in Vanino delivering alumina we could be fitting out a converted bulk carrier with the necessary equipment of our own and substitute our own floating silo in place in about ten months. In the meantime we would already be delivering alumina to the smelters.

We would have our own crew on board who would stay on board to operate the ship and the equipment. They would prepare their own food and have their own cabins on the vessel. Once alongside, the ship would not move. It would be permanently moored on the quay. The port and the technicians were very happy. The representatives of the smelters were very happy. It was a simple and elegant solution which would get us into the alumina import business in a matter of weeks, not months.

On the third of December 1992 the Vanino Port signed a protocol "for the construction, operation and maintenance of a terminal for the receiving, storing and handling and shipping of alumina and aluminium." This was signed with Trans-Cis Commodities (a Trans World Group company) Niksa Lazaneo; the Vanino Economic and Transport Association, Vladimir Pogodin; Bratsk Aluminium Plant, Yuri M. Schleifstein; and Krasnoyarsk Aluminium plant, V.I. Cherbinin. The aim was to deliver Australian alumina to the Bratsk and Krasnoyarsk smelters through the facility at Vanino. They adopted my plan for a floating terminal with the provision that a permanent land-based storage system might eventually be required. The contract specified "The project of the terminal provides a gradual development of the facilities for the discharge of the imported alumina...including the installation of a floating silo."[ix]

I was very pleased. There is a cardinal rule in logistics that says that the system that is built must contain redundancies in case of problems. That means that you should look at where the potential problems might occur and prepare the facilities to cope with them if they happened. There were two fundamental weaknesses implicit in building any import system for Russia. The first weakness was that there were no facilities to store a full cargo of 25,000 metric tons of alumina arriving on a vessel from Australia. There were no bulk storage facilities in the port so some buffer storage had to be created so that the incoming vessel would not be delayed in discharging its cargo in the Russian port. A bulk carrier delivering alumina from Australia must be guaranteed an agreed period for the discharging of its cargo in the port. This time period for the discharge makes up part of the hire agreement (charter party) of the vessel. If the discharge took longer than the period agreed we would have to pay extra for every hour this vessel was delayed ('demurrages'). This would be very expensive. We were obliged to discharge the vessel as soon as practicable. Without a buffer store it would not be possible to do so.

As we were delivering the imported alumina into railcars, the speed of delivering into railcars was the defining variable in the discharge process if we didn't use a buffer storage. We couldn't load railcars as fast as we could unload the ship. Therefore we had to separate the process of discharging of the bulk carriers from the loading of the railcars. By using the floating silo with its own equipment to discharge the cargo from the bulk carrier into the buffer store of the holds of the silo vessel we were able to separate the discharging of the bulk carrier from the loading of the railcars. These became two separate, but related processes. This separation was crucial to our success.

The railcars could be brought alongside and loaded without reference to the incoming bulk carrier. If we were to import the 800,000 metric tons a year of alumina this would mean importing around 66,000 metric tons a month into and through the facility. That would mean two and a half deliveries of alumina each month from Australia. Each delivery of alumina to the silo would require around 460 railcars to be loaded, or about 38 railcars every day, seven days a week.

That would be a very difficult rate to maintain as each rail car had to be moved along a single track. Using the floating silo with the three dischargers meant we could load three railcars at a time which should have given us plenty of time to complete the shifting of the cars. I was very unsure if the BAM had that many railcars available as once loaded they had to be transported to Bratsk or Krasnoyarsk smelters thousands of kilometres away. The journey would take time and the journey back would take time. It was crucial that the whole system didn't depend on the provision of rail cars. That would be risky and potentially very expensive.

This seemed a difficult concept for many of the metal traders to understand. However, it is a very simple concept familiar to most of the female population, at least. If your washed clothes are in the drier and there is no place to put them, you can only clear the drier by folding and ironing the dried clothes as fast as possible. Your ability to clear the drier, and by inference the washing machine before it, lies in folding and ironing the dried clothes. However, if you had a safe place to put the dried clothes from the drier before folding and ironing you could empty the drier at one go and fold and iron whenever you were ready. The logistics of washing clothes and delivering bulk alumina into railcars are not very different

Having received the go-ahead for the floating silo from the port and the smelters I then went on to examine the way in which the smelters were handling their supplies of bulk materials. I travelled to Bratsk smelter and was taken by the chief engineer, a Korean, to look at the facilities. It was a very impressive smelter with twenty-four pot lines, most of which were working. The smelter received its major ingredients in one receiving shed with a hole in the floor into which the boxcars discharged their load by allowing the base of the box car to open. I was appalled to see that the shed was filled, almost knee high with alumina powder, and cryolite, with a trace of black carbon coke. There was no segregation of products. Everything went down the same hole. This was not very efficient and certainly unhealthy for the workers who worked in the receiving shed.

Even more importantly the admixture of extraneous products in the raw materials made it very difficult to control the exact quality of the raw material bath inside the carbon shells through which the electric current was passed to produce aluminium. Smelting takes place in large, steel, carbon-lined furnaces known as reduction cells. The carbon lining is called a cathode. Alumina is fed into the cells where it is dissolved in molten cryolite, a liquid which can dissolve alumina and conduct electricity at around 970°C. Two tonnes of alumina are needed to make one tonne of aluminium metal. Electricity is introduced into each cell through carbon blocks manufactured by the smelters, called anodes. The carbon anode is bonded to a metal rod using molten cast iron. This rod allows the anode to be suspended into the reduction cell during the smelting process. This is one end of the electric circuit. All of the reduction cells are connected in series by an aluminium busbar which carries an electric current and these cells form a reduction line. A continuous electric current of 100,000 to 320,000 amps (depending on the smelter) flows from the anode, through the alumina - cryolite mixture, to the carbon cathode cell lining, and then to the anodes of the next cell, and so on. The electrical current enables alumina to react with the carbon anode to form aluminium and carbon dioxide. Between 13,000 and 15,000 kilowatt-hours of electricity are used to make one tonne of aluminium. The aluminium, in a molten form, sinks to the bottom of the cell. It is siphoned out in a process known as tapping and is transported to a holding furnace to be cast into products.

Unless the mixture is correct there will be impurities in the finished primary metals. Aluminium is traded primarily on the London Metal Exchange market. The exact specification for the aluminium which can be traded on the Exchange specifies primary aluminium (A7) of minimum 99.7% purity with maximum permissible iron content of 0.2% and maximum permissible silicon content of 0.1% in lots of 25 tonnes in ingots, T-bars or sows. This is LME-grade material. When I visited Bratsk smelter only a small proportion of the primary aluminium produced was 99.7% pure (the 'A7' standard). The rest was 'off-grade' (99.6%-A6; 99.5%- A5) or lesser purities. This had a marked effect on the prices as off-grades traded at a discount from the A7 standard. All the costs were the same in making the aluminium but the reward was less because of the impurities.

There were other problems associated with increasing the production quantity and quality of the Russian smelters which would need to be addressed by metals specialists who the TWG brought to the smelters, but improvements in some of the physical handling aspects were made by me. What shocked me more was the lack of concern for the welfare of the workers in the smelter. There are a number of very hazardous and toxic substances in use in an aluminium smelter. Exposure to high levels of cryolite, for example, produces nausea, vomiting, gastric pain and osteosclerosis, (hardening of the bones). I had done a major research study for the International Metalworkers Federation a few years earlier entitled "Occupational Health Hazards in the Aluminium Producing Industry" which examined in detail every step in the production process. It also included a detailed list of all the substances found in the smelters and the limits allowed for human exposure to these substances.

The Russian workers had no such information available to them and their union was a political organisation not very interested in worker safety and health. I asked the management of the smelter and Trans World if they would mind if I had my study translated into Russian for them. They were very upset that I would even think of doing such a thing. They feared that the Russian workers might demand changes which could save their lives and health. That would cost the management and Trans World money. This was not attractive to them. Fortunately I had brought a copy of my study with me in English and in Japanese (the International Metalworkers had translated the study in many languages). I left these copies with the worker's committee in the smelter before I asked if it would be okay. I made a point of carrying copies with me whenever I visited an aluminium plant and left them there.

This kind of attitude about workers' health and safety prevailed throughout every aspect of the Russian workplaces I visited. It was curious in that there was no one, no organisation, no authority and no union who felt it was its responsibility to protect the workers from the hazards of their working environment. It seemed a bit strange for the Worker's Paradise to have built in no programs of occupational health. I found this through my entire period of working in Russia. I expected this in the labour camps of the Gulag but not in the factories, ports and offices of the New Russia.

This was no different in Vanino. After my second trip to Vanino, when I watched the first aluminium being loaded on the ships I noticed that the stevedores on the docks had only makeshift gloves. I was surprised as it was by then late fall and a temperature of -16° C. It was very inefficient. On my next trip to the port I bought 30 pairs of waterproof gloves which I gave to the stevedores working with our metals. These were very cheap cotton gloves which had been dipped in plastic. They cost less than half a dollar each but they saved us a lot of wasted time. Later I brought hard hats, down-stuffed jackets and goggles for our workers. Not only did they work more efficiently, they had some pride in working for us. We found that many in the port shifted their workstations so that they could work on our projects. This ultimately saved us much more than it cost.

The port authorities were surprised but welcomed this; however they didn't duplicate this in other areas of their domain. They called me the 'Amerikansky Narodnik'. The term 'Narodnik' derived from a group of socially conscious middle-class Russians in the 1860s who were concerned with the rights of the peasants. Their children formed the revolutionary party "Narodnaya Volya" (the 'Peoples Will'); Russia's first organised revolutionary party which sought to spark a great peasant's uprising. This didn't happen but sporadic acts of terror were conducted by the Narodniki. On March 1, 1881 they succeeded in assassinating Tsar Alexander II. They later evolved into the Social-Revolutionaries and the Popular Socialists who helped bring about the 1905 Revolution. I was happy to be called a Narodnik.

For my part I characterised much of what I found on the ground in the Far East as the "Kholkoz Krasnaya Lapas". This is hard to translate exactly but it means a Red State Collective Farm with 'lapas'. Lapas are the footcloths that Russian and Soviet soldiers used to wrap around their feet, often in lieu of boots. It was a term which referred to the hangover of primitive Soviet habits operating in the modern world. It was not really a derogatory term; it was more of a chiding for not adopting modern practices and methods.

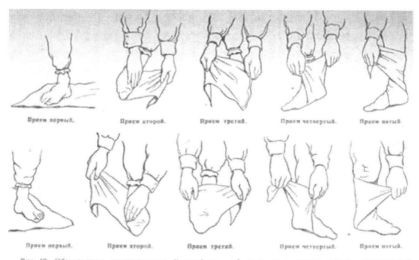

Рис. 18. Обёртывание ног портянками. Верхний ряд — обёртывание портянкой правой ноги; нижняя ряд — обёртывание портянкой левой ноги.

Russian Army Instruction on Lapas

In some cases, however, it was more than just quaint; it was horrific. I was in the port of Bolshoi Kamen, between Vanino and Vladivostok at the Zvezda Shipyard. There they repair Russian Navy nuclear-powered submarines, There were, at one time, twenty scrapped nuclear submarines in the port. There were sailors working on an open barge off-loading radioactive waste from these subs by hand and taking them out to be dumped in the Sea of Japan. It was horrific. I wonder how many of these sailors are still alive. I saw the same thing in the North, in the Kola Peninsula at Zapadnaya Litsa and Severomorsk where sailors were moving nuclear assemblies from the subs of the Northern Fleet in and out of storage without protection. Even in the 1990s it was a hard life being an ordinary Russian or a member of the armed forces. "Kholkoz Krasnaya Lapas" hardly did it justice. I recommended to the Croatian port agents we engaged

(Inspection Services of Vienna) working in these ports that they wear their lead underwear but to no avail.

In order to staff the various functions in London, Moscow and Vanino we had to hire people. In Vanino we set up with the port a joint venture company, Trans Vanino Corporation (TVC). This was headed by Port Director Shengeliya and I was the Deputy Director. The port presented us with a number of people who would make up TVC in Vanino. The lead officer of this was a Mr. Zhivanos, along with two young ladies, Irina and Sveta, and another chap named Oleg. Later there would be some additional workers, primarily in the accounts department. Zhivanos was a pleasant person who was well trained in the art of Soviet activity. That meant there were endless discussions and planning but not a lot of actual work. Irina and Sveta showed up and did virtually all of the work. Oleg we saw from time to time but never when there was a ship in port or a project which needed to be completed. When I chided them for their relaxed attitude towards performance they answered me that I didn't understand the Russian system of work. As they informed me, the Russian system meant "They pretend to pay us and we pretend to work." However, it was very friendly.

Until TVC was formed we had been using the port agency FEPCO as our port agent and cargo agent. FEPCO was a joint operation between the Port and the company Inspection Services, a Croatian company based in Vienna. FEPCO was supervised by Mr. Savinov (who had a stake in the business) and Mrs. Valentina Tsareva who had good ties with the railroad. Both Savinov and Tsareva were hard-working and responsible. The local Croatian representative in Vanino when we started was Zlatko Manojlovic. By chance he was a friend of Niksa's from their hometown Split and I had met him when I was loading, years before, a cargo of cement from Dalmacia Cement in Split. Zlatko was a true professional and was a great help setting things up. He was soon transferred to a port further south and his replacement, Robert, was too fond of establishing close personal bonds with Russian women which angered their boyfriends/spouses and limited his ability to work out in the open without fear. I was quite happy with FEPCO but the exigencies of the port situation meant that we had to work through the company TVC instead of FEPCO.

Since TVC was not structured to handle the various demands of a port agency we continued to use the FEPCO services but through TVC.

The job of a port agent is very important. Its tasks include: making port arrangements, cargo arrangements, dealing with the masters' requirements; filling in customs forms; arranging bunkers (fuel), water and tugs; preparing ship's documentation; conducting and supervising vessel and cargo surveys and monitoring work time used for timesheets; preparing the bills of lading from the mates' receipts; supervising the stevedoring and handling disbursements in the port as needed; *inter alia*. There are standard fees for this and often amount to over USD$20,000 per port call. It is a serious business. We were sure that the team led by Mr. Zhivanos were not really trained in this type of business (except for Irina). The TVC team would work with us on the import facility rather than on the export side.

In Moscow, Niksa was permanently assigned to the Vanino project and monitored what was happening in the port. In London I was successful in persuading David Reuben, with some difficulty, to allow me to implant into the Trans World office my ship manager, Sunil Malhotra. Sunil was someone with whom I had worked for some considerable time and who managed my chartered vessel "Al Jabalaine" and the two smaller vessels which we owned "Kabedi" and the "Thios Victor". Sunil had been working with Voigt Maritime but left them to work with IBT within the Trans World office. He was active in the chartering of vessels for Trans World cargos as IBT in all their business areas, not just Vanino. I also hired a young man, Alex von Moll, who was the son of a friend and who was studying shipping at university. His father asked if I could give him work experience so I hired him. He proved to be an excellent choice and a fast learner. He learned so much about metal trading that he went on to take up a successful career as a metal trader with a large international bank.

A few months later David Reuben came to me with a request. David's wife, Debbie, had been pressing David to find a job of sorts for a man who often played golf with David and who had spoken frequently with Debbie about asking for her assistance. David's wife Debbie is a lovely, kind and generous woman. I had known Debbie long before I knew David as David's son and my second son were classmates at school (Westminster Under) and they frequently visited each others' house to play. I had never met David but I did meet Debbie. It was Debbie who spoke with my wife at a school sporting event when my wife was bemoaning the fact that my eldest son who had graduated with honours in economics from Edinburgh was having difficulty finding a job. Debbie volunteered to speak with her husband to see if the job he had been advertising was filled. She called us later to say that the job had been filled but that if we dropped off my son's resume she would give it to her husband to consider. She did and my son was given a job at Trans World. We were very grateful.

Debbie's ears must have been burning for months. David and I travelled together frequently in Russia over the next year or so and we often were invited to dinners and parties by our Russian hosts. As might be expected there were always unattached women as part of these parties. David was careful to forestall any inappropriate requests by regaling the hosts with stories of how wonderful his wife was and how he was hoping to bring her with him on his next trip. Within the bounds of decorum I added my support to the stories of Debbie. I remember we were at a dinner party with Yuri Kolpakov of the Krasnoyarsk smelter and his girlfriend Oksana. Oksana took me aside and asked if there really was such a person as Debbie with all those wonderful qualities that David described. I assured her that it was all true and that I was grateful to her as well for her kindness to me.

This time Debbie had chosen to sponsor a man I knew, Victor Parness. I had met Victor years before when we were working in Nigeria at the same time. Victor was working in the Nigerian ports importing a variety of goods. He and his partner were very successful until the partner was jailed after a change of government. Victor was able to leave Nigeria and returned to London where he continued his business. It didn't prosper and despite the fact that Victor had left Nigeria with a lot of cash it slowly diminished in the pursuit of a high life style. I had met Victor again about two years before I went to work with Trans World. Victor had introduced me to a Ghanaian businessman who was interested in financing a cargo of cement which I would bring to London on the Al Jabalaine to begin operations in London. This Ghanaian financed the cargo but couldn't or wouldn't pay his bank that had financed his cement purchase so we had problems clearing his cement out of our ship. It cost us £2.3 million which we never got back despite a court judgement in our favour after a lengthy law suit. So I was a little ambivalent about starting a new relationship with Victor. However, if this was something Debbie was promoting I had a debt to repay. David didn't want Victor to be part of Trans World and asked me to hire him in IBT. He would pay us for his salary. I agreed and Victor came to work for IBT.

Victor had many skills and knew his way around ports and trade documentation. He was a nice person and very dedicated to making the system work. His only problem was that, for some reason, he had the ability to antagonise people. It was hard to say why because he was usually cheery and jovial. However, he seemed to rub people up the wrong way. I took him with me to Vanino and asked him to stay there for part of the time as I couldn't stay there for any extended period as I was busy in getting the bulk facility going and in setting up shipping for the aluminium in other ports. In a very short while the people from the port, from TVC and from FEPCO asked me if I didn't think it was better that he left the port to continue his work in London. In a matter of weeks he had antagonised several key people. Victor wanted to return to London anyway. He arranged to hire a young Bulgarian in the port to stay there and look after the TVC business. The Bulgarian did not last long there. He left abruptly and took the laptop computer I had brought down for him with him as he left. We never recovered it or found him. It was not a brilliant start. Victor returned to London.

A few months later my lawyer recommended her new boyfriend to me as another person for my team. He had just left the British Army and taken a degree at a notable business school. I met him and was very impressed. Hugo Barrett was the most organised person I had ever met. He took notes, kept every bit of paper in order; followed through on communication and projects; and was a wonderful person for me as I never took notes nor kept papers in order. He was a gem. With him my team was complete.

Having this staff allowed me to travel to other Russian ports and negotiate the rights to export Russian aluminium. With the assistance of Zlatko, Niksa and I travelled to the ports of Zarubina and Posyets on the Russian, Chinese and Korean border to create further outlets for the supply of aluminium that was pouring out of the smelters. I travelled north to the port of Tixsi at the mouth of the Lena River in the Arctic and the port of Anadyr on the Bering Strait opposite Alaska. I visited Dudinka, the Yenisei port near Norilsk in the Far North where nickel and platinum were being shipped and I visited the famous Gulag town of Vorkuta.

I shall always remember Vorkuta. I went down to the small restaurant in the middle of town, near the hospital. It had sawdust on the floor but I was told that the food was supposed to be okay. I sat down at a table. Near me there was a table with two couples sitting. Behind them a lone man sat at another table. There were others scattered around. I had just been served my plate of pelmenyi (Russian ravioli) when a man sauntered in. He pulled a gun and shot one of the men from the table with the two couples. The lone diner stood up and shot the man who had killed the other diner. There was a lot of noise and soon three policemen rushed in. They took out the two bodies and apologised to us for the fuss. We all kept eating and finished our meals; after all we had to pay for them and I, for one, had no idea where else I could get a meal in Vorkuta.

As the work progressed in Vanino and ships were being loaded efficiently for delivery to Japan, Korea, Taiwan and Singapore we had another opportunity which presented itself in the port. This project is still relevant as the workers in the Far East are fighting Moscow's attempt to promote the sale of Russian-made cars in the region.

Since late 2008, the Russian papers have been full of the mass protests in Vladivostok and other centres in the far Eastern region of Primorye Krai against the raising of taxes on imported automobiles. When, Prime Minister Putin announced he would not go back on his plan to protect the Russian auto producers; the civil disobedience continued with riot police and soldiers attacking the protesters.

Like everything else in Russia there is more to this story. This not just a protest against taxes on foreign cars, it is an attack on an entrenched commercial practice. I must confess to being one of the architects of this problem. In the early and mid 1990's I was busy shipping primary aluminium from the Far East port of Vanino to Japan. The journey was short (about two or three sailing days). We used smaller vessels of about 4,500 dead weight tons for the journey. Japanese port charges were very high. When we delivered the aluminium to the Japanese rolling mills we returned to Vanino or, sometimes, Nahodka and Vladivostok empty (in ballast). Travelling in ballast added to our overall expense.

At time there was a thriving business, run primarily by one of the major Yakuza groups (Yamaguchi-Gumi) , to sell used Japanese cars (US$600 each) for export from Japan. These, for some strange reason were almost always white, right-hand drive vehicles. The local Russian Mafia in the major centres of the Far East wanted these cars to fill the shortage in Russia. It was a natural business. As soon as we delivered the aluminium they filled the holds of our vessels with refrigerators, motor cycles, other white goods and white cars. The decks were covered with cars. When we arrived back in Russia the local people took them off and sold on the refrigerators, etc. However, the cars were sold at an auction on Saturday morning. Vanino was the biggest auction because most of our vessels went there to load. It was held in the parking lot outside the 'Vanino Hilton'. Our freight for the return journey from Japan was paid from the auction proceeds.

This went on for a while but soon we were confronted by Evgeny, the local customs officer. He said that what was going on was getting him into trouble. We didn't want to harm a friend so we negotiated a compromise. We would legally import forty cars from Japan and pay all the duties and would get Russian license plates for these right-hand drive cars. After that we could import as many cars as we liked but would pay $100 to the Customs people for license plates for each car. At the auction the buyer paid $100 for the plates and honour was saved. The problem was that we had only forty plate numbers to play with so there were scores of white Japanese cars in the Far East; all with the same number license plates.

This system has continued long after I stopped shipping there. The reason that this business thrived was that it was very difficult to actually get cars from Eastern and Central Russia to the Far East. The roads were rotten. One could choose to drive through mud or snow. There was no other choice. The railroads were more expensive than the taxes on the cars and, although one could get the Russian cars as far as Khabarovsk without difficulty, moving South and South-east from Khabarovsk was more complicated. This system survived without difficulty until Putin decided to intervene.

Relations with Trans World remained good and I was very active in a range of activities within Trans World proper. I still hadn't had the go-ahead to charter the floating silo to get the alumina import in motion but it seemed imminent. I met with Sunil who pointed out to me that our efforts to charter vessels for the transport of aluminium from Western Russia, Latvia, Estonia and Lithuania for Trans World were not as successful as they should have been. We decided to monitor the negotiations for a number of trades. We found that our negotiations with the various owners for the hire of the vessels for these shipments were being frustrated by a group of traders who were employed at Trans World. The same people who would trade the metals would then contact their shipbroker in Spain and use that shipbroker to fix the vessels for the carriage of these trades. They were always more expensive than the rate we obtained from the same shipowner but the traders controlled the business. We were outraged. We documented their backstairs dealing for three ships and went to the management to complain that Trans World was being cheated. We went to Mike Boggs, the comptroller, and laid out our evidence. He said he would take it up with David.

The next day he called us to his office and said that he had presented our findings to David who said, on reflection, that he needed the traders, especially Jeremy North, the head trader, and that we shouldn't make a fuss about them making a few bucks on the shipping. I pointed out that we were specialists in the shipping business and could get good rates for Trans World. It was foolish to pay more for nothing. Our arguments made no impact on the situation. That afternoon Jeremy North came to my office and said that he knew we were upset. He said that they regularly added on a dollar a ton for themselves and another dollar for the Moscow office. He was a fair man and offered IBT another dollar for ourselves so that we wouldn't feel hard done by. I thanked him for his candour and told him that I had an agreement with Trans World to get them the lowest price and that I couldn't cheat the company. I left it at that and said no more.

However, the next week I was in Moscow and had a meeting with Lev Chernoy, the Russian partner in Trans World, and with Iskander Makhmudov who was an assistant to Mischa Chernoy, the other partner. I pointed out that they were losing two or three dollars a ton on all the metals they were shipping by allowing the traders, including Tolya in the Moscow office, to take a commission on each shipment. They were less relaxed about the situation than David Reuben and suggested that they would have a consultation with David about allowing this to go on in London. Lev also said he would have word about career guidance for Tolya personally. Apparently their powers of persuasion were very good and the practice of backstairs commissions ended fairly abruptly.

I had great difficulty in understanding in why David would even consider allowing such a practice to go on but I guess that, on reflection, having good traders for the metals made up for being cheated on the shipping. The bottom line would be preserved. I, and his Russian partners, thought that allowing oneself to be cheated gave off the wrong message. Later, when a steel trader hired by David tried to get me to conspire with him to make some extra cash through falsifying the shipping price I reported this to David as well. This time he fired the steel trader.

There was a strange morality which was endemic in many of the businesses in which I found myself. When I was arranging the purchase of equipment for my Nigerian partners, for example, they expressed complete surprise when I insisted that I had not taken a personal commission on the purchase from the suppliers. I was expected to cheat and they didn't care. This happened to me quite frequently in business dealings. I am probably stupid and naive but I cannot bring myself to do such a thing. It's not a fear of being caught because no one really expects any different. I can't do it because it is wrong and I would hate to have anyone in my business try to do it to me. It is an aspect of the business mentality which has always appalled me. I realised that I was not really cut out to be a businessman. I carried wads of cash with me everywhere in Russia and I never even thought to pocket any of it personally. I would have never been caught because no one signs receipts. However, it would have been wrong to do so.

Over the years I have suffered greatly from a lack of personal corruption. With a little bit of flexibility I would have been rich. Perhaps I am the fool as it would have been nice to be rich. It only reinforced in my mind what I was taught at an early age; businessmen are corrupt and big businessmen are very corrupt. It was imbued in the very nature of the capitalist system. There was a level of moral relativism which prevailed and people were applauded and praised for their deviousness and venality. It was a world I wasn't used to and I didn't like very much.

Perhaps the best example of the business mentality is the story of the two partners in the garment business in New York. At the beginning of the season they decided to make Madras plaid jackets. They made 10,000 of them. A week before the season opened the *Womens Wear Daily*, the bible of the garment trade, published an article saying that plaid jackets were 'out' for the season. The two partners were in despair. They knew that if they couldn't sell the jackets they would lose the factory and probably their homes and cars. It was a nightmare and they worried and worried. One day a week later a man knocks on their door. He says "Hi, I'm in from Australia.

Your friends said you might be able to help me. I am looking to buy some plaid jackets". The partners smile and say "Sure, we can help. How many do you need?" The man says "About 10,000". The partners say "Well that's a big order but we'll check with our contacts but we can assure you a supply". They negotiate price and delivery terms and shake hands on the deal. The Australian says, "Ok, we have a deal, but I must check with my partners in Australia. I'll check with them. If you haven't heard from me by noon on Friday, you can go ahead and start shipping the jackets." They wait all day Wednesday. They waited all day Thursday. They waited Friday morning. All of a sudden at 11:45 a messenger comes to the office with an urgent telegram. He gives it to the partner who passes it to the other partner saying "Sam, you open it. I can't stand it. I know we've lost everything; we're finished" Sam opens the telegram and jumps around laughing and shouting "We're saved. Thank God. It's terrific!". His partner asks what the telegram says. Sam says, "Don't worry it isn't from Australia". "So, what does it say?" "It says your mother has died!".

Because of my naiveté I was unprepared for the bombshell that exploded in early 1993. The Trans World partners had decided that I could not go ahead with the floating silo in Vanino. I would have to devise another system.

CHAPTER SIX

The early stages of the privatisation of the aluminium industry in Russia were dominated by three major influences: the political consequences of the changeover from Gorbachev to Yeltsin; the explosive growth of criminal organisations; and the growth and expansion of an effort by police and investigative organisations seeking to control the excesses of this process of privatisation. All of these were an influence on its development. They took place in an economic climate which had never really accommodated free enterprise and was not prepared for its emergence. Still less was it prepared for the influx of foreign businessmen and their methods of doing business.

The communist economic system was never the system of choice for the capitalist control of the means of production in Russia. However, even the earliest efforts at reform during Tsarist Russia ran up against economic and political inhibitions which predated communism. The father, or perhaps the godfather of Russian capitalism, Nikolai Khristianovich Bunge, who was made Minister of Finance in 1881 and then became Chairman of the Cabinet of Ministers, tried to release Russia from its feudal economic structure. He restructured the banking system, opened a peasants' bank and reformed the tax system. He invested in railroads and spurred the growth of Russian industries coupled with the first laws on workers' rights. The Tsarist system wasn't ready for this and he was forced out of office in 1887 by the conservatives and the boyars. The feudal system was continued.

The next reformer fared little better. Pyotr Arkadyevich Stolypin was also Chairman of the Council of Ministers (under Nicholas II) from 1906 to 1911. He took office after the 1905 Revolution and had to spend a lot of his time fighting the terrorists and agitators. However, as a response to the pressures from the countryside he engaged in a massive program of agrarian reform. Stolypin was convinced that if he could separate the peasant movements from the urban proletariat he could regain control of the political system. His reforms empowered a new class of market-oriented smallholding landlords. However when he dissolved the Second Duma (the elected legislature) and changed the rules to promote the election of landed gentry and the aristocracy to the Third Duma, these elected members were so conservative that the value of all the previous Stolypin reforms was vitiated. Stolypin attempted to expand the role of decentralised elected local governments ('zemstvo') but was defeated and, in 1911, assassinated. This was the last attempt at reform before World War I and the October Revolution.

The hostility of Marx towards capitalism is well known. His "Das Kapital" spells it out clearly. The Marxist Russian revolutionaries of the Bolshevik wing were determined to fight against the evils of capitalism. The Bolsheviks did not take power after the February 1917 revolution although they were an important political force. With the ouster of the Tsar the new Russian Government was formed by the Mensheviks (Martov and Kerensky's party), a social-democratic party which entered in a number of alliances with the non-Marxist liberal parties. This new government allowed many of the exiles to return home to Russia. Stalin, Kamenev and Muranov returned from Siberia. Lenin returned from Switzerland and Martov from Germny.

The Right and the Left of the socialist party competed for control of the government. In the October Revolution in 1917 the Leninist Left wing faction finally took over total control in Moscow, although the Mensheviks retained control of Georgia until the Kronstadt Uprising in 1921 when all opposition parties were banned by the Bolsheviks.

The two sides were fighting over a vision of how the new Russian state should deal with the economy. The major gulf between them lay with the socialists' view that Marx's labour theory of value was wrong as was his predictions of the imminent demise of capitalism. The key figure in this analysis was Eduard Bernstein, a German Social Democrat. Bernstein pointed out that Marx's notion of the increasing centralisation of the capitalist system wasn't actually happening. Capitalist industry, while significant, was not becoming overwhelming and that the ownership of capital was becoming more, and not less, diffuse through stock exchanges and public markets. Bernstein contended that socialism could be built by reforming capitalism. As capitalism was improved then workers' rights would expand and this would gradually introduce a socialist political structure on a thriving capitalist system of industry. Bernstein and his followers said that rejecting capitalism would leave nothing as its replacement other than a highly centralised authoritarian and dictatorial system which would restrict the liberties of workers and peasants. That would not be an acceptable system. The Bolsheviks rejected Bernstein as a

"Revisionist". This argument has been the core problem for the Bolsheviks and their Communist Party descendents to deal with because Bernstein was right and the Russians took seventy years to admit it.

They key consequence of the triumph of the Red Army Bolsheviks in their war with the White Army was that Russia passed into the hands of ideologues who rejected market forces as an instigator of economic and political change. They governed through authoritarian control and central planning. The traditional Russian explanation lay in the story of a man who is told by his comrades that when the revolution comes they will all eat strawberries with cream. The man complains, "But I don't like strawberries and cream!" His comrades tell him "Comes the Revolution you will like strawberries with cream!"

Russia had passed from neo-feudalism to communism without ever having passed through a stage of economic pluralism. That has been the key weakness of Russian economic history. There has been a strong party dominating a weak state. The Communist Party exerted its political control to supervise the functions of a parallel state bureaucracy. The fundamental weakness was that the party's targets became the goal not the efficiency of the system. The central administrative control of the system was performed by people who had no experience in such an administration and the sheer size of the country being governed meant that information flow was slow and inaccurate.

The incentive system of this structure was a factor in its failure. Rewards came from fulfilling the tasks, projects and instructions from above, irrespective of their utility or reflection of local conditions. If there had to be a choice between fulfilling the demands or quotas as opposed to efficiency and obeying local rules, it was these quotas and demands that the officials chose to fulfil.

Almost anything was considered as acceptable if the demands were satisfied. If those demands were not satisfied there were severe penalties. This could mean demotion or enforced job change; perhaps early retirement. If the job was of sufficient importance failure could mean liquidation or transport to the Gulag as a 'saboteur'. The easiest solution was to lie or exaggerate minor successes. The central planners knew that a large amount of their information was based on convenient fiction, partially, at least, because they knew that they had allocated insufficient resources to actually fulfil the tasks.

It was a common practice to bring in "shock workers" (udarniki), people who worked at a very high pace, to set the operative timing for the labour content of a job or a workshop. These udarniki would work flat out for two days or so and their work rate would become the norm for all the other workers in that job for the foreseeable future. After a couple of days these udarniki were moved to another job to perform their tasks again. The quotas based on their exaggerated work rates were impossible to match by ordinary workers.

An even more bizarre practice was introduced in 1935 when Aleksei Grigorievich Stakhanov mined 102 tons of coal in less than 6 hours (14 times his quota). The Communists instituted a Stakhanovite Movement which attracted emulators across Russia and in various industries. Stakhanov was awarded a medal as the first "Hero of Socialist Labour". Soon the Communists encouraged the Stakhanovite Movement through 'socialist emulation" and produced dvukhsotniki (workers who produced twice their quota in a single shift) and even tysyachniki (workers who produced ten times their quota in a single shift). This madness was exposed as a fraud after Stalin's death but it still has a resonance in the Russian workplace.

It was abundantly clear to the planners and factory managers at every level that Soviet efficiency was a sham and a delusion, but the fiction was maintained as the consequences of failure were very severe. It was a Potemkin economy. Prince Grigori Alexandrovich Potyomkin-Tavricheski was a military commander and protégé of Catherine the Great who was sent south to subdue the Ukrainians and to take the Crimea. Catherine went down to the Crimea in 1787 to see her conquests. To impress her, Potemkin had hollow facades of villages constructed along the banks of the Dnieper River in order to impress her. There were no villages but there were elegant facades. In Soviet industry there were high levels of production reported but these, too, were a facade (the Russians use the term 'pokazuka' for this type of charade). This existence of this fictional economic structure had three major consequences.

The first consequence was that in order to survive in this kind of system it was vitally important to have a circle of friends and acquaintances that could use their influence to provide the group with the necessities of life; the permits which were endlessly required for every aspect of life; and access to people with influence. In short, blat[x]. The members of the informal group pooled their influence and managed things that no individual could achieve on his own through networking and informal exchange. Children got their places in school through blat. Jobs were obtained through blat. Apartments were allocated through blat. This system extended to enterprises as well. Most enterprises had their own 'tolkach' (a 'pusher'). He, or she, was a professional blat dealer. They renegotiated contractual norms for the enterprise, they reduced expected outputs, they obtained additional resources without official allocations, etc. The tolkach was the lifeblood of the enterprise. These professional and private traders in blat, created a comfortable system which protected the citizens and the enterprises from the exigencies of the Soviet system. When one was part of this system of mutual interdependence there was usually a 'top person' or organisation at the centre of this web of self-help. The blat system operated under the 'umbrella'' or 'roof' ('krysha') of this central figure or organisation. To survive and prosper it was always best to have a 'krysha' or to have access to one. The most important thing to understand about blat is that it was almost entirely a non-monetary exchange. In the planned Soviet economy money played a very small part in peoples' or enterprises' life. Results were achieved through mutual exchange of influence, not cash.

The second consequence was that this informal system of mutual interdependence which prevailed had very little to do with the monopoly of power of the Communist Party. The Party was a closed shop of appointed functionaries who owed their loyalty to the Party and not to the civil institutions in which they were employed. The 'krysha' of the communists was the leadership of the Party, the Politburo and the Central Committee and, occasionally, regional parties. Discipline was maintained within the party structure by occasional purges, terror and expulsions. However, the Party was able to maintain discipline and obedience throughout the rest of the Soviet Union through the 'control organs'; especially the KGB and the MVD. These extra-bureaucratic organisations were used to instil fear and obedience in the Soviet population. It was like the sign that used to hang in the Washington White House in Chuck Colson's office "When you have them by the balls their hearts and minds will follow!" This was often arbitrary power used to instil loyalty to the regime through the exploitation of the fear of an internal and an external enemy. It was a power that reflected the will of the top leadership and often had nothing to do with any organisational or economic concerns.

The depredations of the Chekists and the fear that they instilled with arbitrary arrests, executions and enforced imprisonment in the Gulag were so arbitrary and capricious that the bulk of the population could not believe that their activities were actually sanctioned by their leaders whom they admired. The Gulag was full of letters, scraps of paper, and missives of every sort addressed to Stalin trying to tell The Great Leader what was being done in his name. They said "If only Comrade Stalin knew". Well, Comrade Stalin did know and he added extra names to those being tormented or sent for liquidation in his own hand in the margins of the proscription lists that were found in the archives.

The role of the Chekists is crucial to the understanding of how Russia moved into the era of private capitalism. One of the difficulties in understanding the role of the Chekists, especially the KGB, in the modern era (post 1980) is that there should be a clear distinction made between the KGB thugs and the KGB planners. A large portion of the KGB was engaged in the security of the state; they did this by acting as border guards, as surveillance officers (7th directorate), transport officers (4th Directorate), security officers at government installations (15th Directorate), government protection service (formerly 9th Directorate), protection of the constitution (formerly 5th Directorate), Many were engaged in technical functions: communications and cryptography (8th Directorate), in technical operations (OTU), sigint (16th Directorate) archives (10th Directorate) and schools. These were active, almost entirely within the boundaries of the Soviet Union.

On the other hand the First Chief Directorate (Foreign Intelligence-FCD) was made up of a different type of professional. Most of these were engaged in the normal business of spying (illegals, case officers, counter-intelligence, 'active measures', disinformation, covert action, communications, codes, computers and technical services.) and were engaged in essentially covert work. These professionals were mainly chosen from the ranks of the party elite and were the graduates of universities and technical schools. A few others were part of the Directorate of Intelligence Information and had been principally drawn from the ranks of many who had served abroad and were familiar with the political and economic operations of Western and Third World countries and academics. These were the 'academics' of the service and the thinkers. They were a 'different' KGB than the border guards and security people; they were engaged in mainly overt work.

However the heads of these KGB directorates and departments were often drawn from the Party rather than from moving up through the KGB ranks. They reflected the political directions and loyalties of the Party leadership, If that changed they were often replaced. Their task was primarily in fighting for budgetary allocations and following the 'Party line'. The production and evaluation of intelligence lay elsewhere. Over the years I got to know several of these overt KGB intelligence officers who had been stationed or served abroad. They were often quite sophisticated analysts of the world scene and very well-informed. They frequently recognised the Emperor's lack of clothing but, as they were employed by the Emperor's tailors, they restricted their fashion analysis in missives home.[xi]

The reason why this is important is that in October 1988, with the replacement of Chebrikov as the head of the KGB, Vladimir Kryuchkov became its Head. General Kryuchkov (to give him his quasi-military rank) was not a career intelligence officer but a Party bureaucrat. He was put in charge of the First Chief Directorate of the KGB in 1974 by Andropov. He was an Andropov man who had worked with Andropov in the Komsomol and the Party,[xii] He later became friendly with another Andropov man, Mikhail Gorbachev who in 1988 raised Kryuchkov from the First Chief Directorate to the Head of the KGB. This was the first time in the history of the KGB that someone from the First Chief Directorate (Foreign Intelligence) had risen to the top of the agency. It also marked the spread of the "Saratov Mafia" of Andropov and his friends.

Kryuchkov, although learning a great deal from listening to his staff, was as paranoid as the rest of the Soviet leadership. With the US maladroit handling of the shooting down of the airplane KAL007 over Russia the Soviets became obsessed that this was the precursor to a NATO first strike with nuclear weapons on the Soviet Union. They postulated an Operation RYAN in which scenario the Soviet Union would be premptively bombed with nuclear weapons. This happened on Andropov's watch and involved Kryuchkov, then still in the FCD, as the chief analyst. Andropov issued blistering denunciations of Reagan's policies and took to his bed in a prolonged period of vituperative decay. The Soviet government was in turmoil. In October Lech Walesa had just been given the Nobel Prize and the U.S. invaded Grenada. The next week

NATO began a routine exercise, Able Archer 83, which the KGB took as proof of an imminent surprise attack. Nothing happened and, as Able Archer 83, concluded and everyone went home tensions lessened. However, the arrival in the UK and Germany of Cruise and Pershing missiles drove the tensions back up again.

These were relieved slightly at the death of Andropov in February 1984 and the accession (for a year and a bit) of Konstantin Chernenko as General Secretary of the Party. Kryuchkov's FCD kept up the pressure internally within the KGB to find out more about Operation RYAN, with little success largely because there was no Operation RYAN. The dismissal of Army Chief of Staff and Defence Minister, Marshal Orgarkov and the death of Marshal Dimitry Ustinov (two of the most obsessed with the nuclear war scenario) led many in the Politburo and the Central Committee to believe that RYAN was not an urgent matter. This is the context in which Gorbachev took over at the death of Chernenko. The Soviets had passed through a major crisis in the belief that the West was about to attack. The concern was not only for the safety of the USSR but a deeper concern that there was very little the Soviets could to stop it other than Mutual Assured Destruction. It was too expensive to continue on this path and they were rapidly running out of options.

One of the reasons that it was too expensive was that the Soviets were fighting a desperate and debilitating war in Afghanistan. In defence of a Communist government which the Soviets had installed in Kabul, the Soviets sent its troops across the Afghan border on Christmas day 1979. They rapidly occupied the area around the capital but their opposition, the mujahidin scattered to the rural areas. Initially the Soviets had overwhelming firepower and air supremacy. However, with the introduction of "Red-eye" and "Stinger" missiles and modern equipment the mujahidin were able to shoot down Soviet helicopters and to destroy Soviet tanks. These were largely supplied by the U.S. in Operation Cyclone ("Charlie Wilson's War"). The mujahidin began a war of attrition with the occupying Soviet troops. This was very expensive in men, material and propaganda. It was bleeding the Soviet military dry and winning no friends around the world. Equally as important it distressed the parents and families of these soldiers who were suffering and dying in Afghanistan, creating a major gulf between them and the Andropov, Chernenko and Gorbachev Governments.

The Afghan War, in particular, engaged most of the resources and efforts of the other major Soviet intelligence agency, the GRU or Glavnoye Razvedyvatel'noye Upravleniye is the acronym for the foreign military intelligence directorate of the General Staff of the Armed Forces of the Russian Federation, The full name is GRU GSh (GRU Generalnovo Shtaba i.e. "GRU of the General Staff"). The GRU was founded by Leon Trotsky in 1918. The GRU, which is subordinate to the General Staff, is organized into Directorates, Directions, and Sections. Most of the work of the GRU concerns military intelligence (gathering information about foreign armies, orders of battle, communications links, etc.) The tasks are divided operationally by function and by area (e.g. Africa, Asia, etc.) An area with which I had some contact was the Institute of Information which studied open source materials. I also met several people who were part of the Army, Navy and the Air Force as officers in their services who co-operated with the GRU specialists.

Its headquarters, the 'Aquarium' is located in Khodinka Airfield, right near the Ilyushin Design Bureau, just outside Moscow. The GRU has always been independent of the KGB. Indeed the KGB had to ask permission to visit the GRU or to attend its functions. The GRU was larger than the KGB and had its own "Special Forces" spetznaz troops. Unlike the KGB, it has been largely unchanged in the post-Soviet era. Since it was less 'political' it had offended fewer people. It kept its structures, its officers and its tasks. Despite the dissolution of the USSR at the start of 1992 and the reduction in manpower within the GRU engendered by Russia's reduced economic might, the GRU remains largely unchanged from the Soviet era. In the former Communist bloc their military intelligence arms also remain largely unchanged despite becoming democracies. The GRU today is a cohesive, highly efficient, and professional military intelligence agency. There was a good esprit de corps between the regular military officers and the GRU. I remember entering the Main Airforce Building for a meeting in 1996 with some friends. Standing on the steps was a young man, slightly chubby, in an airforce uniform without a hat. He was being greeted and cheered on by almost everyone who walked in the door. I was introduced and shook his hand. I asked my friends who this hero was. They told me he was the guy who traced the satellite phone of Dzhokhar Dudayev, the Chechen leader, which allowed the

Air Force to send two laser-guided missiles to where Dudayev was speaking on his phone and blew him to small pieces.

By the time of Gorbachev's accession to power the war in Afghanistan was deteriorating badly. Resources were draining from the USSR budget and military progress had stopped and containment was the policy. Gorbachev told the military that they had a year to sort things out. They embarked on a policy of creating an Afghan Army which would notionally take over from Soviet troops, who would then be free to return home. This did not work so, at the end of 1986, they prepared to bring their troops home. The first contingent returned to the USSR from May to August 1988 and the rest from November 1988 to February 1989. It was an expensive and humiliating experience.

After the war ended, the Soviet Union published figures of dead Soviet soldiers: the initial total was 13,836 men, an average of 1,537 men a year. According to updated figures, the Soviet army lost 14,427, the KGB lost 576, with 28 people dead and missing. Material losses included: 118 aircraft; 333 helicopters; 147 tanks; 1,314 IFV/APCs; 433 artillery guns and mortars; 1,138 radio sets and command vehicles; 510 engineering vehicles; 11,369 trucks and petrol tankers[xiii] It was a very costly business.

The reason for this description of the security services and the challenges which faced Gorbachev is to point out the inner stresses of the Soviet system ripe for reform under Gorbachev and the fear and hostility which had been engendered by the 'glavni vrag' (the main enemy – the USA) in the Operation RYAN business and the Operation Cyclone resupply of advanced weapons to the Afghan mujahidin. Gorbachev knew that unless the system was reformed and modernised it would collapse, and yet he also knew that despite the praise from the West for his reforms, the West held little trust in Soviet institutions and leaders and would be very wary of assisting him in modernising the country. The new State Constitution introduced in 1977 under Brezhnev attempted to remove the ability of leaders like Khrushchev from dictatorial reverses of state policy but effectively blocked off initiatives under a blanket of requirements which demanded peer agreement and review. The political system seemed stuck in aspic.

The Soviet economy continued to decline and the emphasis on heavy industry left a great gap in the satisfaction of the country with the levels of consumer goods. This gap in consumer satisfaction led to the growth of a widespread and thriving black market. The growth of the black market in consumer goods, in particular, was an important factor in the spread of organised crime across the USSR. This explosive growth in organised crime was one of the most important adaptations to the Soviet system and had a major role in the aluminium business. Crime and corruption are intertwined with the changeover of the Soviet Union to a 'market economy'.

One important factor in the analysis of crime, criminality and corruption is the controlling variable of time or 'time horizons'. The poorer the person the shorter his time horizon. A government can plan and function on a relatively long time horizon. It has a five-year plan; a series of three-year pilot projects, regional development schemes, etc. Its time horizon stretches out into the distant future. Most major international corporations operate on a similar time scale. They can make 'long-term' investments; position themselves to take advantage of a market which is emerging over the medium term; build in 'loss leaders' for the short-term to buy long-term market share. Middle class professionals, civil servants and white-collar workers can plan their lives and career prospects in years. Blue collar employees can plan in units of years, quarters or months. Poorer people on the dole or receiving supplementary assistance can plan in weeks. The truly poor can only plan on days or even shorter intervals. The shorter the time horizon, the more immediate the need for satisfaction of basic needs - food, shelter and protection. It is this time horizon disparity which has been the seed bed of corruption in societies across the globe. Governments, political parties, aid and social welfare agencies cannot minister effectively to the needs of the poor because they do not and cannot operate in the same time zone as the poor. Those who can deliver in the short term - deliver money, extend credit, provide food or craved illicit substances, protect households or shops from attack, arrange employment opportunities, and punish enemies - are almost exclusively criminal organizations and often receive in return the political, religious and economic powers of those whom they assist. Those who take these powers in exchange for material goods trade them for more valuable considerations with governments, corporations or international agencies. This exchange is the beginning of the trail from criminality to corruption.

What has been most important for the survival and expansion of these criminal institutions was that they were better constituted to adapt to changes in their environment than the political organizations and structures within which they operated and for which they substituted. Criminal institutions, by definition, usually are composed of the outcasts of the society (even though they may be closely allied to the mightiest in the land). They are self-elected and self-sustaining. This has meant that they are much more able to adapt to the challenge of change than the 'regular' political organisations. This has been a particular feature of Russian organised crime.

Russian organised crime is not a new phenomenon. It emerged in the Gulag as criminals were mixed in with political prisoners. The criminal leaders, urkhas, dominated the lives of the prisoners in the camps (and often the guards). They developed an elaborate society of criminals who agreed to be bound by a code of honour. Their leaders were vory-v-zakone or "thieves within the law". They kept discipline among themselves. They even spoke an argot, fenya, which isolated them from the others. The prison argot was used quite frequently in conversations with me during my visits to the Far East. I had to learn who was a 'pakan' (boss), who were the razboiniki (heavies), who were the byki (bodyguards), and to avoid the baklany (punks) the suki (traitors-bitches) and the stukachi (informers). There were elaborate rules about behaviour and propriety. It was very similar to the rules governing the borgata in New York except for the first rule; there should be no co-operation or fraternisation with the Chekists. The Chekists had never made it to Castellemare Del Golfo or Palermo so it wasn't an issue or part of the U.S. rules.

These criminal prisoners and their code of conduct were particular to the Gulag and some urban prisons. Its impact on ordinary citizens who managed to avoid imprisonment or internal exile was small. The populace were not afraid of them in the way they feared the NKVD, the OGPU and the KGB. The crook could only rob you or kill you. The Organs could do far worse things and did do so arbitrarily, on a regular basis. If you are poor there is not much you can lose to a bandit while you could lose your liberty, family and future to the Chekists. A lot of this changed dramatically during the Great Patriotic War (Second World War). Stalin needed every able-bodied man he could find or capture. There were thousands of these in the Gulag. While he couldn't trust the 'politicals', he felt he could appeal to the patriotism of the criminals. He offered remission of sentences and similar perks to criminals who signed up to their patriotic duty.

This abandonment of the cardinal principle of the vorovskoi mir (thieves' world) – no co-operation with the Chekists –led to a war within the criminal community at the end of the Great Patriotic War. This war was between the zakony (loyal thieves) and the suki (bitches) and was called "The War of the Bitches" and went on for a number of years. When the prisoners who had taken up the pardon and then were returned to the prisons or the camps after committing further crimes their lives were made difficult for them by the zakony. They retaliated by working with the prison authorities as stukachi. There was a lot of violence and many were killed na piku (carved up) or degraded to opuschiny (raped). The prison authorities didn't care much as there was insufficient food so culling the population was a welcome relief.[xiv]

Until the late 1940s, at the end of the War of the Bitches, Soviet organised criminality was mainly low-level and regional. It dealt with the usual prostitution, protection, illegal substance procurement and parallel trading in goods rackets. Criminality fitted in well with the system of blat and tolkachi which dominated the economy. During the postwar world many of the officials of state companies operated as quasi entrepreneurs on their own in selling their products to the criminal world in exchange for resources needed to continue production. These were often smuggled abroad and cash, usually hard currency, became a medium of exchange in the business world. A class of criminal traders arose (criminal only in the light of their operation on the fringes of the law) who bought and sold resources like coal, pig iron, and alumina from state-owned enterprises and arranged their delivery abroad or to the domestic users who had difficulty in getting 'planned' access to these resources. In addition, the whole range of consumer products demanded by the population and unavailable in the Soviet system, were offered for sale by the criminal gangs.

Some of these traders ('deltsy') became very sophisticated and built large trading organisations which acquired goods and transported them around the world. This type of activity was replicated in the Eastern European states forced by the presence of the Red Army to remain in the COMECON. I learned a very important lesson dealing with them. I had an agreement to buy Polish cement for export to Malta (and then, I believe, on to sanctioned Libya). I also had an agreement with a Maltese denim blue jeans factory operated by the President of Malta's daughter which she had acquired somehow from Levi Strauss. I made a very ambitious deal with the Poles and the Maltese businessmen. I would buy Polish cement and deliver Levi Strauss blue jeans to Poland. This was easy and there was an almost inelastic demand for both products. The only thing I forgot to do was to put some sort of a payment mechanism in place which would turn the transaction into cash. I needed to set up a countertrade banking operation that would allow me to make money from the trade. As I had set it up I delivered a certain number of blue jeans to Poland in exchange for a certain tonnage of cement. I sent over 30,000 tons of cement to Malta and delivered several hundred thousand pairs of blue jeans to Poland before I stopped. My profit was in cement and blue jeans, not cash. I could sell some of the extra cement in Malta which helped me pay for the shipping and some of the extra blue jeans to some Russian deltsy. However, the returns were negligible. I told them I didn't want to continue and that they should do it directly with each other without me. I stopped my side of the business. My accountant went through the trades and informed me that my great cement-for-blue jeans deal which I was certain would make me a fortune, netted me US$16.50. My children and friends, however, had loads of Levi Strauss blue jeans as gifts. The Poles, Russians and Maltese made money; not I.

By the time of Brezhnev these informal economy's commercial leaders were firmly locked into the supply system. Many became very wealthy. Among the most prominent of these was Galina Leonidovna Brezhneva, the President's daughter. Galina was a special case. She was in close touch with many of the top criminals in the USSR. She had four husbands. In 1981 she married Deputy Interior Minister of the USSR and Lieutenant General Yury Churbanov, a man run by the Uzbek Mafia. Yuri Churbanov, Brezhnev's son-in-law was convicted of accepting more than US$1 million in bribes from Uzbek officials during the late 1970s and early 1980s. Eight other officials were in the dock with him including the former Uzbek Interior Minister and several regional police chiefs. Churbanov was sentenced to twelve years in a labour camp.[xv] Churbanov's wife Galina was linked to a Moscow diamond-smuggling ring through her lover "Boris the Gypsy" (Boris Buriatia). The anti-corruption campaign of Andropov while he was in the leadership of the KGB netted many of the top Party people[xvi]

By the end of the Andropov era, despite his efforts to crack down on official corruption, the Soviet economy was characterised by a failure of the central planning system and the rise of a symbiotic process of enterprise managers establishing a long working relationship with the leaders of organised crime.[xvii] By the time of Gorbachev there were four major players in the Soviet economy; the state–appointed factory managers and their political contacts; the new class of traders and middlemen; the zakony; and the bitches. The government's anti-alcohol program in 1985, like Prohibition in the U.S., added immense wealth to the criminal classes (manly zakony) and did little to reduce alcohol consumption.

Gorbachev's reforms continued to support and develop the criminal penetration of Soviet industry, even if inadvertently. The 1987 Law of State Enterprises gave independence to state enterprises and allowed them to make joint ventures with the traders and the organised criminal gangs. Shortly thereafter Gorbachev passed the 1988 Law of Cooperatives which lifted the restrictions on types of activities of companies, profit, size, and pricing. These new cooperatives were empowered to establish joint ventures with foreign firms, which in turn opened legal access to Western banks. The combination of new laws, access to foreign capital, and infiltration of organised crime into the formal economy gave rise to a formation of elite mob entrepreneurs and their successful and powerful gangs.

One of the fundamental problems was that there really was no law; or at least one which specifically dealt with title to goods or land. After the Law on Co-operatives was introduced there was a deluge of often overlapping and conflicting laws and decrees emanating from a variety of jurisdictions. The ultimate validity of laws was difficult to establish because the same subjects were often covered by many different and mutually contradictory rulings. Presidential decrees, which were often not consistent with each other, coexisted with and often contradicted parliamentary legislation. "The weakening of hierarchical links and the collapse of the Communist Party destroyed the former network of administrative co-ordination. Administrative offices have overlapping jurisdictions, each pursuing its own agenda. One of the consequences of such confusion is that titles of properties—such as the ownership of a newly privatized flat—can be registered by different offices. This allows for multiple sales and frauds of perspective buyers. "

The tax system was similarly confused. Until January 1999, Russia did not have a tax code, and taxes were levied by decree for a total of eighteen Federal levies. Presidential Decree No. 2270 of 22 December 1993 freed regions and cities to levy taxes. According to this decree, local government could establish up to eighteen local taxes. It became the duty of the taxpayer to sort out taxes according to the budget to which they accrue, share the money between different budgets if necessary, and monitor changes in tax regulations, since many new taxes were retroactive

A tax inspection was followed by a tax police inspection, followed by a tax inspection by a higher tax office. Moreover, the audit of the same object (e.g. the VAT tax base), for the same period of time, was made several times. Tax authorities often used on-site visits to the same taxpayer to punish him for appealing his fines in court. No one really knew what the law meant; only that it[xviii] probably existed.

This was equally true for private transactions. I had shipped some steel from the Ukrainian port of Mariopul to China for a St. Petersburg trader. Because of problems in the port there were delays and the trader owed me US $56,000 in demurrages (delay fees) I presented him with my bill and asked him to pay me. He turned to me and said "How do I know that Russian law is the same on demurrages as English law? If I don't pay you, what can you do; sue me?"He pointed out that it would be difficult to get a lawyer who would press the claim and a judge who could not be bought for a lot less than $56,000. I explained to him that it would not be necessary to hire a lawyer at great expense or bribe a judge. For $200 I could have him killed in St. Petersburg. After that I would bill his wife and offer her the same deal. He was a Russian and understood that this was a Russian way to settle the problem so he paid me the following week.

Russian organised criminal groups, generically referred to as the 'Mafia' grew up alongside nascent Russian capitalism. Its growth paralleled the growth of legislation enabling private ownership of factories; the private ownership of banks; and the private ownership of stocks and shares. All of these were absent from the Russian economy for seventy years and, as they returned or were permitted, the Mafia was in a good position to take a piece of the businesses being transacted. The Mafia should be considered as relatively low level players in these businesses. They were largely the muscle in the protection rackets and the carriers or wood and water in the major transactions. The business brains in the rise of organised crime came from the ranks of the intermediaries; the traders and deal makers who were associated with several of the Mafia families but who were also independent of their structures. It was these intermediaries who consulted with the Party officials or the plant managers. It was these intermediaries who travelled abroad and made deals with foreign businessmen.

There were two kinds of intermediaries in this development. The first were the top level traders who arranged the purchase of products or resources and offered them for sale to others. They used the Mafia family to which they were affiliated to assist them and to share the proceeds, but they considered themselves separate and apart from their associates. They considered themselves businessmen, not criminals. Some worked at the very top of the state-business structure; they were 'institutionals' like Semyon Mogilevich and Grigory Luchansky. They set up their financial empires with the active participation of the Russian political elite. Despite being associated with a Mafia Family, their deals were often legitimate and the structures they built genuine businesses. The Mafias infiltrated the banks but didn't actually do any banking. They mainly used their positions to obtain the lists of depositors and shook them down for cash and shares in their businesses. A large number of Russian bankers have met a violent death. The Russians joked that they would send a petition to the World Wildlife fund to have Russian bankers declared an endangered species.

The second type of intermediary was the young men who were taken from the universities and assisted in setting up banks and financial institutions. These young men, Khordokovsky, Aven, Fridman, to name a few were, set up by the political establishment (Silayev, Korzhakov, Soskovets and Kasbulatov) to provide a legitimate banking system that could channel the funds coming in and out of Russia and to be the intermediaries in businesses with the new overseas financial investors. These later expanded to stock brokerages as privatisation moved forward. Occasionally they had to provide financial services to the local Mafia families.

As might be expected with all this Mafia activity, there was also a Russian and overseas interest in prosecuting and preventing criminal elements in the society. One of the most determined of these was the Senior Investigator for Special Cases of the Investigation Committee of the Russian MDA Lt. Colonel Sergei Glushenkov.. Glushenkov was particularly interested in the developments in the Russian aluminium industry. He started the prosecution of the alleged criminals in his famous Case No. 009 of February 21st, 1994. Over the years, Case No.

009 swelled and split, marking out and separating more and more new people involved; it changed numbers and turned into a six-digit one from a three-digit one, and on its pages a scene of the contemporary history of Russia of that period unfolded, [xix]

Another lawyer, Bruce S. Marks of Philadelphia filed several suits against leading figures in the Russian aluminium industry in U.S. courts and research on the Russian organised crime became a growth industry in the 1990s. There were reports after reports issued about the tie-ins between organised crime, Russian industry and the political leadership of Russia under Yeltsin. A great of what was being written was true. However this did not cause a lot of sleepless nights among the Yeltsin circle, the "Family". Most of those who were engaged in this massive privatisation of Russia and the use of these intermediaries felt fully justified in doing so. They felt justified in doing this their way because they had no trust or faith in the U.S. or Britain or Germany or France. They knew, from Operation RYAN and the Operation Cyclone deliveries of sophisticated weapons to the mujahidin that the West posed a danger to Russia. They saw that Reagan pushed his advantage over Gorbachev to agree arms reductions treaties with Russia that many conservatives could not agree with.

They were particularly afraid that all the boasting of first world status and stature as a major power would disappear if they let everyone know just how weak and fragile the economy was and how ill-equipped the military was to resist an attack. One evening I was enjoying a banya at a military base in North Moscow with a very brave and impressive man (twice a Hero of the Soviet Union) who volunteered to supervise the helicopter deliveries of sand and concrete to cover the Chernobyl site immediately after the explosion with no effective protection against the radiation. He was a General in charge of the Soviet/Russian fighter aircraft. He told me that he was frightened that the Russian air force pilots were limited to flying one and a half hours a month because the air force couldn't afford the fuel. A cosmonaut who was with us in the banya said that the Russian Federation of Cosmonauts had complained that their training schedules were severely reduced. Later, when I visited Star City (the cosmonaut headquarters north of Moscow) I was surprised to see how little activity there was.

Even more bizarre was what was revealed to me at a meeting with the Northern Fleet. We had been working with Anatoly Filatov (the last "Red Director" of Norilsk Nickel) and the Northern governors on a plan to deliver foodstuffs from Africa to the Arctic area. I asked how they were delivering the food themselves. The admiral told me that periodically they would take the missiles out of the tubes in the nuclear subs and fill the voids with potatoes. They would use the nuclear subs to deliver these potatoes to the isolated bases on the Arctic coast and the islands. He warned me that if there was a confrontation with a US submarine he would bombard the sub with fresh potatoes.

This wasn't just embarrassing, it was dangerous. The men I met who were involved in creating a new order for the new Russia were, if nothing else, patriots. They feared for their country and the buffeting it was receiving from its enemies and its former friends. They knew it was dangerous to allow the massive money laundering operation to take place; they knew that they were risking a great deal by selling off their gold supply; they knew that allowing criminal elements to grow and expand might be difficult to control in the future; but they also knew if they didn't do everything they could on their own, there was nobody else who would help them. I could understand that. I am a patriot myself and if my country were in such a dangerous predicament I would do the same as they. It would be a grave miscalculation for anyone to doubt that even after years of oppression by the KGB, by the economic shortfalls, the disorder, the chaos and the tyranny that the dissidents in Russia were not also patriots.

This generation of Russians have all been through a system of education that instilled the value of patriotism and loyalty. The children of the Pioneers and the Komsomol have all been taught from the same script. Even the doubters, in my experience, still believe the core values if not in the practice. I learned this when I made a maladroit attempt at humour. I was asked to design a storage system for grains in the port of Vanino. I produced some drawings and called the installation the 'Pavlik Morozov Memorial Grain Store'. This was greeted by wry smiles and frowns,. It was a subject about which that they didn't seem ready to accept humour. Pavlik Trofimovich Morozov was the young 13-year old Soviet boy who denounced his own father to the authorities for hoarding grain during the repression of the kulaks. His own family turned on him and killed him when the Organs arrested his father. This became a celebrated case in the Soviet Union and there were songs, plays and operas written about Pavlik's loyalty to the State. It became part of every Soviet child's education. I probably should not have made a joke of it as they seemed to think it was in bad taste. This surprised me as they were uniformly hostile to the State and had suffered from the State's activities. It was poor judgement on my part.

With all these forces at work it was now time to start to create the alumina import facility.

CHAPTER SEVEN

I was shocked to be told on my return to London that the TransWorld partners had decided not to allow me to use a floating silo to import alumina to Vanino. I couldn't understand this and asked why such a decision was made. David said that it was very important to show the Russians that TransWorld was serious about investing and staying in Russia and that the floating silo was too 'temporary' and not a firm commitment to the country. David said that we must look as if we were putting in twenty or thirty million in the project so they knew we were serious. I replied that having the floating silo was a good way of protecting TransWorld's interest as, if there were a problem with the port or with the railroads we could pack our bags and move off to a better place in an hour or so. It would be a "floating asset". If TransWorld invested twenty or thirty million in a facility it would give the initiative to the Russians who could hold the investment as a hostage. I also pointed out that if the alumina was held on the ship before passing over the rail to the quay then maritime law stated that title to the alumina had not passed from TransWorld to the receiver. TransWorld could still claim title to the alumina if something went wrong with the receiver or the port. As each arriving ship contained around 26.000 metric tons of alumina that meant that delivering it to the quay risked around US$ 3.6 million unnecessarily. They disagreed. I was told that I should come up with a plan that didn't involve a floating silo and which would look as if it cost twenty or thirty million but which shouldn't really cost more than one or two million.

The reasoning behind this was that the Bratsk smelter had invested through its Vladivostok joint venture, Dalso with a Mafia-connected family, *Zhem*, into a facility at Rajin in North Korea, using the same Vigan pneumatic equipment as was chosen by Meshin in Nikolayev in the Ukraine. Meshin had said that his cost for the equipment in the Ukraine was supposedly twenty million dollars (which is what he and Kravchuk split between them from the stolen bauxite left at Nikolayev) and the 'college of Alexanders' (everyone in Dalso seemed to be an Alexander) said it had supposedly cost them twenty-five million to set up in Rajin. The actual cost of each of their installations was under US$250,000. Marc Rich was planning on setting up something similar in Murmansk. It was important to look as if we were matching their announced spending plans.

I did the calculations and pointed out that this would be a folly as it would add at least two or three dollars per ton for the imported alumina. I was told not to worry. I thought about the instructions and decided on a new system that would continue the ability to divorce the discharging of bulk carriers from the potential delays of the rail cars.

Vigan Unloader

If they didn't want to use a floating silo I would devise a system which discharged the incoming bulk carriers into the holds of a 'mother ship' permanently moored at the quay using conventional grabs on board the mother ship. I would build a receiving hopper above the rail lines on the quay which would load directly into railcars moved below the hopper. I would move the alumina from the holds of the 'mother ship' to the hopper using a new piece of machinery recently designed for the purpose of discharging bulk commodities, the "Pneuma-Grab".

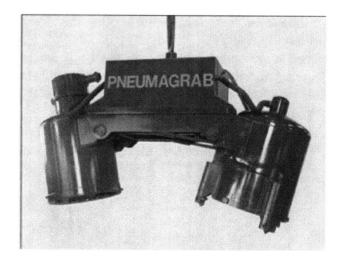

This grab is lowered onto the bulk cargo. It closes its hinged sides and compressed air is pumped into the grab and, when full pressure is reached, a valve opens to push the bulk cargo with the compressed air down a pipe to a storage facility. This can be a silo or a hopper which loads railcars.

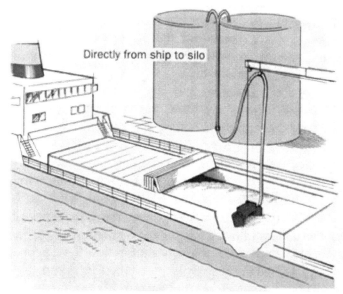

Directly from ship to silo

Initially the Pneumagrab would be mounted on the 'mother ship' between the arriving carrier and the quay. It would discharge into the hopper I would build above the rail lines. Eventually I would build a land-based storage facility to replace the 'mother ship' if I was forced to by TransWorld.

It seemed a very quick and efficient system. I would use two normal alumina grabs; that is ship's grabs with a rubber lip to stop the very fine alumina from running out. These would be placed on the 'mother ship' and would discharge the bulk carriers.

I realised that my tasks were clear: (a) construct a hopper for the railroad carriages; (b) arrange for the hire and purchase of a PneumaGrab; and (c) arrange for the delivery of two rubber-lipped grabs. I explained this to David who said that as long as I was not using a floating silo I should go ahead.

I contacted the designers and engineers of the PneumaGrab in Sweden and told them of my plans. We agreed to work together to design and build the facility (the hopper, the filters and the installation of the PneumaGrab and its compressors). Victor Parness, who had been sent to Vanino, worked hard to find the best place for us to actually construct the hopper and consulted with the port in getting permission to use Berth 20. We hired the Scottish engineering firm, Morrison's, to help us do the civil work and supervise the project. They sent two engineers to the site. I joined them with two Swedes and we made ready to begin.

I thought I would see if the port actually had these rubber-lipped grabs on hand. I asked the head of the port if there were such grabs in the port. He said he thought so but that I should ask Sergei. I went to find Sergei, who was an old, retired worker from the port. I asked him if he knew if these grabs existed and where they were. He said to come back the next day. I went back the next day and Sergei asked me to accompany him. We walked down to the port and, just behind the refrigerated shed; Sergei pointed to the ground and said "They are buried here!"

I was a bit dubious but the port director brought a front end loader and we dug. Sure enough, there were two very good grabs with rubber lips; exactly as I had requested. Being very naive, I asked why they were buried. I was told that in the Soviet Union everything belonged to the State. Equipment could not be sold, traded or used as collateral. All equipment had to be accounted for in the assets of the port. Even if something was broken it had to be accounted for. Therefore, since everything had to stay on the port's property, it was easiest to bury it and dig it up when it was needed. All over Russia, in ports, factories or transport depots there were things buried. It meant they could be accounted for but took up no valuable space.

I asked how they remembered where everything was buried. They told me that every place had a 'Sergei' of its own who was in charge of remembering. Whenever something had to be found, Sergei would remember where it was. I then asked the obvious question, "What happens when Sergei dies or forgets?" The answer was "Then Russia will have lost some very important assets."

The Swedes came out and we decided on a design for the hopper which would be placed above the rails on the quay so that two trains could be loaded side by side. The hopper would have four outlets, with a dust-free connection. The railcars would be positioned underneath the two discharge teats for each car and the valves would be opened and the railcars filled.

This might sound straightforward but it wasn't. We were guaranteed railcars but there were four different types of railcars for bulk carriage in use in Russia; each with a different set of openings (hatches) on the roof of the carriage. To fill these openings we needed flexible bellows and a plywood template with appropriate openings to correspond with the opening hatches on the railcars. This would allow us to fill the carriages without dust or waste.

The next question we had to deal with was the stowage factor of alumina. The stowage factor of a cargo is the ratio of weight to stowage space required under normal conditions. It indicates how many cubic meters one metric ton of a particular type of cargo occupies in a hold. The stowage factor of bulk alumina (the sandy variety) is 0.61 cubic meters per metric ton. In short, one ton of alumina would require 0.61 cubic meters of space. Obviously lighter goods, like one ton of wheat, would take much more space than 0.61 cubic meters required by alumina. This was important as the Russian rail cars were designed to hold 55 metric tons of grain and we wanted to make sure that these rail cars would hold at least 55 tons of alumina.

The next problem with filling the railcar was the angle of repose of bulk alumina. The angle of repose is the maximum angle of a stable slope in bulk granular materials determined by friction, cohesion and the shapes of the particles. We all know this from our own homes. When a substance like sugar or salt is poured onto a flat surface; it forms itself into a conical pile.

The internal angle between the surface of the pile and the horizontal surface is known as the angle of repose. Materials with a low angle of repose form flatter piles than material with a high angle of repose. In other words, the angle of repose is the angle a pile forms with the ground. This applies to alumina as well. Alumina has an angle of repose of around 23 degrees; alumina forms a fairly flat pile. This meant that we would have no problems of space in loading the full 55 tons into each railcar. As the railcar moves on its journey the shaking and jolting of the cars will lower the angle of repose in the railcar.

We then examined the four types of rail cars we were promised.. We had worked out how to fill them efficiently but noticed that the discharge of the railcars was a bit trickier. The discharge system for the Russian rail car was a 'bomb bay' flap on the base of the carriage. The two flaps would open and the bulk cargo would flow out. However, because the rail cars were very old and slightly decrepit these bomb-bay flaps didn't always produce a stable seal. The alumina would just pour out of the base of the rail car and, like an aluminium Hansel and Gretel, would leave a trail of expensive alumina across Russia to the smelter. It was crucial that we find a quick way to seal the flaps for the journey that would be watertight, resistant to jolting and which would not freeze. Also it would have to open when it reached its destination through the sheer weight of the alumina which was being released.

I did some research and decided that the most efficient system was to use a polyurethane sealant in a hand-operated aerosol can. We used an aerosol that dispensed a one part, liquid urethane foam which expanded 200% to 300% and cured to a durable, hard foam, insulating sealant. It filled the cracks between the flaps on the bomb-bay doors by expanding to fill the void. It dried tack-free in 15 to 30 minutes and cured completely in 8 to 24 hours, depending on humidity.

We used a convenient aerosol that dispensed a one part, liquid urethane foam. I decided to take out a couple of cartons to test how much it took to seal a railcar and how long the whole process took to complete. I arrived in Vanino and went to see the lady who ran the rail services at the port. She gave me two railcars to test. I entered into the railcar through the hatch and climbed to the bottom using a flashlight. I hung, head-down, into the bomb bay base and started to apply the polyurethane. It worked very well but the fumes in the sealed railcar were very noxious and unpleasant. I exited the boxcar and waited a day. I returned the following day to test the seal with a hose to see if the water would run out. The seal worked well. However, I was concerned that too long an exposure to the polyurethane foam and the aerosols would be too much for the port workers on a continual basis. I realised that some of the rail carriages could be sealed from the bottom as well as from the top as it expanded. I tried to seal the next carriage from the bottom and it worked almost as well. I told a couple of the workers to try it out. They did and were very impressed. I went back to London to travel on to Sweden to deal with the design of the hopper. About four days later Victor called to tell me that my sealant was a big success. Every can was missing as the workers had taken them home to seal their houses.

This was not what I had intended, but you couldn't blame them. It was the winter and their houses leaked. The port authorities asked me if I would like to fire them and hire new people. I said that there was no guarantee that the next lot wouldn't take the sealant as well so we needed a new system. I went back to Vanino with another load of sealant. I explained how important it was for us to have the railcars sealed before they were filled and asked for their co-operation. I suggested that for every twenty cases of sealant I brought in I would give them a case for themselves. They would get half at the beginning of the sealing of the carriages and half at the end. If there were any missing from what we agreed then they wouldn't get the second half and I would take that job away from them and give it to the railroad crews to do. That seemed to work and we didn't lose any more sealant.

I need not have worried about the toxic effect of the polyurethane foam fumes. The workers loved it. It was a cheaper intoxication than alcohol and they fought among themselves as to who would do the inside boxcar sealing. They told me they were surprised to see me dangling upside down inside the boxcar testing the sealant and crawling around on the ground testing it from below. Apparently this was something their management wouldn't do. I explained that my father always told me that I should never ask or require someone to do something I was not willing to do myself. It wasn't fair or proper. However in this case I hadn't given it a thought. It wasn't some form of gesture. It was plain curiosity. I just wondered how the foam would work.

Tore Manson, Lars Elestam (of Hagglunds and Botexa in Sweden) and I discussed the best way to build the receiving hopper on the quay. We examined the various design constraints and inspected the rail layout at Pier 20. We came to an agreement on the design. It would be too expensive to build this in Europe as it would cost a fortune to transport. The Swedes were concerned that they didn't know of facility in Russia that could build it. Mr. Shengeliya was dismissive of their concerns. He said that the metal contracting company which worked in the nearby Port of Sovyetskaya Gavan (where our plane landed) would be perfectly capable of building the hopper. He and Victor contacted them with our design and they assured us that it would be no problem.

The Swedes asked if they had the specialised steel forms, like angle bars, to assemble. The Russians said that they would fabricate everything that was needed. The Swedes sent me a thorough list of all the materials other than the steel that would be required and the equipment they would need to assemble the structure. This amounted to over US$60,000. I passed the list (not the prices) over to the Russian who told me they had everything already A deal was agreed. The Russians would build the hopper for US$42,000 (less than what the Swedes wanted for labour and tools alone). They said it would take ten weeks which was very quick. I contacted David and told him. He said to go ahead but not to tell anyone about the price as he had told people it would cost over a million dollars for the installation and the design. I told the Russians to go ahead. I gave them US$25,000 in cash to get them started and they seemed pleased.

One of the reasons they were pleased, I was told by Mr. Sandler, was that this was their first commercial contract. They hoped that if they did this well there would be other orders. They said they had the expertise and the facilities but no one knew of them. This contract would change their lives.

Occasionally in life what seems a very small thing can change things in a big way. I was regularly stuck for a few days in Khabarovsk when the weather was too bad to fly on to Vanino. I had to either hang around for better weather or take the twenty-six hour train ride to Vanino. I had tried the train once and it was a Hogarthian nightmare of thieves, bandits, hookers and commerce that covered all tastes. I was sure that I could catch every communicable disease known to my species on that train if I didn't stay awake and vigilant. I vowed never to do the journey twice.

On my days waiting to go to Vanino I walked around Khabarovsk. When I first got there it was fairly derelict but, as the winds of commerce swept in from Asia (China, Japan and Korea) and from the West, the city prospered. New restaurants popped up. No longer were little old ladies selling shrivelled apples in the street. Soon they were dressed in Chinese down jackets and vests and they were selling ice creams, Western sweets and computer books. The change was dramatic. I even spent some time at a contemporary art show which was excellent.

I walked along the market and looked in the shops. It was very impressive. Even the young lady selling 'kvass' (a fermented bread drink) out of a twenty-foot tanker looked happy at the new surge in business. The only woman who seemed sad was the young lady in the food shop selling "smetana" (sour cream). I always bought some smetana from her and asked why it was fermenting instead of fresh. She told me that her boss insisted that she sell the old stock first so no one ever got to buy fresh smetana. This upset her as other shops were starting to sell smetana which was fresh and she was losing business. That made her smetana even older. I asked her how much smetana she had left of the old stock. She showed me three big boxes. I told her I would buy all the old smetana from her so, thereafter she could sell fresh smetana like the others. The whole transaction cost only around US$16. I bought all the smetana and gave it away in the street outside and told everyone that they would only get fresh new smetana at the store. The girl's face beamed; I had never seen anyone so pleased. I met her a few months later and she smiled and told me I had changed her life.

I got news that the constructors had finished the first part of the hopper construction at Sovyetskaya Gavan. I asked if I could go and inspect it. There was a hesitation. They said that I couldn't go and inspect the hopper because the site was off-limits to foreigners. I replied that I couldn't pay for something I hadn't seen. They said they would compromise. They would take me to see the hopper but I would have to be blindfolded part of the way. I agreed and got into the car. We drove to Sovyetskaya Gavan and approached the shipyard. They stopped and put a blindfold on me. They then drove into the shipyard. When the car stopped I was instructed to get out of the car and to face south. I did and they took of the blindfold. I was looking at the hopper and the sea.

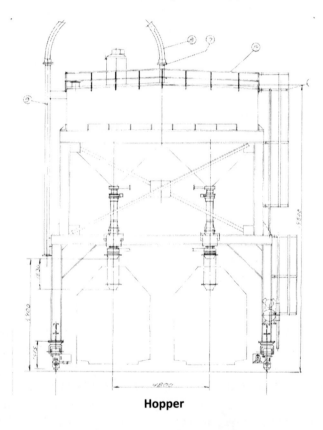

Hopper

I was given firm instructions not to turn around or to walk around the hopper. I looked at the hopper they had built and had almost completed. It was excellent. They had done a brilliant job and done it quickly. I told them what a good job they were doing and looked forward to its completion. They had built everything from scratch on the basis of our drawings. We had asked that they check the stiffeners on the base and they had adjusted the design of these to a better configuration than we had suggested as they were more familiar with the requirements of running on Russian rails. It was an excellent piece of work. They blindfolded me again and we left the shipyard.

I was very puzzled why I had to be blindfolded. I did some checking. On my next trip to see the hopper they did the same thing. This time I asked them if I could look around. They said "No, it is impossible" I asked if they didn't want me to see the "Thoughts of Lenin Collective". They panicked and asked me where I had heard about the Collective (a euphemism for where the Russian nuclear fleet was built and serviced). I reached into my briefcase and drew out a satellite map of their port with everything clearly labelled and a sonar map of the marine approaches to the port. They were shocked. They asked me where I had found such a map and charts. I told them that these were prepared by the US Department of Defence and were available in bookshops in Washington, NY and London. I also had the US bombing maps of the area; the Tactical Pilots Chart and the Operational Navigation Charts for their region which included all the radar stations and their frequencies. They threw their hands up and said I could look wherever I wanted. There were no secrets left in the new world. They built the hopper very well and delivered it to the port.

Later they were able to win a multi-million dollar contract to work with Hughes Industries and the U.S. Government in scrapping excess Russian nuclear submarines there. I spoke with Erasto Borisov who was the U.S. interpreter on this classified contract and he mentioned that my name came up in the negotiations. I had given then them a great recommendation.

The reaction at Vanino port to my gift of the Tactical Pilots Charts and the Operational Navigation Charts for their region was also interesting. The chart is surrounded by many references to the U.S. Department of Defense and similar markings. The Port Director and his colleagues looked at the map and expressed great surprise and delight. They worried that if the KGB saw such a map they would be concerned and might take offense.. Yet they liked the maps. Mr. Sandler suggested that he get a scissors and cut away everything but the map. Honour was saved and the trimmed map was stuck on the wall.

Gordon Calder, the head of the Morrison's team had made several adjustments to the berth and the area around where the 'mother ship' would moor. The Morrison engineers were all Scottish. Indeed most of Eastern Russia was filled with Scottish engineers working in the oil industry in the East and on Sakhalin Island. Some were upgrading the mining facilities in the Sakha Republic and Chukotki. They were, I believe, the largest group of engineers in Eastern Russia. When I went to Baku in Azerbaijan the place was also wall-to-wall Scottish engineers as well. It made for interesting conversations on the trips from Moscow to Khabarovsk as we were able to discuss the events of Scottish second and third division football. They were mainly Montrose, Forfar and Albion supporters. I was the lone Cowdenbeath supporter. The Russians were not as well-informed about the lower ranks of the Scottish League so were unable to participate. It was a source of constant amusement to me to hear Russian spoken with a heavy Gaelic overtone by the Scots.

The export of finished aluminium was progressing very well in Vanino. The quantities were handled by a specialised team from the port and there were few bottlenecks. There were problems elsewhere which were causing concern. In June 1993 TransWorld had a serious problem with the Port of Ventspils in Latvia. TransWorld had been shipping aluminium through Ventspils for over six months, spending between US $ 20 and US$ 30 million a month in Latvia. All of a sudden, the Port stopped the export of TransWorld aluminium, locking in around US$ 17 million's worth on the quay. There was no reason given, only that they were 're-evaluating Russian transit shipments". In fact the Latvians were trying to put some pressure on the Russians who had made some problems for them in the port of Riga. Alan Bekhor used British diplomatic channels to explain that this aluminium was the property of a British company, not a Russian one, and sent a strong note to Mr. Goodmanis, the Latvian President. It took about six days but this was worked out. Periodically we had these problems in the ports of the former Soviet occupied countries.

On my return to London I informed TransWorld that all of the civil engineering projects were almost completed and that the hopper would soon be ready, I suggested that we prepare to ship the European equipment to Vanino to test out the PneumaGrab. I also suggested that we start searching for an appropriate 'mothership' which we could send to Vanino to be moored on the quay and to prepare the grabs for when the bulk carrier arrived with the first alumina.

In my absence in Vanino the TransWorld people in London and Moscow were getting nervous. They asked what would happen if the new system didn't work. I explained over and over that there was no reason it should not work but, if they were insistent, we would build in a redundant system. That meant we agreed to buy a used hopper from Hacklin in Finland. I also agreed to buy a Neuro pneumatic unloader which we would keep in the port in case the grabs failed, the Pneumagrab failed and the Devil decided to attack our installation with fire and molten brimstone. The Neuro would sit on the hopper and we would have a backup system.

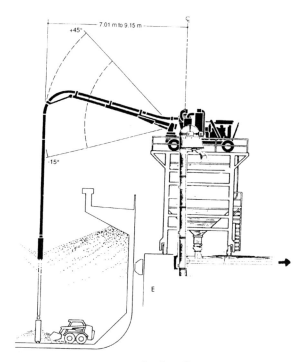

Backup System

This seemed to appease the amateur engineers; Gordon Calder of Morrisons and Tore Manson of Hagglunds, who were real engineers, told TransWorld that the system was fine and well thought out.

Before I could leave London again to prepare for the arrival of the equipment in Vanino I was taken aside by David who told me that he had heard from his Russian partners that we needed to have a permanent storage system at the port. Using a 'mothership' was too much like using a floating silo. They wanted some sort of building. I told them that this was an excellent idea and one I could support. We would use the 'mothership' in the port until the storage building could be completed. We would not be delayed.

I was very familiar with the use of inflatable air structures in a variety of configurations: tennis courts, sports arena, warehouses. In fact I was the managing director of ASATI International, plc in London which designed and created air-supported structures for the bulk storage of commodities. I was a specialist on these buildings and had incorporated some of my own patented technology in the creation of a storage system for grains and powders.[xx]

I prepared a design for an air-supported building for Vanino which would receive the imported alumina in the area behind the rail lines on the quay and which would deliver the alumina to my hopper above the rail cars. This would solve the problem of delayed railcars and would keep a store of alumina in the port at all times.

Air-Supported Dome

I contacted the supplier in New York and worked out the specifications with them. We agreed to build a dome 147 feet in diameter and 60 feet high. This would easily hold over 60,000 tons of alumina in a protected, dehumidified and heated enclosure that would discharge automatically from its base through a mechanical conveyor to the hopper.

An air-supported structure is an engineered building formed from one or more layers of continuous flexible membranes anchored to the ground so that a leak-proof seal is formed and which is inflated and pressurized by the constant supply of air inside the structure. This air-supported structure, in its least sophisticated form, is very much like an inflatable tent, which uses a constant supply of air to support the fabric membrane as opposed to wooden or metal tent poles. Most air-supported structures are far more sophisticated than these, with air locks, revolving doors, a steel bias cable harness, air conditioning, heating, humidity controls and a wide range of product handling equipment built into them, but the principle is the same.

For most installations which require heating and/or air-conditioning, it is customary to provide a packaged heating and pressurization system integrating the heating and cooling system with the pressurization system. This inflates the air structure to its full shape and pressure while automatically heating or cooling the interior to the desired setting. This heating and cooling system re-circulates warm or cooled air, eliminating heat stratification and passing the air through a lithium chloride wheel which dehumidifies the air stream..

I was sure this would be perfect for Vanino. We only needed to build a concrete slab in the port and a concrete ring beam to which we would tether the membranes which made up the dome. It would store all the alumina we needed and would keep the alumina warm, dry and ready to flow when the railcars arrived. Most importantly, I could have it ready within twelve weeks and airfreighted to Vanino in another week. The installation time would be three days. It might take the Russians longer to build the concrete base than I would take to build the building.

David seemed impressed at my solution and asked how many millions this would cost so that he could tell his partners. I told him the cost for the whole building and its related equipment would be US$ 235,750. Erection would add another US$ 5,000 with specialists from the US and we would have a ten-year guarantee. I checked this concept with the Port of Vanino who were overjoyed to have such a structure, particularly when I explained that we could do the same kind of storage for grains and fertilisers afterwards. I sent the news to New York and John Ligas came out from NY and advised the Russians and the Morrison engineers how the base and ring beam should be laid. We placed the order.

I was very pleased that I was allowed to use this type of building. It was perfect for the climate. These structures are as permanent or as temporary as may be required. One such structure was used as a 'temporary' international arrivals hall at Los Angeles Airport. This 'temporary' structure was used for twelve years when planning permission for the permanent hall was delayed. When the Alaska Pipeline was being constructed it was clear that warehousing for equipment and for human shelter would be required under severe weather conditions. Forty-six air structures were erected along the path of the pipeline and moved from site to site as work was completed. These were quick to erect and move, even in ambient temperatures of -49° C and high Arctic winds. As might be imagined, the thermal Integrity of these structures was a great part of their success.

What is most important is the use of air-supported structures is that the inflation system which supports the building is also the heating, cooling, and drying system. Any conventional building or tensioned-fabric building requires a separate heating or cooling system. Often these also require a system of insulation. The air supported structures have these 'built in' rather than as extras. They are part of the very nature of the structure rather than an add-on. I thought this was an elegant solution for Siberia.

I spent some time with Sunil reviewing the shipping operations of the metals across Russia. We had good facilities and operations running in the Baltics (Liepaja, Ventspils, Riga, Klaipeda, and Tallinn) but we were under some pressure to take more product through Russian Baltic ports (Vysotsk, Vyborg, and St. Petersburg). However the internal rail connections to these ports was poor and they had much more ice than the non-Russian ports.

In addition there was a lot of bureaucracy in places like St. Petersburg where the local political leadership had turned against Anatoly Sobchak, the St. Petersburg mayor (1991-1996) and tried to make life difficult for him. The city was run, under Sobchak, by his two close companions, Vladimir Yakovlev and Vladimir Putin. Unlike

Sobchak, who financed a range of admirable cultural projects, Yakovlev and Putin engaged more directly in commerce, with some of the less admirable of Leningrad's business community. Our shipments were directed to the Exportles side of St. Petersburg port which we found restrictive. Yakovlev ran against Sobchak for mayor in 1996 and won by a narrow vote. Then Sobchak was persecuted with a variety of criminal investigations and charges of corruption (most of them trivial). He fled St. Petersburg for Paris. When Putin took power in Moscow in 1999 many of the charges against Sobchak were dropped. He was able to return home. A few months later, in early 2000, Sobchak had a heart attack and died; his two aides also died of heart attacks with him. There seemed to be a lot of that going around. Many suspected poisoning but the charges were never proved. Business and politics frequently overlapped in Russia.

I had been warned about St. Petersburg by some prominent Russians who were in a position to know. While I was working on setting up Vanino Port I had also been working to assist a group of Russian military officers who were anxious to set up a relationship with their U.S. counterparts. I became involved as part of "Operation Jeremiah" which brought a selected number of Russian officers to the U.S. (the first meeting was at West Point) to set up a permanent liaison committee of retired U.S. and Russian officers. These were serious people and included among them: General A Burlakov (head of the Western Group of troops in Germany); Marshal. E. Efimov (Marshal of Aviation); Admiral V. Konevski (Deputy Commander-in-Chief of the Northern Fleet); General S. Kostomin (Army Chief Engineer); General V. Lobov (General of the Army and Professor of Military Science); General G. Smoilovich (Head of Military Science); Admiral V. Sidorov (Commander of the Pacific Fleet), General A. Vashin (Presidential Adviser on Military Affairs); Admiral Shalatonov (Deputy of the Marine Centre); and Marshal N. Skomoronov (Head of the Airforce Academy) Several were Heroes of the Soviet Union and Skomoronov was twice Hero of the Soviet Union and Chairman of the Heroes of the Soviet Union Club. There were others as well.

We helped arrange a reception for them in the U.S. through liaison with the Pentagon with several current and retired U.S. generals and admirals. This Operation Jeremiah was not designed for public attention but it did establish a good connection between the two sides and smoothed over many possibly uncomfortable misunderstandings. The Russian officers I met were very well-qualified professionals and extremely aware of the importance of maintaining this direct link with the U.S. They were very pleasant to be around and well-informed. Unfortunately, this Operation was short-lived.

Shortly after the beginning of Operation Jeremiah I also was involved in a parallel activity. There were several important KGB officers, or former KGB officers, who had been exploring expanding relations with their U.S. counterparts. Among the most prestigious was General Victor Budanov, a former chief of counterintelligence for the KGB, who formed a joint venture with Gerard Burke, who was once assistant director of the National Security Agency. Budanov headed his own firm, Dzericho Associates, as well as the Moscow office of Parvus International, a business intelligence firm in Silver Spring, Md., founded by Burke that employed former CIA, KGB and Soviet-bloc agents. The head of Parvus was my friend William Green, who later formed his own company TDI International of Washington D.C. for whom I have been a consultant for many years as well as, earlier, for Parvus.

In my discussions with these various gentlemen from the military and intelligence communities we were able to exchange views on the political and criminal aspects of the New Russia. They were very concerned that the elaborate plan to preserve Russia through oligarchs and criminals was bringing about changes that no one could control. It was changing the fundamentals of Russian order. I explained what we were doing in the aluminium business and mentioned some of our problems. It was interesting as, when I mentioned St. Petersburg (Leningrad), they warned me that this was a local regime run by "snakes and weasels". They told me that a group of relatively low-level Chekists had left their services and moved on to take power there and that they resented the power which was retained at the centre in Moscow. I didn't ask if this was the Centre or the 'centre' but I supposed it meant the same thing. They feared that these ex-Chekists were younger and more greedy and would eventually pose a problem to the establishment. They had ambitions to become like the oligarchs; oligarchs in epaulets. They didn't know much about business but that wouldn't be an impediment. The phrase they used echoed one told me by my grandfather "When cobblers make pies we are all in trouble."

They pointed out that aluminium was a critical industry to Russia and one that they had tried to rescue themselves. The shortage of raw materials suffered at the end of the 1980s had caused great problems to the aluminium industry's biggest customer, the military-industrial complex, particularly when a number of production facilities began downsizing production. They thought they had resolved this in 1991 when the USSR Council of Ministers allocated 480,000 metric tons of aluminium for sale through the state trading company Razno on the world market. They had earmarked this sale to procure the raw materials and equipment required by the facilities. They thought that this would resolve the supply problem.

However, the break-up of the Soviet Union made the supply of raw materials even worse. The Nikolayev alumina refinery in the Ukraine; the Pavlodar alumina refinery in Kazakhstan and a small alumina refinery in Azerbaijan were lost to Russia; a net loss of around 2,5 million tons of alumina (or 1.25 million tons of aluminium). The Russian alumina production facilities at Achinsk and Pikaleva were only able to meet 40% of the aluminium business demand for raw materials.

These were already stretched to capacity as the break-up of the Soviet Empire in Eastern Europe saw a sharp reduction in alumina supplies from refineries in Hungary and, Yugoslavia. The USSR had long-term contracts with Yugoslavia and Hungary for 1.65 million tons a year. By 1990 these supplies were gone. There was no slack to take up. The Hungarians through the company 'Hungarlu' found a more profitable market in Western Europe and the Bosnian aluminium smelter expanded to use up a larger portion of Yugoslav alumina.

The reformist government of Yegor Gaidar set up a state company "Aluminium" to supervise additional sales of aluminium in the world market to raise funds for the purchase of raw materials. 'Aluminium' distributed quotas for metal sales and purchases.. However, the 'shock-therapy' of letting the market determine policy hit the aluminium smelters very hard and impeded supplies to the military-industrial complex who could not afford to buy Russian aluminium at world prices.

This is when the Russian leadership decided on the policy of allowing Western capitalists in to take over a large part of the industry and to take over the raw material supply business through 'tolling'. Large private companies from the West, Marc Rich, AIOC and TransWorld among them, began fairly large-scale tolling. This tolling saved the productive capacity of the Russian smelters but added less to the Russian economy than was expected. Under the tolling scheme the imported alumina and the exported aluminium were duty-free. The separation of the metal sales from the profitability equation did not allow the working capital of the plants to increase. These Western companies had little interest in allowing the smelters to grow financially secure. Very little direct investment, other than raw materials, went to the smelters and the technology and modernisation were talked about but rarely performed.

In fact these companies, like TransWorld granted credits to the plants through their own off-shore companies and banks making the Russian smelters dependent not only on raw materials but also on credits. Even the sales of the metals that the smelters were allowed to produce for their own needs were used to repay the loans of TransWorld. In 1993, when privatisation was allowed companies like TransWorld used these debts and obligations to become a co-owner of the Russian aluminium smelters. They took over the responsibility of selling Russian metal on the LME. There was little true transparency in these sales even among the partners. The non-LME pricing of aluminium is usually fixed on an average price of the day, the day previous and the day subsequent to the actual trade. So, by manipulating the date of putative sale, it was possible for one partner to gain an advantage over the other. In the case of TransWorld it took the Chernoy brothers several months to figure out that TransWorld London was shaving around five percent on every trade. London explained it was the result of a clerical error but Mischa was not convinced and this led to friction in the partnership.

To add to the confusion, there were suddenly purchases available of small quantities of metals. Hard-faced young men with shaven heads and gold teeth showed up with 10 tons, 100 tons and once even 300 tons of primary aluminium. The provenance was obscure but their existence was real. We were constantly being offered these metals, primarily in European Russia. We bought them for a fair price and, because of tolling, could export them duty free from Russia. I arranged to have them loaded on the vessels and documented by their inclusion on the mate's receipt and the bills of lading as if they came from tolling. I met these young men everywhere I went.

Another oddity arose. The Russian government found that the depressed economic climate meant that the various charitable organisations were unable to raise money to do their needed work. The government couldn't supply the cash they needed; so they agreed to give a quota to these charitable and sports organisations of primary aluminium which companies like TransWorld would take and market for them internationally. The profits would be delivered to the charities and the entire transaction would be duty free. We would ship for charities like the Widows and Orphans of Chernobyl, the Russian Lawn Tennis Federation, etc. In many of the sports charities we were guided by 'sportsmen' like 21st Century Association Anzor Kikalishvili and the Tennis Federation's Shamil Tarpischev. There were many rumours that they were not entirely playing by the rule book but we only wanted the metal. We didn't involve ourselves with their other businesses; they were also very amusing and pleasant people.

So, by mid-1993 I had prepared everything at Vanino to import alumina in volume through a modern and efficient system; with backup. I had travelled to many ports in Russia and the Baltics to make more effective our shipments of metals. Sunil and I had chartered around fifty vessels which we used to deliver these metals and supplies to North America, Rotterdam, and ports in Japan, China, Hong Kong, Singapore and Taiwan. I had travelled with two young and ambitious Irish businessmen to the port of Novorossisk and Tuapse and arranged for our own berths at these ports on the Black Sea. Everything seemed to be in order and ready to progress.

At the same time I had established contacts with a group of top military leaders who were very interested in the success of the aluminium business as aluminium was key to the production of military equipment and with several important KGB and GRU officers who shared their interest. The new Yeltsin government was making ready to start an intense period of privatisation and an opening of the Russian market to the world. Things seemed very propitious and our goals seemed attainable.

CHAPTER EIGHT

When Yeltsin helped remove Gorbachev from office on December 25, 1991, the Russian economy was in desperate straits. During the last two years of Gorbachev's rule the Russian economic growth rate had actually turned negative[xxi]. According to calculations by the US Central Intelligence Agency, in 1990 GNP for the whole Soviet Union fell somewhere between 2.4 and 5 percent. The following year, in 1991, the GDP for just Russia also fell 5 percent.[xxii] It was clear that the Soviet economy was failing and, despite shedding fourteen republics and regions, the new Russia was not doing much better.

The key failing was the Soviet Union's inability to keep pace with the rapid technological changes in the West; in communications, computers, and military technology. Innovation and adaptation were not bywords in the Soviet planners' vocabulary. The satisfaction of consumer demand was even more remote as a policy driver. Many of these technological innovations in the West arose from small, private companies like Apple or Microsoft with a low capital base which were effectively self-starting. This was the practical opposite of Soviet central planning models. The Western consumers were the engines of change as they bought and adopted the computers, mobile phones, electronic games, microwave ovens, etc. as part of their normal lives.

This is not to say that Soviet, and later Russian, industries were not productive. They just produced goods that no one wanted. Equally important was the concomitant end to the Cold War. The new spirit of co-existence and disengagement was devastating to Russia's main industry, the arms industry. The figure admitted by Gorbachev of the military-industrial complex's share of the national GNP was 20%. In some cities like Perm, Novosibirsk, Krasnoyarsk, Bratsk or Irkutsk the figure was closer to 65%. The reduced tensions with the West created the chance to reduce the wasteful spending on arms. However, although they were wasteful, there were no other industries which the state could introduce to take their place. Military production offered a stable element of Russian consumption and kept many other industries alive. As military spending decreased industries like steel or the aluminium industry foundered. Domestic demand for aluminium dropped from almost four million tons a year to 200,000 by 1992.

It was a very inefficient system. What sheltered the Russian economy from the full impact of this systemic failure were the vast supplies of oil and gas which they could sell on the world market.

The Yeltsin regime decided that the only way to make a dramatic change to the system was to wholeheartedly embrace private capital as the cornerstone of the economy. Yeltsin's decision to privatise the Russian economy was bold, and destined to cause many unforeseen consequences. In October 1991 he entrusted this privatisation project to Yegor Gaidar and Anatoly Chubais, both with experience in the West and in contact with specialist advisers from Western financial institutions. In November 1991 Chubais became a minister in the Yeltsin Cabinet handling the portfolio of the Committee on the State Properties responsible for the privatisation of the Russian economy.

Chubais convinced Yeltsin that there was an urgent need for cash to save the system. Yeltsin was not convinced that a mere blanket sale of assets would be the answer so they opted for a voucher system, similar to that of the Czech Republic. The voucher scheme was proposed and adopted on 11 June 1991 by the Supreme Soviet and the actual program was started by the decree of President Boris Yeltsin on 19 August 1991. The reformers thought that if they sold off the shares in the state enterprises the workers couldn't afford them and only the Mafia, the Red Directors (those who had led the factories under the Soviet system) and foreigners would be able to afford the shares.

Under the voucher privatisation plan, the government distributed vouchers; each corresponding to a notional share in the national wealth. These were distributed equally among the population, including minors. They could be exchanged for shares in the enterprises which were scheduled for privatisation. Most people, however, weren't well-informed or were very poor so were persuaded to sell these vouchers for cash. The vouchers themselves did not represent cash. They represented a notional value in the aggregate worth of the country. They might represent a cash value in the future when an exchange was developed in which these vouchers could represent a portion of the capital stock of a company; and then only if the company made a profit. It was a lot like planning using the Middle Eastern definition of "tomorrow". The basic Arabic translation is "bukra" - an unspecified period in the future meaning "tomorrow". It could also be translated as "bukra mumpkin" –an unspecified period in the future; perhaps. The best translation would be "bukra fiy mishmish" – tomorrow at the time of the apricots; but the apricots don't always come. These Russian privatisation vouchers promised cash, "bukra fiy mishmish". Most people tried to do what they could to exchange them for something they could use.

At that time there were scores of pyramid and Ponzi schemes promising fabulous returns and instant wealth. The most famous was the MMM Company of Sergei Mavrody who stole millions and millions from its Russian investors, leaving them with nothing. Meanwhile the actual vouchers were bought and accumulated by the Red Directors and the mafias whose previously captured banks now also became stockbrokers The was a poor start for the privatisation plan and reflected badly on the introduction of capitalism in Russia. The Russians used to say that "Everything Marx told us about communism was false but everything he told us about capitalism was true"

Gaidar's and Chubais' privatisation scheme relied upon the pre-existence or rapid development of Russian financial institutions to handle the cash and shares of the new corporations which would take the burden of subsidy from the central government and which would produce a capital pool which could provide for the buying of raw materials and the selling of intermediate and finished products based on market demand. The government would not do this gradually but would "shock" the system by jumping into the privatisation wholeheartedly. Unfortunately there were no residual financial institutions in existence in Russia which could do their part of the bargain and none were developing. So when government eliminated price controls and prices rose this didn't necessarily lead to higher profits or encourage others into the market as producers; it led to stagnation, decreased production and unemployment.

One of the most pernicious theories was the reformists' belief in the Coase Theorem. "Coase argued that once property rights became private, regardless of how irrational the initial allocation, those property rights would ultimately be traded until they found their highest and most productive use. Therefore, even if the 'wrong' people became owners of privatized assets that had once been state property, ultimately these owners and their inept directors would be fired in favour of better-trained, more competent owners and managers. If the stockholders of the company settled for something less, other investors would sooner or later seek a takeover by more efficient managers, as often happens in the capitalist world."[xxiii]

Only someone who was inexperienced with the Soviet system could advance such an argument. The notion of stockholder rights is usually a polite fiction in the West. Under a decentralising communist state it is an oxymoron. Those who had power or an advantage prospered, irrespective of privatisation.

Under Gorbachev's Enterprise Law (1987) many of the plant directors saw an opportunity to break away from the state system and use the states' resources to set themselves up in a parallel system. They used the Cooperatives Law to lease the factory premises to themselves. Many of these new companies foundered as they produced goods which they couldn't really sell. The Soviet system was geared to heavy industries and arms production. There was no way a factory owner could make his fortune in selling arms or machine parts. Many found they could only pay their wages to their workers in the goods that they produced. I remember driving down the roads in eastern Russia and seeing groups of people trying to sell sewing machines that their bosses gave them in lieu of wages. Moscow and St. Petersburg became giant barter markets. There were exceptions. Those plants which produced exportable natural resources, oil, gas, ores, beneficiated ores, pig iron, etc. suddenly became extremely rich. They were selling their inventories, even if at first they couldn't produce anything more than they had in stock. Not only did they grow wealthy but they empowered the tide of middlemen who could take their goods and sell them in the West or Asia and return the roubles or hard currency to the plant operators.

This was the fundamental problem with privatisation; a problem not recognised or wilfully obfuscated by the scores of Western advisors brought in by Gaidar and Chubais to assist them. If the factories didn't produce goods that people wanted before privatisation, changing the ownership didn't accomplish much. Soviet factories rarely produced consumer goods of any quality or which conformed to fashion. They made components for the varied industries and very little for the consumer. There were no Russian brands or products with any consumer loyalty. Everything 'good' was imported.

I only knew of one major exception to this rule. The Soviets produced a very heavy gauge condom, known in Russia as "galoshes" (rubber boots) which had a big market among Western homosexuals. Apparently their attempts at safer sex in the wave of fears about Aids led them to try to reduce the risk of tearing or abrasion by using a heavier gauge condom unavailable in the West. I was frequently asked to bring in quantities of these galoshes on my return from Russia. They gave me, in exchange, two Western condoms for each Russian. On my return to Russia I would give these Western condoms to my contacts (almost exclusively women) who would give me two galoshes for each Western. I never made any money on this but was amused by the looks on the customs officers' faces as I passed through inspections with substantial quantities of condoms. They all wished me a happy visit.

Many small intermediate hustlers filled the gaps between failing factories and consumer outlets; with uncertain success. The classic story is a man who finds twelve cartons of tinned fish and offers them to his contact at 100 roubles a carton. The buyer then sells this to someone else for 150 roubles. He then sells the cartons to another for 200 roubles. He sells the tinned fish to a supermarket for 250 roubles. They are put on display. Someone buys one, opens the tin and finds the fish is rotten. He demands his money back from the supermarket. The supermarket pays him and goes back to its supplier and complains the fish is rotten. The man says, "Don't be stupid. This fish isn't for eating. It is for trading".

This rush to shock privatisation was spurred on by Chubais and his Western economist friends. They had no plan for the Russian State to invest its funds for the conversion of these privatised industries into functioning businesses. Privatisation became a free-for-all. This was not a universal failing among the Russian economists. One of the most important of these was Yuri Yaremenko, whose book Structural Changes in the Soviet Economy is probably one the best descriptions of the working of the system. Yaremenko disagreed fundamentally with Gaidar, Chubais and their Western advisers. He stated that the essentially primitive state of non-defence industry in the Soviet Union would not allow it to adapt to a wholesale, shock, privatisation. It needed a gradual program with heavy state subsidy. The demilitarisation of the economy should involve engaging the military productive base to start programs of construction of social housing and the transformation to consumer goods.

The end of the Cold War had taken the burden off the back of the Soviet Union and allowed, finally, the state to start looking at modernising the economy. No one paid any attention to Yaremenko and his views were overlooked. His fears were the same fears expressed by the convocation of Red Directors in the late fall of 1992 at a meeting in Togliattigrad near Samara which was called to address the problems of conversion. They raised their two fears of being unable to provide for the millions of families that relied on them for employment if the factories failed and the fear that their ability to make an effective conversion of their plants to a competitive standard would be thwarted by a lack of state investment in the conversion process.[xxiv]

Their fears were ignored by the young, fresh-faced Westernisers and the apparatchiks of the Yeltsin inner circle. Several of the Red Directors pointed out that adopting, willy-nilly, an economic plan introduced by Russia's main enemies might prove to be a poisoned chalice. They were overruled and ignored. The Red Directors understood that if there was to be some security in the process of privatisation it would have to come from arrangements reached outside the normal channels of business-government relations.

The services industry wasn't much better. The Russians tell of a man who wanted to buy a car. He goes into the showroom and orders the car. He asks when it will be delivered. The salesman takes out his book and says it will be delivered exactly three years from that date. The buyer asks, "Morning or afternoon?" The salesman asks why this is important. The buyer says "Because I have a plumber coming in the morning."

Not only were the managers of the factories effectively divorced from any effective input in the debate over privatisation, the working people, whose standard of living was dropping daily with the effects of high inflation, devaluation of the rouble and their savings with it, were dissatisfied and disempowered. The effects of privatisation were felt first by the workers who financial cushion was minimal. Privatisation meant moving into the money/cash economy at a time when factories were three or four months behind in paying the workers. There was great unrest. The Russian government feared their disquiet. The role of labour in the fall of Gorbachev and the rise of Yeltsin is very rarely discussed or understood.

What are often missing from the discussion of the effects of privatisation on the Russian economy were the psychological and political effects of the destruction of the Berlin Wall in November 1989. All of a sudden there was a whiff of freedom in the air. This turned into a breeze and then a hurricane in short order. The East Germans threw out their leaders and their Stasi. The Poles and the Baltic States ('Pribaltika') asserted their independence. The dissidents of Charter 77 took over Czechoslovakia. The Hungarians demanded their Soviet comrades from 1956 leave the country forthwith. The Warsaw Pact was in tatters and the Russian troops started on their long journey home. The COMECON fell to pieces as the economies of the former satellites did privatisations on their own which didn't involve the Soviet Union.

What little commerce there was between Russia and its former satellites disappeared as their consumers preferred Western goods. The Russians had to bring home their troops from Europe as well as bring home their troops from Afghanistan. There was no provision for such an implosion of the Soviet Empire. There was no money or reserves to sustain a slow transition. Gorbachev and later Yeltsin were bereft of any workable plans. One of the most important reasons for their hesitation was that the Russian citizens demonstrated that they, too, wanted to try out the freedoms which the Germans, Czech and Hungarians were enjoying. The KGB made a last ditch effort to restore the *status quo ante*, but failed to make their coup work. The genie was out of the bottle. The Russian people realised that the *nomenklatura* had feet of clay and supported Yeltsin in his crusade against the old order. It was heady times. However, they soon found that you can't eat freedom; democracy doesn't mean a full belly. The old system under which the factory provided food and goods to even remote areas faltered. There was a mass migration from much of rural Russia to larger towns and cities. When I trudged along the BAM looking for sidings I saw people packing their bags and moving away. By mid-1993 many of the small towns near Tynda and Chita were ghost towns. In Yukutia (Sakha Republic) there were scores of abandoned villages. It was hard enough to live in the cities; life in the rural areas was impossible.

It wasn't impossible for only political or economic reasons; the Russian roads made life impossible. In the winter they were covered by heavy snows, often drifting over the roads to high peaks. In the summer they were giant pools of mud, potholes and steep edges. There are, to this day, more than 30,000 towns and villages without a year-round road link to their nearest administrative centre. Russian roads have declined since 1989. Today there are only about 400,000 miles of roads, most of which are unpaved, for the whole country. In Siberia at Chernyshevsk, the road actually disappeared for eight or nine hundred kilometres. All cross-country drivers had to load their vehicles onto Trans-Siberian Railway car- and truck-carriers in order to traverse the essentially roadless stretch by rail. The Russian railroads were, except for the BAM and the Trans-Siberian, non-existent in Russia east of the Urals. Even then they never double-tracked much of the BAM and never finished the upgrade to a key bridge.

Typical Siberian Road

With the fall of the Wall and the breakup of the Soviet Empire it became clear that what little consumer and machine goods the Russians could produce they would never be able to compete against the goods produced in Poland, Czechoslovakia and East Germany. The Russian market was the Far East, but this was for its insatiable demands for raw materials and metals. They had better and cheaper manufactured goods of their own. There was a very bleak outlook for maintaining manufacturing jobs and it was these jobs that they had to deal with in privatisation. The rising expectations of a working class who saw the dead hand of the Chekists being lifted from its back was a power motivator. The publication and circulation of Solzhenitsyn's account of the Gulag was a rude shock, even to the True Believers. The Gulag was still in business. The last camp for 'politicals' (at Perm) wasn't closed until 1992. The Russian government was afraid of what the ordinary Russian workers might do. It reflected on an earlier time when the government found itself in conflict with its citizens.

In the planning for the privatisation of the Russian economy the average citizen was largely removed from the equation; both as a worker and as a consumer. This was a very foolish omission as it had been the spontaneous actions of working people which had sparked the end of the Soviet Union and the Soviet Empire. The spark of freedom was lit by the Russian people themselves, inside Russia; the unsung heroes of Bloody Sunday of June 2, 1962 in Novocherkassk.[xxv]

In May 1962 Khrushchev and the Politburo decided to place Soviet nuclear missiles in Cuba to demonstrate to the Americans what it was like to have nuclear missiles on its borders. The leadership knew that this policy would have serious consequences and ordered the military-industrial complex to increase armaments production. They chose guns over butter. This dramatic shift of the national resources away from the satisfaction of consumer demand towards expanded military capability was a watershed in the development of the USSR.

The country had to tighten its belt again. The relative improvement of people's material standard of living achieved in 1955-60 was brought to a halt. A period of unrest began. In early 1962 in the city of Aleksandrov the authorities opened fire on a crowd of protesters. This marked the beginning of a series of clashes between the people and the state over food and prices; the people's trust in the authorities had been unfounded.

On 1 June 1962 a price rise for meat, butter and eggs was announced. As usual the 'necessity of important economic reforms' was advanced as an argument for this attack on ordinary people's basic standards of living: "Everyone must grasp that if we don't implement measures today such as an increase in the retail price of meat, tomorrow we will see a shortage of these products and there will be queues for meat," said Khrushchev, describing the essence of the reforms. Actually meat had already disappeared from the shelves in small towns and villages. People there had to purchase meat and other foodstuffs in the cities, or at private markets. At markets, however, the prices depended on those in the public sector and they shot up after Khrushchev's announcement, thus making the supply situation unbearable.

The economic crisis of 1960-62 had created an explosive situation. The price reforms sent shock-waves through the entire country. Indignant workers held discussions to work out what was happening, but in the end they kept working all the same. In Novocherkassk it was different.

Hardest hit by the price rise were those workers whose enterprises had just cut wages. Among them were the workers of the 'Budyonny' Electric Locomotive Factory in Novocherkassk. The workers got together in groups and began discussing how they were going to make ends meet.

The situation was made worse by the arrogant attitude of the management who ordered the workers to fall in line with the policy. Large groups of workers formed as a unit and a strike for food was prepared. The metalworkers' union put up signs 'Give us meat and butter!' and 'We need flats to live in!' The slogan 'Eat minced Khrushchev!' became very popular. The factory siren sounded bringing in more workers from the nearby workers' suburb. They held a series of mass meetings.

That night, when the mass-meeting was over, tanks arrived. Workers began fighting their own Soviet Army and 'blinded' the tanks by covering up their vision slits. In the course of this battle, a tank crashed into a pylon, knocking it over and tearing down a power-line. The tank rolled into a trench and was unable to get out. That same night the KGB carried out its first series of arrests, taking into custody many of the speakers at the rally.

On the morning of 2 June a demonstration of between 10,000 and 30,000 participants began in front of the electric locomotive factory and set off towards the city centre. People carried placards with slogans calling for the maintenance of social justice; there were also portraits of Lenin. At the front were Pioneers (members of the Party children's organization).

When the demonstrators approached the bridge over the river Techa separating the workers' suburb from the rest of Novocherkassk, they found tanks on the road ahead of them. The crowd of thousands began to chant: "Make Way for the Working Class!" The tanks did not move, nor did their crews give any sign of life, and the workers passed between them and continued on their way.

Finally the crowd reached the buildings of the city council and began demanding that the administrators come out. The square was full of people, old and young. The administration had fled through the back door. At that point in time soldiers armed with automatic weapons were brought in. They forced back the crowd and cleared the city council building of demonstrators. The bulk of demonstrators then headed for the police headquarters and began demanding that those arrested by the KGB be set free; nobody was released from the cells. Then the assembled demonstrators stormed the building.

Suddenly there were sharp reports of machinegun fire. The soldiers had opened fire on the people near the police station. The machine-gunners stationed on the rooftops around the perimeter of the square were clearly given the order to open fire. There were bodies everywhere, including a large number of children. However, the people were not to be intimidated so quickly. They began coming back to the square almost straight after the massacre, but were met by a terrible sight. The square was awash with blood, and the trampled white sun-hats of the children.

The workers weren't intimidated. The majority of factories in the town stopped work, the streets filled with people. Cars with workers drove up from all directions. The workers filled the streets in a massive demonstration, even though armed soldiers could be seen in the distance. There was a sea of people on the square in front of the city council building; almost twenty thousand workers and their families. The tanks there tried to move off the square, but people wouldn't let them. "Tell Khrushchev! Tell Khrushchev!" the crowd chanted, and then: "Let him see this! Let him see this!"

Koszlov and Mikoyan were in the town during the riots and tried to make empty promises to the workers. The workers continued the protests and their mourning. That night the KGB struck again. During the events of the previous two days the KGB had taken thousands of photographs so as to keep track of everything that happened in detail. These were used to identify the 'leaders' and agitators. Everyone who was arrested was interrogated and shown the photographs. Under threat of punishment they were forced to reveal the identity of people they recognized. The movement was thus deprived of its leading participants. At the same time a curfew was imposed on the city and food supplies were improved - a stick and carrot strategy by the authorities.

Although the revolt was hushed up and the trials not reported the Procurator-General's report makes it clear that the top levels of the Soviet state were involved."In the morning of 2 June comrades Kirilenko, Kozlov, Mikoyan, Il'ichev, Polyansky, Shelepin and responsible staff of the central organs of the country arrived at the building of the City Party Committee and City Executive Committee. Frol R Kozlov informed N S Khrushchev about the situation and requested, through the Minister of Defence of the USSR, that the commander of troops I A Pliev be instructed to use troops to break up any possible pogroms in the city". General Shaposhnikov, who was there from the beginning, had been relieved of his command for refusing to allow his men to shoot at the workers. Late on 2 June internal troops were brought from Rostov-on-Don and all were given weapons and ammunition, and by 10 o'clock all divisions of these troops were in a state of battle-readiness."The authorities admitted to the deaths of 22 workers and the wounding of 39 more." This was a gross understatement according to witnesses. About sixteen children were murdered and many more were hurt or arrested.

The Soviets were unable to suppress dissent in Novocherkassk despite the troops and the killings. They relented and decided to make Novocherkassk a 'Hero City'; a designation which would allow it to have better rations than before. As a result of "Bloody Sunday" in Novocherkassk the Soviet system had been rocked by this city-wide protest. The news of this protest travelled all over Russia through the grapevine, as well as to the neighbouring states. The working people, united, had forced changes from the USSR apparat and the Party. Change was in the air and the state was shown to be vulnerable. The vulnerability of the state to massed workers' protests was an inspiration to the working people in Poland, East Germany, Czechoslovakia and Hungary. It was the spark that set organisations like Solidarnosc in Poland in motion. The heroes of Novercherkassk opened the first crack in the wall of oppression.

Although the Chekists were able to regain control of the city the waves of dissent spread across the Soviet Union. The failures of the Soviet economy to satisfy the basic needs of the workers led to the spread of underground dissent and the undermining of the traditional Soviet trades union organisations.

Under the Soviet system, there was no independent political action allowed to be taken by workers, and their unions were one means of ensuring that. Soviet unions were part of the government and Party apparat. The official trade unions functioned as a branch of government. Their main duty was ensuring the fulfilment of the several 'Plans'. They were "transmission belts" between the government and the workers. Union leaders were chosen by the nomenklatura system and their primary function was to improve labour productivity, not to promote the interests of the workers. Since, in theory, the state belonged to the working class its interests were, per se, identical to the interests of the state. The workers couldn't possibly have a strike as it would be a strike against themselves.

In the Soviet and other communist systems, trade unions played a different role than those in the West. Soviet trade unions had a distinctive relationship to the state. They were government organized, state-controlled bodies which performed "dual functions." They had management and administrative functions and also were charged to protect and defend workers' interests. They were designed both to represent the workers and to increase workers' production. Trade unions controlled housing, day care, health care, access to vacation spots, recreation and cultural areas and, most importantly, social security funds and pensions.[xxvi]

The Soviet working class had made a tacit agreement to trade social security for political compliance, a "social contract." In this contract, the regime promised full and secure employment, low and stable prices on necessities, a wide range of free social services (day cares, hospitals, schools, etc.) and egalitarian wage policies. In exchange for economic and social security, workers accepted the monopoly of the Party on interest representation, agreed to the centrally planned economy and to the dictates of the authoritarian system. The erosion of the social contract during the late Soviet period led to a system in which there were few shared values. The lack of consensus or tradition of discussion on what a society or government should or should not do led to a dramatic rise in labour unrest and political activism.[xxvii]

Unions were organized on an industrial as opposed to a craft basis. There were fifteen industrial unions affiliated to the central union organisation the All-Union Central Council of Trade Unions (AUCCTU). The unions had a state-granted monopoly in their respective industries. This type of organization allowed for maximum

Party control and also precluded any choice on the part of union members. The AUCCCTU was led by high level Party functionaries; Alexander Shelepin, the former head of the KGB, became the head of the AUCCTU. The labour movement was a key part of the Party's control of the government and the economy.

This breakdown of the 'social contract' was an important part of the failure of the Gorbachev reforms, as was the gulf between ordinary working people and the official union structures. Perhaps the best example was the Miners' Strike of 1989. The coal mines of the Donbass in the Ukraine were always a source of dissent in the Soviet Union. The working conditions were appalling. The safety record was worse and the living standards were primitive. The seeming opening of 'glavnost' and 'perestroika' led the workers in these coal mines to seek an improvement in their lifestyles through their official unions. These official unions were powerless, they said, to make any changes and rebuked the workers for trying to organise themselves outside the established union structures.

The miners formed independent strike committees ('stachkomi') in July 1989 and prepared for major coal strikes that summer. The stachkomi demanded to discuss improvements in health and safety and an increase in the wages of the miners. Their strike was successful in that instead of ordering in troops to suppress the strikers Gorbachev and his Politburo met with the strikers and listened to them. A compromise was reached and on October 9, 1989, a new law on strikes was passed in which strikes in key industries like defence and the railways were banned but which allowed for the balloting of the members and arbitration procedures in other strikes. The law came into effect on October 24, 1989. However, the cat had already escaped from the bag. The 1989 strikes were undertaken outside the existing union structures. The strike committees were made up of only working miners; no managers were allowed. The leadership was largely under the age of thirty-five.

During the strikes, the strike committees met in almost continuous session and took responsibility for the provision of public services. They insured order and maintained and monitored the mines. The power to meet on their own and to negotiate with the government and the Party was a cathartic event after seventy years of repression. Miners' strikes became shock waves helping to topple

Gorbachev, bringing Boris Yeltsin to power, and ending the Soviet Union.

As a result the AUCCTU's Nineteenth Trade Union Conference decentralized the union structure and turned the AUCCTU into a looser confederation: the General Confederation of Trade Unions of the USSR (VKP) under Vladimir Shcherbakov. Despite this, worker protests increased. There were an estimated 2,000 strikes during the years of 1988 and 1989, including the nationwide miners' strike in July 1989, with a loss of over 7 million work days. Strikes grew in intensity and in length. Strikes were widespread in 1989 – the official trade unions were totally bypassed and new alternative unions (initially strike committees) were established, predominantly in the coal regions of the Donbass (Ukraine), Karaganda (Kazakhstan), Kuzbass (Russia), and Vorkuta (Komi ASSR within Russia). Bus drivers, railroad workers, metallurgists, air traffic controllers, and others also struck. These strikes were precipitated by changes in work and compensation rules, coupled with a declining standard of living. Workers were being penalized through bonus reductions for outmoded and broken equipment, lack of inputs, and transport delays.[xxviii]

The old Soviet trade union federation was dissolved in 1991 and a new one created by its affiliated unions, the Federation of Independent Trade Unions of Russia (FNPR). It called itself independent to underline its autonomy from the Communist Party, which Yeltsin banned later that year. The FNPR was the only mass national organization, apart from the military, to survive the transition from socialism

The growth of commerce between Eastern and Western Europe which swelled during the early days of perestroika played a role in the institutionalisation of labour dissent. Although the history of dissidence and unrest within East Germany, Poland and Czechoslovakia in the late 1970s had a dramatic effect on the internal policies of these nations, the trade unions there were still dominated by their Soviet-style trade union organisations. Initially the union structures were not radically altered by these protests, but with the gradual liberalization of the COMECON (as in the Helsinki accords) a new type of Eastern European unionism emerged; outside the existing union structures and were allied to political dissent rather than party loyalty. Surprisingly the first of these dissident labour efforts arose within the USSR itself when, in November 1977, Vladimir Klebanov and five others called a press conference in a Moscow flat to announce the formation of an Association of Free Trade Unions of Workers in the USSR. These unionists were among those millions of workers in the USSR who, for a variety of economic and political offences, were sentenced to imprisonment, 'treatment' within the Soviet psychiatric centres, or who faced general demotion to lower grades because of their efforts to pursue trade union grievances. Klebanov himself had attempted to form a union of miners in his native Donetsk area to press for shorter hours and safer working conditions which landed him in a psychiatric ward and then prison. Klebanov, and most of the new unionists, were unemployed and were considered unemployable. They petitioned the International Labour Organisation (ILO) to hear their claim to be recognised as a genuine union under ILO Article 87, signed by the USSR, which guarantees the universal right to organise unions. Their call was picked up by Western union bodies. The ICFTU made a formal complaint to the ILO against the USSR for its violation of Article 87; a complaint joined in by most of the ITSs and numerous national centres. The Russians denied that such an organisation existed. They stated that "All this is twaddle from beginning to end. There are not and have never been any such trade union 'associations' in the Soviet Union". Nonetheless, the authorities began to arrest all the signatories to the union's petition. Klebanov was returned to his psychiatric ward.

Following the crackdown on the leadership of the Free Trade Union Association, the dissident workers expanded their union to include a wide variety of trades. They formed the Free Interprofesional Association of Workers (SMOT), which attempted to gain international recognition of their right to represent workers in Soviet industry. In August 1979 the KGB arrested the three most prominent members of the SMOT executive, Vladimir Borisov, Nikolai Nikitin and Albina Yakoreva, on charges of hooliganism and resisting arrest. This was followed by a wave of protests by unions in the West. Borisov, in fact, had been invited by George Meany of the AFL-CIO to address the union's convention, but the authorities would not grant him a visa. The US Machinist Union (IAM) leader, Bill Winspisinger, cancelled his planned visit to the USSR because of the arrest of the SMOT leaders. Other unionists cancelled or postponed visits for the same reason.

Union dissidence spread beyond the USSR. In February 1979 the prominent Rumanian dissident, Paul Goma, announced that a free trade union had been formed in Rumania. The leadership, Dr Ion Cana,

Georghe Brasoveanu and others come from a wide range of occupations. Their union, the Rumanian Workers' Free Union (SLOMR) concentrated primarily on labour relations, rather than politics, and complained of Rumania's high unemployment rate, poor working conditions, long hours, low pay and the burden of political favouritism in promotion. The SLOMR petitioned the ICFTU for acceptance as an affiliate. The Rumanian government soon cracked down on the SLOMR and the president, Ceausescu, called its leaders "betrayers of their country". Many SLOMR leaders soon found themselves behind bars, unemployed or otherwise punished by the authorities.

In mid 1979 the Polish unionists made common cause with the political dissidents to protest at the low wages, shortage of basic foods and the repression of dissent in Poland. They formed an Organising Committee for Free Trade Unions in Silesia and a free trade union committee (KOR) to press their claims for recognition. A prominent leader of this movement, Kazimierz Switon, was arrested in April 1979 and others in the KOR were seized and put on trial. This later grew into Solidarity.

In Czechoslovakia, the dissident group surrounding the Charter 77 movement included a large number of trade unionists. Most, when their protests were reported in the West, were fired from their jobs. The ICFTU petitioned the ILO to hear the case of the dismissed Czech workers on the grounds that the Czech government had ratified the ILO's Discrimination (Employment and Occupation) Convention of 1958 and these firings violated this convention. The ILO decided to publish the ICFTU's petition and the Czech government's reply. Most damning, however, was the complaint by Jiri Hajek to the Federal Assembly of Czechoslovakia accusing the government of the persecution of dissident unionists and also accusing the Czech official unions of participating in this persecution. The head of the URO (the Czech Central Union Board) issued a directive ordering all unions to expel all Charter 77 signatories. All appeals to the employment board were ruled out because the government has decided that Charter 77 was a subversive document.

Protests against poor working conditions, low wages and poor management occurred in Eastern Europe through unofficial or wildcat strikes. In Yugoslavia, the home of self-management, these strikes were numerous. It was a policy of the Yugoslav government to tolerate these strikes, or "work stoppages" as a good indicator of trouble spots in the economy. Through this they were able to prevent the intense politicisation of worker unrest which characterised the dissatisfaction in East Germany and Hungary.

The increase in East-West investment and trade in the early 1980s established greater links between the workforces of Eastern and Western Europe. The growth of East-West trade union unity was, for the communist states, a two-edged sword. On the one hand, the pressures for unity among union movements which transcended the cold war divisions offered the communist unions in the West a new legitimacy and opportunity to play a far more important role in international unionism than previously. The unions linked with the communist parties of France, Italy, Spain and Portugal saw a broader base for creating local pressure groups within the EEC and the multinational companies. They pressed for 'Eurocommunism'. On the other hand there was always the danger of contagion. The unionists of Eastern Europe who met Western unionists for discussions on a shorter work week, better conditions of health and safety, more adequate pensions, unemployment and the control of the multinational companies were frequently tempted to apply these lessons at home. The growth of unrest within the Eastern European economies and the crisis of unemployment and inflation which threatened the economies of the East inevitably led to further demands that the unions actually be seen to function as a vehicle of workers' demands.

The contact between East and West provided these Eastern unionists with support and advice as to how best to act to defend their members. The Czech metalworkers' union during the Prague Spring sent out delegations to many Western nations and hosted frequent delegations of metalworkers from the USA and Europe. Many of these exchanges consisted of advice on how Western unionists handled key policies relating to collective bargaining and contractual demands. Other meetings encouraged the unionists in their pursuit of legitimate demands from the Czech government. It is small wonder that the fiercest opposition to the Russian occupation of Czechoslovakia came from those unionists in closest contact with their Western colleagues in the metal and transport unions. Following the ousting of Dubcek the union leadership was itself purged. The lesson to the Russians was clear; contacts between East and West were not without risk for the East.

One vital reason for Western unionists to visit the East and to promote higher wages, better working conditions and shorter hours in Eastern Europe was that there was a real economic payoff for this activity. Along with the strong political motivation to build free unions in Eastern Europe, West European unions had become increasingly upset by the flow of cheap products into Western European markets from Eastern Europe. As more and more multinational companies invested and produced in Eastern Europe they used this manufacturing base to supply Western European markets. This trend started in the metalworking industry with the growth of Russian and Eastern European manufacture of motor vehicles under licence to companies like Fiat. This expanded to include large Swedish imports of Polish and Baltic softwood products marketed as Swedish-produced and designed. In the mid-1980s there were moves to establish huge chemical, especially petrochemical, plants in Eastern Europe which the multinational chemical corporations used to replace or threaten to replace existing Western European chemical plants as they became obsolete. These developments alarmed West European trade unionists who saw in the low wages, unhygienic conditions, and long working hours of East European labour a threat to the jobs and benefits in the West.

This interaction was not only the province of unionists. Intelligence agencies on both sides of the border used their influence to infiltrate the unions of the other side and to control or report on the resources engaged in the struggle. Josef Frolik, the Czech defector, spent years in the UK in the service of the Czech intelligence organisation targeted primarily on trade union affairs. In his subsequent testimony he revealed numerous contacts with leaders of the British trade unions and exposed the intense rivalry between the Czechs and their Russian masters for access to British unionists. A principal actor in the Russian efforts to penetrate and influence foreign unions was Boris Averyanov, head of the International Affairs Department of the AUCCTU, executive board member of the WFTU, and colonel in the KGB. Averyanov served in the London embassy as labour attaché and later as an adviser to Allende in Chile. When Shelepin left the KGB to take the leadership of the AUCCTU, Averyanov was his deputy and right hand man. Another figure well known to trade unionists from the Third World was Timor Timofeeyev who headed the Institute of the International Workers' Movement, a research organisation specialising in analysis of political trends in the world labour movement. He was a frequent lecturer and questioner at the AUCCTU's Higher School of Trade Union Studies, which was loosely attached to Moscow University.

In the U.S. the international affairs department of the AFL-CIO was still led by Jay Lovestone, purged as Secretary of the U.S. Communist Party as a result of the Bukharin purges, and now a fierce and rabid anti-communist. With the support of George Meany, Jay Lovestone and Irving Brown the AFL-CIO set itself up in the foreign policy business. It put Phil Delaney in the State Department to be in charge of U.S. labour policy. With US government support the AFL-CIO engaged in labour projects across the globe, financed and supervised by the CIA. Initially the funding came through Cord Meyer's shop at the agency but later, after the exposure of the CIA's links with the 'charitable foundations' which donated so freely to the AFL-CIO, funding came through AID sources and the State Department. Several of the US unions objected to the AFL-CIO becoming an agency of the U.S. government and disaffiliated from the AFL-CIO on this issue. I was proud that the UAW was one of those and we carried on our international programs without any ties to or financial support from the government.

I must say I was very amused one day in Moscow, years later, when I had a chance to see the Russian specialist on international labour, Timor Timofeeyev at a meeting. I looked at him and recognised him immediately. He may have called himself by his Russian name but he was Gene Dennis, the son of Eugene Dennis the General Secretary of the US Communist Party who took over the Party after Lovestone left and Earl Browder was replaced. I hadn't seen him in years since I dropped him off in Dobbs Ferry with Freddy Magdoff before Bobby Magdoff's funeral. I didn't want to embarrass him so I didn't go over to see him. It is a funny world. I also learned that the budding capitalist, William Browder of the Hermitage Capital Management fund was making an impact on Russian capitalism. Browder was the grandson of Earl Browder who had taken control of the CPUSA after Dennis. I did tell Jay when I saw him next about the continuing role of the families of the US Politburo and enquired if he thought we could expect a child of Max Schachtman to show up as Metropolitan of the Orthodox Church.

The AFL-CIO was adamant that they would allow no contact between Western "Free" unions and the unions of Eastern Europe, especially those in the Soviet Union. With the outbreak of the 1989 miners' strikes the new President of the AFL-CIO, Lane Kirkland, decided that the US unions should offer its assistance to the striking miners to help prise them away from the Soviet state. As he had done earlier with Solidarnosc in Poland, he invited the Soviet coal miners to the US and gave them substantial financial support.

"In April, 1992 the Free Trade Union Institute established an office in Moscow, and organized the Russian American Foundation for Trade Union Research and Education. RAFTURE sought to encourage the formation of a new labour centre to replace the FNPR, and trained organizers for raids. It was a creature of U.S. foreign policy, guiding resources to those unions which supported Yeltsin and privatisation. The FTUI paid the salaries of administrative staff in certain independent unions, and started a newspaper, *Delo*, with $250,000 from the National Endowment for Democracy. *Delo* campaigned for Yeltsin and for business/labour/government partnership, urging workers not to demonstrate against non-payment of wages"[xxix]

The Free Trade Union Institute set up training programs in Russia and Eastern Europe. These offered practical courses in unionism along with a strong political direction designed to support Yeltsin. The FTUI funded a database of union activists and "different anti-democratic union groups," paid for television programs and a labour education program, and set up a public relations operation and an advisory council of trade union leaders. It used $660,000 to set up four radio stations in Russia in 1994. These initiatives in trying to gain control of the direction of Russian labour died when Jesse Helms cut the aid budget which deprived the AFL-CIO of its financial lifeline. Its programs still exist in a small way but they have little direction on the course of Russian labour movements.

Russian workers were suffering under the new shock tactics of privatisation. For seventy years they had been state employees. Their wages, working conditions and leisure were controlled by a variety of Party and union organisations. Life was hard but predictable. With a stroke of a pen they found themselves in the private sector. The Communist ideology had always quoted Friedrich Engels, "After the seizure of power by the working class, the dictatorship of the proletariat will be used to abolish capitalism and, hence, classes. Since states only exist to regulate class conflict, the state will thereafter be redundant and will wither away." Well this state had certainly withered away and no one was sure what had replaced it.

The next years saw the replacement of the withered state by a rising tide of 'oligarchs' who took over much of the profitable sectors of industry and the concomitant rise in organised criminal gangs who controlled, not just crime, but sat on a mighty wave of corruption that was the strongest force in the new Russian society. There was no respite for the working people and they continued to suffer.

CHAPTER NINE

Just as the Russian workers woke up one day to find that they had been moved from the state sector to the private sector, Soviet business found that the same stroke of the pen had moved them from state capitalism to private capitalism. In both cases there was little preparation for such a shift and certainly no guidelines or infrastructural changes introduced to prepare or equip them for the move.

Despite the macroeconomic thinking and highly-researched academic models of how the workers and the businesses of Russia should perform under the new system, there were fundamental, practical, realities at play which precluded the success of the theoretical models. The problems which faced the workers and those which faced the new businesses were congruent and inter-linked. Simply put, the companies couldn't pay the workers from accumulated earnings because there weren't any. They could not continue producing goods because they had no money to buy raw materials. They couldn't ship these goods to and from the factories because no one knew who was financially responsible for supplying the railroads with coal, diesel, rolling stock or electrical power. The regional governments had no funds to invest to shelter the costs of the transition phase and no one was collecting taxes which could allow the state to set up transitional funds and no one had any idea about pricing.

More importantly, Russia realised that pursuing a policy of promoting internal trade was adding to its dilemma, not resolving it. The currency situation was grave because there was no apparent support for the economy other than the gold reserves which were dwindling and the attempts by the new ex-state enterprises to continue to sell raw materials like oil, gas, ores and primary metals into the world market. It is easy to say "selling its goods on the world market" but the realities of the international system for the trading of goods are sophisticated and strict. It is a formal, practical, and well-established system which is highly sophisticated and deals primarily with the exchange of documents, not actual goods. The heart of an international trading system is the link between commercial banks, international insurance agencies, international inspection agencies, regulated transport providers and large dollops of cash. These were missing in the new Russia.

Under the Soviet system there was a level of regulated interaction within the nations of the CMEA (Council for Mutual Economic Assistance) and the COMECON[xxx] for mutual assistance and in co-ordinating the Soviet and Soviet Bloc trade with each other and with the rest of the world. This trade was controlled by the central ministries of trade in the COMECON countries and was backed by the treasuries and central banks of the Eastern European nations. The currency problem was resolved by "rouble clearance"; that is the rouble served as a clearing mechanism among the several countries. There were several non-COMECON countries associated with rouble clearance, the largest of which was India.

This rouble clearance zone was an attempt to remove the Soviet trading system from the exigencies of trade with the Third World and within the Soviet Bloc. Oddly enough it was very beneficial to some of us who operated outside this system. My company used to be the agent for Stroyimpex of Bulgaria in trading Bulgarian cement to countries like India. We were no economic powerhouse but we operated outside the rouble zone. That meant that, as a foreign company, we could trade in US dollars. In fact, because I was trading in US dollars I could charter Russian ships at a far lower price than the Bulgarians could and I could sell cement to India for dollars, not in roubles for clearing. That meant that I had cash dollars to pay the offshore commissions to the Bulgarians, the Russians and the Indians. They could set whatever price they notionally wanted for the transaction. My company would charter Soviet ships which would load at Varna-East in Bulgaria and sail to one of four Indian ports. After taking my agreed profit I would deliver the excess cash to London banks for the Soviets; Austrian banks for the Bulgarians and Bahrain or Dubai banks for the Indians. Our company was not unique in this business. We even got involved in selling Vietnamese fruit juices to Scandinavia as Bulgarian juices which they had received as counter-trade from Vietnam for goods delivered by the firm Kintex to Vietnam. These companies with whom I traded were all State-owned enterprises. As I told the Bulgarian Foreign Trade Minister "Communism contains the seeds of its own destruction". As in most aspects of commercial life there are always practical aspects of theoretical economic models.

No matter how sophisticated the trade in goods; no matter if the traders are state entities, private companies; thieves or prates at some point in the transaction actual physical goods have to be picked up from place A and delivered to place B. There is no theoretical way to do logistics. This fact is often missing in the construction of academic models. The logistics are the hard part as they deal with real people, real ports or airports and real goods. The ability to know the rules, the pitfalls, the dangers and the opportunities is crucial to the success of the enterprise. When the Soviets became Russians they were unprepared to do what was necessary to carry out their transactions.

The most striking thing about the many academic analyses of the changeover from communism to capitalism is the apparent inability of the observers to see why the new Russian state was completely unable and unprepared to take its place in international commerce and why the system of 'tolling' was so crucial to Russia's development. This was not some ideological conflict or covert intervention by corrupt politicians and Western capitalists. It had to do with the actual way international trade takes place. This is crucial to any understanding of the transition.

When you go out to the shop and buy something as simple as a Mars bar you probably don't consider the complexity of getting together all the materials needed to make it and deliver it to the point of sale. There is cocoa from Africa, honey from Spain, sugar from Mauritius, and chemical preservatives from four European countries. These are all bought and transferred to the manufacturing plant at the right time and then packaged and delivered from the manufacturing plant to a shop near you.

This is a microcosm of international trade. As the world grows more complex, trading is becoming ever more global. The notion of international trade cannot be understood without understanding the more elemental notion of specialisation. When man emerged from the apes he was a hunter-gatherer. He was responsible for acquiring the food and goods he needed to survive. All men were the same. Then, as cultivation of crops was begun, many men moved to agriculture. They made an arrangement with the hunters that they would give the hunters some of their crops in exchange for some of the game they caught and for their protection. The hunters could specialise in hunting because they knew that the cultivators would give them food, and conversely.

This bargain on specialisation is what has brought man to his current level of development. Very few people spend their time growing food or hunting; but the doctors, lawyers, priests, teachers and others know that society has evolved this system in which, in return for their work, they will have access to what is necessary to live and thrive. It was the ancient Phoenicians who found the way to facilitate this development. They invented money.

Today we all go out to work at our specialities in the knowledge that we will be paid for our labour. 'Paid' means we receive a piece of blue paper or red paper or green paper with pictures of monarchs or dead presidents on it which we accept as payment for our work. We have faith that we can turn these pieces of paper, or bits of stamped metal, into food, shelter, goods and services. We believe in money; we trust currency. If we were not sure that we could turn these pieces of paper into food, we'd have to stop what we were doing and go back to being a hunter or a farmer; or perhaps, trade our crops with someone nearby who has something we need. Our sophisticated modern society is integrated through the medium of money. It allows us to specialise and develop new techniques or professions. It is largely a voluntary system in which we can choose what we want to be as we grow up without worrying about our crop. The greater the money, the greater the choice. When, as happened on a number of occasions in Russia, especially in 1998, there was a lack of faith that the Russian rouble had any value greater than the value of the piece of paper it was printed on, a crisis of confidence took hold. Desperation led to poor choices.

The development, growth and expansion of international trade are a part of man's economic and social development. It depends, ultimately, on the belief that there are rules and procedures which, if followed, will allow often complex transactions in many countries to take place in a relatively risk-free environment. This system of economic interaction has been a necessary and logical step in the evolution of modern economies.

Modern international trade consists of the interchange of documents which describe the goods, their specification, their place of production, their mode of transport and their place of delivery. The risk is diminished in such an interchange by adopting certain, recognised, procedures. These procedures are contained in agreed international rules and regulations which describe, in great detail, the methods of carrying on international trade. The International Chamber of Commerce ('ICC') produces regular updates of "Incoterms"; a document which lists and explains the terms and abbreviations used in international trade so that everyone is agreed about the meaning of the terms. Another publication, the "Uniform Customs and Practices of Documentary Credits" specifies the rules and practices of presenting documents for payment. The various international shipping authorities, like the Baltic and International Maritime Conference ('BIMCO') have standardised Charter Parties and Booking Notes so that they are uniform. Agencies like SITPRO are designed to simplify international trade by 'aligning' the documentation so that it is comparable or identical internationally.

Not only is it vital that the documents which describe the vital parts of the transaction are the same and uniform; it is crucial that the goods being bought or sold exactly match a specification which is universally recognised and interchangeable. There are many trading nations which have set up rigorous standards for goods produced in their country. The British Standards Institute (BSI) produces detailed specifications for a wide variety of goods sold in international trade. If these meet the British Standard, the BSI kite mark is affixed to their description. The ASTM in the U.S., the DIN in Germany or the GOST in Russia do the same. These include methods for testing the goods to see if they meet these standards. So, for example, if one were buying cement from the UK an important standard is BS 12/1978 which describes in detail the chemical composition of the cement, the proportions of the constituents in the mixture, and the physical characteristics of the cement (Blaine or specific surface, setting times, strengths, etc.). If the goods are specified as BS12/1978 then both buyer and seller know exactly what the product offered for sale looks like and does.

The quality assurance is frequently achieved by providing an inspection of the goods before they are shipped and after they arrive. A professional independent testing agency is appointed to inspect samples of the goods to see if they are within the tolerance levels of the declared specification. Their report is one of the documents which make up the transaction. There may also be a requirement for an independent evaluation in the receiving country. Companies like Cotecna, SGS or Saybolt are specialists in this field. In most cases these inspection agencies also weigh or measure the goods being traded and certify their true weight and condition as well as their quality.

Most international trades take place through the mechanism of the Documentary Credit or Letter of Credit. This is the cornerstone of international trade. The buyer and the seller may not know each other. They may be in different parts of the world. They cannot assess the ability of the other to perform or to pay for the goods ordered. The system of documentary credits vitiates these risks. The rules and regulations which generally apply to the use of Documentary Credits are contained in the ICC-issued Uniform Customs and Practices for Documentary Credit ('UCPDC') Publication 500 (as amended)

A letter of credit is a written undertaking by a bank or other financial institution to pay money from the buyer to the seller in exchange for a list of documents. This payment is generally conditioned upon presentation of a draft or other written demand for payment, together with other specified documents describing the goods being sold. If a letter of credit requires certain documents in addition to a draft or demand for payment, it is commonly referred to as a documentary letter of credit. If the additional documents relate to a sale of goods, the letter of credit is a commercial documentary letter of credit.

Commercial letters of credit are a means of paying for goods purchased in international trade transactions. In the typical letter of credit sale, the buyer will request his bank to issue and deliver its letter of credit to the seller directly or through an intermediary bank. The letter of credit will state that, upon presentation to the bank of the letter of credit and certain other specified documents (e.g. commercial invoices, bills of lading; certificates of origin; certificates of quality; evidence of tax paid; certificates of insurance, etc.), the bank will pay the seller the sum of money specified in the letter of credit. The terms and conditions enshrined in the letter of credit are usually found in the Pro Forma invoice issued by the Buyer to the Seller and the Terms and Conditions which apply before the transaction takes place.

The letter of credit protects the buyer because he knows that the seller will not be paid until his bank has presented all the strictly-conforming documents to the bank evidencing shipment of the merchandise. The seller is protected because he knows that he will be

DR. GARY K. BUSCH

paid once the merchandise has been shipped and the required documents have been tendered to the bank.

The letter of credit constitutes the engagement or obligation of the issuer (not the buyer but his bank) to perform as specified. The letter of credit is independent and separate from the contract of sale between the buyer and the seller. It is an engagement of two banks to each other. This is the fundamental point in using a documentary credit. The seller's bank assembles the documents that are required in the credit and presents these to the buyer's bank who checks that they are correct. If all is correct then the buyer's bank pays the seller's bank. Once the documentary credit is issued it has a legal life of its own. This means that international trade, when using a documentary credit, is a trade in documents, not goods. The certificates required are the basis of payment.

Perhaps the most important, because it is a certificate of legal title, is the Bill of Lading. When the cargo is delivered to the export cargo terminal, a Dock Receipt is issued to the entity which delivers the cargo. This could be a drayage company, a railroad, or a waterborne carrier.

The Dock Receipt contains all the information about the cargo, number, dimensions, and weight of pieces. If there is any damage or missing cargo when it is checked at receipt, suitable endorsements will be made to the document. In the case of closed boxes or crates, the term S.T.C. (Said To Contain) is normally used. This is the document used to calculate the freight and any other costs.

When the cargo is transferred to the carrying vessel, the terminal issues a Mate's Receipt, which is endorsed by the vessel's captain or designated officer. Any damage to the cargo is noted on this document. However the vessel normally has to accept the weight and dimensions as given, except in the case of bulk cargoes or homogeneous cargoes, where the cargo may be measured. The Mate's receipt is used to compile the Bill of Lading (B/L). Shipping law requires that the B/L is endorsed according to the Mates receipts. The B/L is a negotiable document and implies ownership of the cargo. The cargo can be redeemed from the ship owner against the presentation of this document at the discharge port and on proof of payment of freight. Copies of the B/L are used for several purposes, but only the original or originals (in some cases more than one original is made) are negotiable.

170

The B/L has three important functions:

1) It is evidence for receipt of the goods on board at a certain date / place and in a certain condition;

2) It is evidence of the contract of carriage between carrier and holder, unless these two parties are the same in the charter party. This would make the bill of lading holder the Charterer of the vessel and thus evidence of the contract of carriage is the Charter Party;

3) It is a document of title to the goods shipped. The holder of the B/L is entitled to the delivery of the cargo. The B/L is a negotiable document, which can be transferred to other parties during the transit time.

Bills of lading are required to be signed and stamped by the vessel's Master.

The shipment of goods by air is different. Most cargo is carried in specialised cargo aircraft but there is a sizeable amount carried in the belly compartments of passenger planes, 'belly cargo'. This belly cargo goes according to the schedule and routing of the airline and is subordinate in preference to the passenger cargos. Very frequently this belly cargo is containerised to reduce pilfering and delay on tight schedules. The document which gives evidence of the flight is an air waybill, a bill of lading for air cargo. Unlike the bill of lading, an air waybill is not a certificate of title.

Another important document in the international transfer of goods is the insurance certificate. This is important in that it speaks to the 'title' (legal ownership) to the goods and where risk passes. It passes along the chain of delivery. It guarantees that someone is always legally and financially responsible for the security and value of the goods.

As important to the exchange is the guarantee that the quality, description and condition of the goods being exchanged are exactly as specified in the agreement and the bill of lading. There is always the risk that the goods presented for delivery do not match, in terms of description, quality, quantity or condition the goods described in the Pro Forma invoice and the documentary credit or bank guarantee insuring payment. The method used to protect the parties to the transaction is an agreement on pre-shipment inspection by a professional, accredited, inspection agency. These pre-shipment inspection agencies inspect the goods before the goods are shipped;

sometimes at the factory or, most often, at the loading port of the marine vessel or aircraft.

An inspection order is forwarded to the inspection company office in the country of export. The inspection company contacts the exporter to arrange the date, time and location for inspection. The inspection is carried out, and a "Clean Report of Findings," is issued confirming the shipment's value, customs classification and that it can be cleared. The goods are shipped onward to the importing country, and the importer uses the inspection report to get goods released from customs.

All of this documentation, inspections, internal transport to the port or airport takes money. The up-front costs of preparing goods for sale on an international basis are quite expensive. One of the most difficult aspects of setting up to carry on international trade is to estimate the money that will be needed to carry on the business up until the point that revenue is produced on sales. The provision of active working capital to conclude the business is one of the most important aspects of international trade. Without that, all the other bits don't really matter.

Many start-up businesses fail to make a profit because they have not accounted for these real costs in advance. Almost every charge and cost of preparing for commerce occurs before any revenue from the transaction is received. That means that the company has to have these funds in hand to make the business work or have access to these funds from a bank or an investor.

There are a range of costs in conducting business which must be prepared for. The cost of the goods is, or should be, well known to the exporter. However, export shipping may require special packaging to preserve the goods through the several handling stages of the transaction and to meet the export requirements of the importer or the importing country. In some cases the trader is not the manufacturer of the goods but a merchant who must pay his supplier. In any case the transport has to be paid as well.

So, if one doesn't have a cash tranche at the bank or an established export history, the bank may require a 100% cover before opening a guarantee of freight to a shipper. This can be very expensive indeed. It is always crucial to know, before the transaction, how the suppliers and shippers can be paid. The incoming documentary credit is only really collateral when it is paid; until then it is a contingent asset. The cost of opening a documentary credit to a supplier, once collateral is in place is about 12.5 basis points (0.125%) per month, with a minimum of two months. So, if one contracts for US$500,000 worth of goods, the charge will be US$635.00 x 2 = $1.250.00. The processing of the documents by the bank ('availment') adds another 20 basis points. So, the original US$500,000 letter of credit will incur a charge by the bank of $1,000 for handling the documentation.

The money which must be used to pay the freight in advance is usually handled by the creation of a Bank Guarantee to the Shipper plus a guarantee for demurrages. The cost of this bank guarantee is usually 10 basis points. In addition, there are fees for amendments (around $50), discrepant documents ($65) and several handling charges. These must all be paid in advance. The figures above are for straight credits (e.g. those which are paid 'at sight'). For usuance credits (those which have a credit period included) there are a variety of finance charges and interest which accrue.

Another aspect of the export process is the 'Performance Guarantee'. In most cases the documentary credit has a clause which states that it will come into full effect only on receipt by the opening bank of a Performance Guarantee of, usually, 10% of the value of the credit. That means, if the letter of credit is not used, or if the documents presented are stale, or dirty or otherwise not in strict conformity with UCPDC, then the exporter will pay to the opener of the documentary credit the value of the Performance Guarantee in compensation. If the buyer opens a letter of credit to the supplier it will have cost him substantial amounts of money. He will pay this to his bank and others if the goods are received or not or if the documentary credit is used or not.

The cost to the opener of a documentary credit is usually about 55 basis point (0.55%) per quarter of the year or part. So, for a Performance Guarantee of 10% of the value of the transaction, the fee will be US$275 per quarter. Amendments cost $40 and there is a $50 charge for handling the documents. If the Performance Guarantee is called, however, the opener must pay the full $50,000 to the bank. If it is not called the value of the Performance Guarantee is unblocked in the account.

The buyer's cash is at risk and he often requires the Performance Guarantee to offset his costs in establishing the letter of credit. His funds are at risk and he needs a guarantee that if the supplier fails, for any reason, to perform, he will be reimbursed. This is a guarantee the seller must make. All this is 'up-front' money for the supplier or the merchant. To this should be added the cost of insuring the goods from the place of manufacture to the port or airport of departure.

There is a great more detail, costs and further commercial elements required carrying on an international trade in goods and which require a practical approach to a uniform international system. It is a general practice in world trade for a bank to require that the opening bank of a documentary credit or a correspondent of that bank in the beneficiary's country add its "confirmation" to the credit. That means that a local bank guarantees the performance of the opening bank. The number of Russian banks which were able to open documentary credits were few and the number of those which had international subsidiaries or correspondent banks were even fewer. This brief outline should indicate why the Russian factories were unable, on their own, to move away from state-owned production to the supply of the international market and to arrange for the purchase of needed materials from abroad. There were no developed mechanisms for factories to import goods from abroad; they had no cash reserves which would allow them to set up documentary credits to pay for them and few traders were willing to trade with the new Russian companies on good faith alone. Even if one believed that Russia itself was credit-worthy (a very rash assumption) it exceeded the commercial imagination to believe that any of the new privatised companies were.

There were, in reality, no Russian banks in 1990-1991 which were equipped to handle the requirements of Russia's private sector trade. The Bank for Foreign Trade (Vneshtorgbank) was established in October 1990 with support of the State Bank of the RSFSR and the Ministry of Finance of the RSFSR to service Russia's foreign economic transactions and encourage the country's integration in the world economy. It was the first and most successful bank for foreign trade. It didn't get its foreign exchange license until January 1991. Vneshtorgbank ('VTB') was able to take over some of the larger, state, trading deals and spread its offices across the globe. VTB was put in charge of handling important government tasks. The Bank was appointed the government's agent for raising and servicing external loans related to funding large investment projects, and was also granted the exclusive right to sell precious metals in the external market on behalf of the Russian Government and the Bank of Russia. VTB was also in charge of servicing the Republican Currency Reserve of the Russian Federation and the Stabilization Currency Fund of the Bank of Russia. It was a state bank, not a private bank.

It was of limited value to the burgeoning crowd of entrepreneurs and middlemen who moved into the ownership and control of the newly privatised sector. This was especially true in the aluminium industry. The break-up of the Soviet Union aggravated the shortage of raw materials. The alumina refineries located in the Ukraine, Kazakhstan and Azerbaijan with their total annual capacity of 2.5 million metric tons a year became foreign operations located in the independent countries. The Russian aluminium production facilities were only able to meet 40% of the aluminium business demand for raw materials. This had a strong knock-on effect with the military industry which was the main consumer of Russian aluminium.

For this reason, the government, headed by Yegor Gaidar authorised further sales of aluminium in the world market to raise funds for the purchase of raw materials. Distribution of quotas for metal sales and purchase of materials was managed by the state concern 'Aluminium' ('Alyuminy'), which was established in 1990 on the basis of the respective divisions of the Soviet Ministry of the Metal Industry. This was unsuccessful. The country was going through a period of hyper-inflation and the value of the rouble denominated working capital of the companies selling the aluminium was diminishing every day. It was becoming evident that in the foreseeable future the industry would simply run out of money and be unable to continue export and import operations.

The earlier consolidation of Russia's aluminium plants into a single holding company, Alyuminy, began to fall apart as it ran out of money. Its director Igor Prokopov tried to get the government to reinstate the subsidised rate for electricity it had abolished in 1968 but he failed. His company, Alyuminy, broke up into several independent smelters and Alyuminy became a state watchdog for the industry.

The Russians were in a dilemma. They needed to buy, in hard currency, the alumina it needed for the aluminium smelters. It didn't have these reserves or the mechanism to guarantee the purchases. The individual smelters (Bratsk, Krasnoyark, Irkutsk, Sayansk, Kandalaksha, Nadvoitsky, Bogoslovsk and Novokuznetsk) had no cash reserves to fund the purchase of alumina (or coal or electricity), nor did they have a line of credit established at any bank which could give them the working capital to produce the aluminium. As a result of this their offers of metals to the world market were not believed; the metal buyers and traders knew that if they agreed to purchase the aluminium and put letters of credit in place the Russian smelters could not be guaranteed to perform, nor could they issue Performance Guarantees as compensation. Still less could they arrange the shipment of the aluminium from the factory to a port as they couldn't pay the railroads or the ships which would produce the bills of lading.

The Russian Government could offer no help. They could offer tax breaks, exemptions from customs duties, etc. but no cash. However the desperate situation in which the Russian aluminium industry found itself was not new. There were many precedents in the aluminium industry when the cash requirements could not be found within the transaction.

The solution to the Russian dilemma can be found in an important chapter of the history of the world aluminium industry, but not in Russia. In 1985, when the world aluminium industry was depressed, Alcoa shut down its Jamaican plant which refined much of the island's plentiful supplies of bauxite into alumina. The export-hungry Jamaican government was desperate to reopen the plant. Alcoa agreed to lease it to the government and keep it running. But Jamaica needed to find a buyer for the output. It found Marc Rich, who had established close ties to Jamaica as part of Phillip Brothers for whom he had worked. Mark Rich agreed to lend Jamaica US$200 million which the Jamaican Government could use to pay Alcoa to keep the plant running and employment steady. As a result, in early 1986 Marc Rich was able to sign a ten-year agreement to purchase most of the output of the Jamaican Alcoa plant which annually produced some 800,000 tons of alumina. The price was reduced to reflect his loan so he was effectively buying the alumina at a discounted price.

Much of this alumina he delivered to the US market. Mark Rich agreed to let Manny Weiss, his metal trader, work with the US affiliate of Marc Rich, Clarendon, to supply US smelters with the alumina. At that time the U.S. aluminium industry was suffering from the high costs of electricity and a depressed market. Many of the aluminium majors, Alcoa and Alusuisse were losing money and were keen to sell their U.S. smelters. The local governments were anxious to keep the smelters going and to maintain employment there. Manny Weiss saw an opportunity. Rather than buy the U.S. smelters and go into the aluminium producing business Marc Rich and Clarendon would assist those who bought the smelters. Clarendon would negotiate good rates for electric power and a reduced wage rate for the labour and would supply the smelters with the cheap Jamaican alumina. In short, for a tiny investment, Clarendon would supply and pay for all the inputs into these smelters and would take the primary metal for sale at a subsidised rate. It would pay a fee, or "toll" to the smelter for the processing.

Clarendon was active in tolling in many smaller smelters as well and took a subsidised interest in others, either in ownership of a minority share or as the off-taker. By 1987, with the boom in aluminium prices, Marc Rich was making a lot of money in aluminium tolling. At that point March Rich, whose metal trading in the Soviet Union with the Soviet state trading company Razno had led to Marc Rich becoming one of its biggest customers for Soviet zinc and lead. Marc Rich was convinced by Felix Posner, a partner in the company, to make a deal with Ivan Russov, Razno's man in London, to offer the same kind of tolling deal for the Russian aluminium industry that Rich was performing with the U.S. smelters. Marc Rich introduced tolling into Russia and the Russian aluminium started to flow into the world markets.

As Mark Rich started to import alumina into Russia he soon found, as in the U.S., that importing alumina on its own was only a partial solution. His company had to make sure that the Russian smelters had electricity, money to pay wages, transport facilities etc. In his co-operation with the Russian authorities they pointed out that they were allowing a new group of Russian entrepreneurs to establish themselves and their Russian companies to help develop the infrastructural needs of the economy outside the state's direct control. Rich had interacted with these Russian traders and middlemen earlier in the late 1970s when he started doing business in the lead and zinc industry; becoming the largest foreign trader in Soviet metals. His expansion involved an association with Grigoriy Luchansky of Nordex (a steel trading company based in Vienna which ultimately had an important presence in almost every Russian port) and with Semyon Mogilevich, active in the trading of Russian and Ukrainian energy supplies. These two were operating as semi-official agents of the Russian leading politicians and were seen as 'institutionals' as opposed to purely private entrepreneurs The introduction of tolling was a major boost to the production and sale of Russian aluminium.

Mark Rich initially prospered in his tolling of aluminium but fell afoul of the Soviet authorities when they completed an audit of Razno's trade with Rich in the lead and zinc market. The KGB investigation demonstrated the Soviets had paid Rich far more for lead and zinc concentrates than Rich's customers in Western Europe had paid. Rich had to pay a penalty and Ivan Russov was removed from his post. The Russian authorities decided it would be wiser to allow in additional Western companies to do tolling as well as Marc Rich. Two Western groups were invited by Russian intermediaries to take part in the tolling of aluminium; Trans World Metals (David Reuben) and the American International Ores Company –AIOC (Alan Clingman). Smaller firms like the Belgian Euromin had minor trading operations with finished aluminium; WORALCO concentrated on Tajikistan and the Balli Group traded primary aluminium it bought from the smelters. However, Marc Rich, Trans World and AIOC were the key players. With the murder of AIOC's main contact with Russia, Felix Lvov, AIOC was driven out of the business and filed for bankruptcy in 1996.

Tolling was successful because the Russian banking system was woefully under-developed and the history of seventy years of communism was an inhibitor of effective commercial trust in the new private enterprises. When Marc Rich and Trans World took on the responsibility of tolling it took on a wide range of problems which had never previously had a solution in the Soviet Union or Russia. While Marc Rich had its ready-made supply of alumina from its Jamaica operations, Trans World had no regular source of supply. Through its Russian partner, Lev Chernoy, Trans World had an important relationship with Achinsk Refinery, a domestic producer of alumina and located by rail near both the Krasnoyarsk and Bratsk smelters. However, Achinsk was not immune to the difficulties of the other recently privatised companies in Siberia so it was clear that some other, external source of alumina would have to be made available to the smelters by Trans World. Trans World decided that the abundant source of supply of alumina in Australia would become its major focus.

The safe delivery of this alumina from Australia to the Siberian smelters was the task I was set by Trans World. Having set up the import facility in Vanino we began to take finished aluminium from the port to deliver to the customers in Asia. One of the first problems we found was that the problems of ice in Russian waters posed a serious impediment to the type of ships we could charter (rent) for our shipping. The charter parties (the rental agreements) of most vessels on time charter specify that the hull may not trade in areas outside the Institute Warranty Limits (I.W.L). That basically reflects the fact that ice is dangerous to the hulls of vessels passing through it. Those areas usually associated with ice, which includes most of Russia's coasts except the Black Sea, require the use of ice-class ships and attract an additional premium as the waters lie outside the Institute Warranty Limits. In effect this mean that we would have to charter Russian ships which were not affected by the IWL.

Unfortunately, many of the good quality Russian ships were stolen from Russia at the end of the Soviet Union and reflagged as Cypriot or similar flag vessels. This would not really affect us as charterers but the ship owners were reluctant to sail the stolen vessels back into Russian waters. We had to deal with FESCO in Vladivostok or SASCO in Sakhalin to charter our vessels as they still had some ships available. The situation was the same in the Baltic and White Seas. Fortunately Vanino was just below the pack ice reach and we could access it all year, although it occasionally required the use of ice breakers. It was always better to use Ice Class 1 or 1A vessels in the winter. The problems we faced were not only the lack of maintenance on these chartered Russian ships but the unhappy fact that they were crewed and officered by Russians. Russians were good sailors and generally competent. The problem was that they were badly paid. The ship owners were responsible for the wages and food supplies for the chartered vessels. Often their pay was delayed. The food supplies the owners arranged with ship chandlers were inadequate and the communications equipment was primitive. We were never completely sure of where the vessel was or what supplies of food, water and bunkers remained on board. We almost always had to advance the funds for food and spare parts in the ports and attempt to deduct these costs from the charter hire due. There was always a fight with the owner who disputed the deliveries, even when they were shown the paid invoices.

More importantly the ship's master (the captain) used his position to squeeze extra cash out of every loading and discharge.

Under the rules the ship's master has to sign the Bill of Lading to make it valid. On the Bill of Lading is a statement of the condition of the cargo. If there is something wrong, say a rust spot or a drop of paint, etc. the master can write a note on the bill of lading describing this. That makes the bill of lading a 'claused bill of lading' as opposed to a 'clean on board' bill of lading Since most documentary credits specify that the bill of lading presented for payment must be a 'clean on board' bill of lading this might mean that the goods could not be delivered or paid for. It was a regular occurrence that a master would refuse to sign a clean bill of lading until he was paid extra ($200-$500) even if there was nothing wrong with the condition of the cargo. As long as it wasn't too expensive we usually paid them.

However, this could go too far. We had a vessel loading aluminium wire rod in coil at Vyborg, north of St. Petersburg which completed late at night. The master demanded a great deal of money and refused to sign a clean bill of lading even though he knew that if we delayed our sailing the port was icing up. We would then have to pay for ice breakers and tugs if we didn't leave quickly. He was adamant. I called the ship owner and told him that we considered the ship 'off-hire' and that he would be responsible for any losses or expenses we had and that we would deduct this from the current hire. I told him we would arrest the ship and charge the master with barratry (fraud by a master or crew at the expense of the owners of the ship or its cargo). He got on to the master who saw the wisdom of proceeding with a clean bill of lading so we could leave. This was not the only time we had this problem.

As time charterers we were responsible for fuelling the ship. That meant that we would have to arrange for a bunkering agent to supply a quantity of fuel oil and diesel at a convenient port. In many cases, if not most, the master and mate would sign for higher quantities than were actually delivered and take a partial payment back from the bunkering agent for the phantom fuel. They then artificially reported higher consumption by the vessel so the loss was not provable. We ordered lubricants to be provided on several occasions. We were surprised to see that the bunkering agent had delivered a very expensive drum of lubricants instead of the simple lubricant we had requested. When we queried this the master said that the vessel required a better grade of lubricant. It turned out that the bunkering agent would put a silver dollar in the bottom of the drum and that master would keep this as his reward for choosing the higher cost lubricant.

There was no controlling these masters. We delivered a load of aluminium to Ben Thuy in Vietnam, on the Ca River. The berth at Ben Thuy is a river berth which meant the vessel stays in relatively deep water as opposed to lying alongside a quay. There was congestion in the port but that wasn't our problem. We had agreed a discharge rate with the receiver and he was obliged to pay us for our lost time getting discharged; to pay demurrages. The vessel was delayed twenty-seven days. I called the master and our port agent every day twice a day to hear what was going on. The port agent said that there was 'heavy weather' so that there were no 'weather working days' as per the terms of our freight agreement. That meant the receiver wasn't obligated to pay. This was nonsense as, according to everyone else in the port and in North Vietnam it was pleasant weather. When we finally discharged the cargo I sent a hefty bill to the receivers for demurrages. They refused to pay, saying there was bad weather. I paid for two surveys of the weather from the British Meteorological Reports and the Vietnamese Meteorological Service who both attested to the fact that every day was a 'weather working day'. It made no difference as the master of the vessel had signed the daily time sheets in the port saying that there was no working time possible. The receivers paid him $5,000 instead of paying me $108,000 in demurrages.

It is a general rule in the international shipping business that in negotiating a charter party through a shipbroker, supplying misleading information or back trading is frowned upon. However, outside of the negotiating of the charter party truth is very rarely encountered anywhere in the shipping industry. However in dealing with Russian ship owners, crew and officers lying reached its apogee. It was an extra burden to an already complicated shipping program.

In many ports the stevedores (the chaps who load and unload the vessel) weren't much better. They, too, were underpaid and sought ways to augment their income. When we were discharging alumina from a vessel in Vanino we were using compressors to pneumatically discharge the holds. All went well the first shift. When we had supper and returned to the discharge we suddenly found that there was no fuel in the compressors. It was late and we would lose an evening's discharging time without the fuel. I politely enquired what had happened to the fuel that I had already provided for the compressors. The stevedores told me it had disappeared. There were 'bad people' in the port. I was in luck, though. The stevedores had a supply of fuel that they could sell me so that discharge could continue. I agreed to buy the fuel and, as if by magic, it arrived back to the compressors in the very same cans that the lost fuel was last seen in. I told them that this was the last time I would do this. In the future I made an arrangement with the local mafia chief in that section of the port and paid his people a relatively small fee to look after the fuel between shifts. I didn't lose any more.

Sometimes the problems had nothing to do with petty theft; sometimes they resulted from sloppy practices. These very same compressors were running low on compressor oil; an internal lubricating oil which is made especially for compressors. I had checked with the chief engineer that the port had this compressor oil in its storage so I wasn't worried. As I ran low I went to the port storage building and requisitioned some compressor oil. They checked their books and said it was there but they had no idea where it was. They asked "What does it look like?" They had about forty steel drums lying on their side full of a great number of things. Some were labelled in Russian, some Japanese and some English. I settled down to look but eventually I could find no clue. I asked if these were the original drums and they said that sometimes they combined drums into a single drum to save space; but didn't label them. I went and took a sample from the compressor so I would know what I was looking for and started to methodically take samples from the forty drums.

Getting the right compressor oil meant getting not just the colour right and the consistency right. It was also important that one got the viscosity right. I took out a pack of paper drinking cups in conical shape (Dixie cups) and laid them in a row. First I looked for red oil (the colour of the compressor oil). I took the samples that I found of red oil and poured a bit down the top of the Dixie cups to see how quickly the oil would run to the bottom. I measured this against my compressor sample. This would approximate the viscosity of the red oil. I narrowed this down to three possible candidates and then tasted the oil to see its alkalinity. Finally I found one that looked right. I had the barrel taken to the compressors and they seemed to work all right. This ritual lasted three hours. As I was testing and sampling the Russians were laughing at me hysterically, especially when I tasted the oil. They said I should put any kind of oil in the compressors as they would likely work. They couldn't understand why I was fussing.

The logistics associated with tolling was complex and aggravating. The internal movements between the ports and the smelters and from the smelters to the ports was worse. It is tempting to think of tolling as the vast logistical exercise carried out by the owners of these giant trading companies and the politicians and Red generals in charge of the smelters. Their role was easy – pay and be paid. The physical movement of the products in and out of Russia was a nightmare and one which required a constant hands-on control and a healthy disbelief of everything that was said, promised and attempted.

CHAPTER TEN

In these early stages of privatisation the new Russian Government realised that it had a very limited ability to control the great swathes of the economy which had been under Party and Soviet control earlier. They knew they had to maintain their interest and controls over the oil, gas and the defence industries; the three major international industries which brought in hard currency. As part of their control of the defence industry they needed to retain some influence on its supplier industries; e.g. aluminium, copper, titanium and a variety of secondary metals. They saw that they needed to develop reliable allies to move into the management positions of these companies to achieve these ends. First, there were the Red Generals, the directors of the Soviet factories, who used this period to take over their factories or industries and operate them as if the factory had been privatised and turned over to them personally. Perhaps the most successful of these was Victor Chernomyrdin. He had been made the Minister for the State Gas Industry under the Soviet system. Under Gorbachev in 1989, the gas industry was transformed by fiat into a joint-stock corporation. Chernomyrdin gave up his title of Minister and declared that he was the CEO of the new company, Gazprom. Unlike in the petroleum sector the state was determined to keep the gas industry as a single entity. Initially it retained the shares in the joint-stock company. When Yeltsin took power he authorised the change in November 1992 of Gazprom from a state-owned joint-stock company to a private joint-stock company. Some shares in Gazprom were sold to the Russian public and some to the Gazprom employees. [xxxi]The majority of the shares were still held by the state. Chernomyrdin was so successful in retaining the unity of Gazprom that Yeltsin chose him as his Deputy Prime Minister and then, in December 1992 as Russia's Prime Minister. When Chernomyrdin went back to government his former deputy, Rem Vyakirev, took over as head of Gazprom. The two of them supervised the burgeoning gas industry and were able to avoid some of the tight controls which the state attempted to use against other industries which were less well-connected.

There were other Red Generals who took over several major corporations and industries, especially in the military-industrial complex. One of the most successful was Oleg Nikolayevich Soskovets.

Soskovets worked at the Karaganda Metallurgical Factory in Kazakhstan from 1971 until 1991 when he became its General Director. In 1989 he was elected to the Soviet Congress of Peoples' Deputies and was made Minister of Metallurgy. After a short spell as a minister in Kazakhstan he was summoned back to Moscow by Yeltsin who appointed him Deputy Prime Minister (to Chernomyrdin) and the man responsible for overseeing all Russian industry. Soskovets and Chernomyrdin worked closely and well together, along with Yeltsin's security adviser, close friend and tennis partner Alexander Korzhakov from the KGB. Soskovets brought with him his talented deputy, Vladimir Lisin, who joined Trans Would Metals in late 1992.

I worked closely with Lisin for a number of years. He not only spoke excellent English, he also knew a vast amount about metallurgy. His postgraduate studies included an MSc in 1989, a PhD in engineering and DSc in economics. He was a very useful person to know and a close confidant of Oleg Soskovets. I was very pleased to see his eventual rise to the status of oligarch as head of Novolipetsk Steel. There was a direct link established between Soskovets and the Chernoy brothers, Lev and Mikhail; and it was the Chernoys who invited David Reuben to expand Trans World Metals into a wider organisation, the Trans World Group. Another major player at this level was Yuri Safranik, the former Minister for Energy and industry, ex-governor of Tyumen and a major figure in the oil business. These Red Directors were an important force in the privatisation of Russia.

They were also important in that they were chosen to be the links between the Chekists and Russian business. In December 1990, when the Soviet secret services became aware of the likely economic disaster approaching the and collapse of the Empire, two top-ranking party members, Vladimir Ivashko and Nikolai Kruchina, along with officers of the first main department of the KGB, organized a new department of the KGB which was to coordinate the transfer of a major part of Communist Party money to the bank accounts of the newly organizing foreign trade enterprises inside Russia and abroad. Arkady Volsky, former assistant to Andropov took over its main control. With the rise of Yeltsin, names like Prime Minister Silayev, Oleg Soskovets, Alexander Korsakov, Ruslan Kazbulatov and Yuri Safranik were added. These were the core people in developing the new Russian business model.

Their first order of business was to deal with the Russian arms industry. Arms, as well as gas and oil were Russia's most reliable earners of foreign cash. It was the need to support this industry which led to their urgent sponsoring of tolling and tolerating the intervention of foreign metals firms. The collapse of the Soviet economy and the Soviet Union itself had profound consequences for the Soviet defence industry and, in particular, Soviet arms exports. The political and fiscal crises which accompanied the fall of the Soviet Union and the collapse of the Warsaw Pact not only gutted the military procurement program that kept arms factories working, but also destroyed the mechanisms that had kept Soviet arms flowing to clients abroad.

Under the Soviet system factories were operated at the command of the state. For example, aircraft frames were produced from primary metals delivered from state-owned aluminium smelters, titanium producers and copper smelters. These primary metals were assembled into armaments in state-run factories under designs produced by state-run planning and design bureaus. "With the fall of communism these state-run factories found themselves on their own. There was no central planning of production; there was no guaranteed supply of raw materials or subassemblies; there was no capital accumulated to buy electric power or to pay for transport or labour. The defence industry was not immune to the problems which beset the rest of post-Soviet industry." [xxxii]

The sensitivity of the arms business, coupled with the need for high-cost engineering, research and development budgets meant that there was a need for a continued level of concentration of the industry under a single umbrella. The Russian arms trade recovered very slowly from the first dark days after the fall of communism. This was achieved by the centralisation and integration of supply by a single entity of a state patronage capital company Rosvooruzhenie. This State Company for the Export and Import of Armaments and Military Equipment was established 25 Nov 1993 by Presidential Decree. Rosvooruzhenie became the Russian state arms export company, and built an alliance among factory directors in the arms industry under its control. Individual companies like Ilyushin, MiG, Sukhoi, Tupolev and Yak retained some autonomy in their design bureaus and suppliers but their management ranks were filled with ex-military personnel attached to Rosvooruzhenie, as were the arms manufacturing and naval equipment suppliers.

There were four major banks assigned to handle the accounts of Rosvooruzhenie in financing arms sales: Menatep, Most-Bank, Intermed, and the Moscow National Bank. Later, in 1995, when Alexei Ogarev, a good friend of Tatiana Dyachenko (Yeltsin's daughter) left his post at Rosvooruzhenie to become deputy head of the Presidential Staff for the problems of the military-industrial complex and military-technical cooperation under Korsakov, he was able to add Yevgeniy Ananyev's MAPO Bank to the list.

The first General Director of Rosvooruzheniye was Aleksandr Ivanovich Kotelkin, a long term GRU officer with experience serving outside Russia. He headed Rosvooruzhenie from November 1994 to August 1997, when he was appointed first deputy foreign economic relations and trade minister. In 1998 he threw his lot in with Yuri Luzhkov, the Moscow mayor and the company, Sistema, and supported Luzhkov in his dealings with the military production centre in the Moscow area. His main job while at Rosvooruzheniye was to keep Gen. Pavel Sergeyevich Grachev, the Minister of Defence, away from any power over the sale of arms.

Initially Rosvooruzheniye hoped to continue its 'captive market' in the former Warsaw Pact nations but this was not to be. Many of the Eastern European states were more attracted to Western aircraft and arms. Those formerly captive markets avoided buying Russian weapons systems because Russian military technicians would come with them as part of the deal. There was a small appetite for this.

One of the additional complicating factors in this was that Soviet aircraft, used in the Soviet Union and the Warsaw Pact, had IFF (identification, friend or foe) cryptographic identification systems designed for command and control. This is a system that enables military and national (civilian) located air traffic control (ATC) interrogation systems to distinguish friendly aircraft, vehicles, or forces, and to determine their bearing and range from the interrogator. The Soviet aircraft transponders recognised as 'friends' other Soviet-built aircraft but set off alarms if the aircraft responded with a different signal. If the Eastern Europeans were going to move towards Western aircraft they would have to re-jig their IFF systems so that 100% of the system was either one or the other or they might shoot down their own aircraft.

As a result, Russian arms exports hit bottom in the early 1990s, dropping from a plateau of $22 billion in 1987 to only $1.7 billion in

1994. Conversion of defence plants to civilian production did not offer a practicable solution. Throwing defence workers out of work in the name of efficiency appeared unacceptable to the Russian government as there was nowhere else for these workers to go. With its markets closing, production falling, and workers unpaid, at the end of 1993 President Alexander Korsakov created the state monopoly, Rosvooruzhenie, to take over the marketing, financing, sale, and delivery of Russian military equipment and thereby re-impose order on the Russian arms industry's chaos

Yeltsin's act cut off the Russian military, the Defence Ministry, and Defence Minister Pavel Grachev from the arms trade by placing Rosvooruzhenie under the oversight of the president's Security Service and his own chief bodyguard Aleksandr Korzhakov (an important ex-KGB figure). The army had shown itself unwilling or unable to stop soldiers selling off their equipment to anyone with cash. Korzhakov, Yeltsin's confidant and the power behind the throne in the Kremlin, had ultimate authority over Russian arms exports and, more importantly, over the billions of dollars in revenue those exports would generate. The governmental measures implementing Yeltsin's *ukaz* were signed not by Prime Minister Viktor Chernomyrdin, but by Deputy Prime Minister Oleg Soskovets, the Kremlin's "grey cardinal," linking him closely to arms exports.

Rosvooruzhenie was more than just a centralised arms business. In many ways it was a club of ex-military officers and GRU retirees. They had all taken up posts in the arms companies and were the liaison between the companies and the military. I had the honour and good fortune to attend some of their gatherings and it was all very comradely. I remember, in particular, the celebration held in the Military Art Gallery to celebrate the 50th anniversary of the Kalashnikov. Mikhail Timofeeyevich Kalashnikov was there along with the leaders of Rosvooruzhenie. I was, I believe, the only non-Russian there. It was very enlightening; enlightening because people spoke frankly. Marshal Shaposhnikov made an eloquent speech and toast on behalf of Rosvooruzhenie praising the work of Kalashnikov and the importance of the military industry in maintaining Russia's military might and commercial power. I was impressed that when Kalashnikov responded he thanked everyone for the hospitality and the kind wishes but expressed his dismay at the widespread dissemination of the rifle. He said that he had invented the rifle to protect the lives and safety of his fellow Russian soldiers and that he was disappointed that the rifle he produced was available in all the corners of the world and had been used to kill his fellow Russian soldiers when they were sold to Russia's enemies or licensed to strangers to produce. I still have my gold Kalashnikov lapel pin from that meeting.

The need for the armaments factories to have unrestricted access to the primary and secondary metals needed for their manufacturing of arms was an important factor in their involvement in the Russian metals producing companies. These same leaders of Rosvooruzhenie (Korzhakov, Soskovets and Silayev) were the architects of Russia's 'tolling' program and the creation of a new system of Russian banking which could handle these exchanges. When the money which was earned overseas returned to Moscow it had to be used and directed for the support of the oil, gas industries and Rosvooruzhenie. The KGB and its allies, under Silayev and Soskovets, set up a system in which loyal and trusted members of the Komsomol system and friendly businessmen could form their own banks; Russian banks. Men like Khodorkovsky, Aven, Fridman and others were chosen and set up in the money business. As this worked and metals or oil were produced and sold, these companies retained a part of the hard currency in their own coffers. As these banks and investment trusts prospered, Russia became more economically independent. They also became less and less dependent on Western capitalists to introduce them to commodity trading. They brought the roubles home and, in the various stages of privatization, they invested these in Russian businesses. At the heart of this restructuring was Rosvooruzhenie and its banking needs.

The new banks were crucial to this development. Perhaps the most famous, indeed infamous in light of his trial and retrial, was Mikhail Khordorkovsky and Menatep Bank. Khordorkovsky was born into a relatively well-off Moscow Jewish family. He went to university in Moscow and stayed on to do an advanced degree in chemistry. He was very politically active since pre-university days. Khodorkovsky graduated in 1986 from the Mendeleyev Institute of Chemistry and Technology (MKhTI) in Moscow with an engineering degree and in 1988 graduated from the Plekhanov Institute of National Economy.[xxxiii]

During 1986 and 1987 he was deputy secretary of the MKhTI Communist Youth League (Komsomol) committee for the Frunze District of Moscow. From this position, Khodorkovsky became director of the Centre for Scientific and Technological Programs of the Foundation of Youth Initiative, where he served until 1989. He got his start in business when Communist Party Deputy General Secretary Yegor Ligachev decided to encourage youth activists to enter business. A technology business centre was attached to each district in Moscow. In 1987, Khodorkovsky was named the head of the centre in his home Frunze district. ("Menatep" is the acronym for Frunze's

"Inter-Branch Centre for Scientific and Technological Programs" the local chapter). The Menatep Group evolved from these business activities, initially through the resale of computers, where profits were made capitalizing on the difference in price between domestic and foreign markets as well as the differential rates of exchange. The young men running Menatep formed allegiances with many of the fringe operating groups in Moscow then entering into the business of "trading" including the local mafia groups and provided the foreign currency exchange function to their businesses.

In 1990 Khodorkovsky was appointed adviser to the Russian Prime Minister Ivan Silayev. In 1992 he was appointed chairman of the Power Industry Investment Fund and adviser to the Prime Minister. In March 1993 he was appointed Minister of Power of the Russian Federation. In April 1993, Khodorkovsky together with Smolensky (bank "Stolichny"), Gusinsky (MOST-Bank), Agapov (Credobank) established a national joint-stock company, which issued credit cards in conjunction with foreign banking partners.

Since his earliest days his partner and fellow shareholder in the banks and investment companies has been Leonid Nevzlin, a graduate of the Plekhanov Russian Economics Academy. He was born in 1959. In 1981 he graduated from the Gubkin Moscow Institute of Petrochemical and Gas Industry. Upon graduation from the institute he worked in the bureaucracy of the USSR Geology Ministry at the department's information division, collecting, storing and processing of information. Later, in 1988 Leonid Nevzlin graduated from the Plekhanov Russian Economy Academy, where he took an MBA in management and marketing. In 1989, along with Khodorkovsky, he became one of the organizers and leaders of the centre of scientific and technical programs that afterwards developed into the MENATEP association. In 1990 he became the first president of the Commercial Bank of Scientific and Technical Progress and, when this became incorporated as the Menatep Bank in 1993, he was appointed its first deputy chairman. It was largely Nevzlin's connections which led Khororkovsky later to expand into the oil business.

These nascent banks were assisted by the passage in 1987 of a law which allowed a private business to start a bank with the rouble equivalent of US$750,000. As inflation got worse and the rouble/dollar exchange rate declined this capital sum was devalued in real terms to less than $85,000 by 1990. This led others, like Mikhail Fridman to turn their small businesses or co-operatives into banks. Fridman's company, Kuryer, like Menatep traded in a wide variety of goods and services and acquired enough capital to start a bank, Alfa Bank. He joined with the overseas Russian, Leonid Blavatnik of Access Industries, to become the first chairman of Alfa Bank in 1991. Alexander Smolensky specialised in construction work as a source of capital by providing *shabashniki* (private building contractors) to the opening markets in Moscow.[xxxiv] With this capital he founded Stolichny Bank in late 1989. He later bought a state bank for the agricultural industry, Agrobank, which he joined with Stolichny as SBS/Agro. Another adventurous Russian, Vladimir Potanin, who had been working with the government to market its metals worldwide, decided to do the same privately and founded a private metal trading company, Interros, which created the Onexim Bank These banks prospered as a funding source for the non-banking businesses of the founders and became the vehicles for the cabal at the centre of the government to channel their business in support of the oil and gas industry and Rosvooruzhenie. Equally, the need for foreign exchange for the emerging mafia businesses and the needs of tolling were catered for by these banks.

We had a lot to do with Menatep Bank in particular as it was Menatep whom we were told to use to effect our payments as tolling began. Looking over our accounts at a random month, August 1993, the major payments we made were through Menatep. What these accounts reflect is that we did not really know to whom the money was going. For example, on the 30th of July we paid $1,832,532.92 to Bank Menatep Transit Account 076.054.001/481 for Bratsk smelter; on the 29th we paid $2,860,000 to Menatep Transit Account 076 054 001/493, also for Bratsk. On the 19th and 20th of July we paid $9,230.000 to Menatep Gibraltar Transit Account 7/009 for Krasnoyarsk. We made a cash transfer through Menatep of $3,000,000 to the Office of Bauxite in Guinea. We were sending around $60 million each month through various banks, but over half through the several worldwide branches of Menatep. There were some payments to private companies we paid through Alfa Bank and quite a number of 'Establishments' of various names in the Bank in Liechtenstein.

These were not insignificant sums. The auditors took me aside one day and asked if I could help them account for these payments. They wanted to know against which invoices they were being made and to whom they were paid. I told them that this was figured out by the tallies of the metals sold, the hedges covered, and from telex instructions via Menatep. Our Russian partners supervised these payments from Monaco as well as London. In a word, I had no answer for them and I had no desire to find out the answer. Occasionally they would ask me about 'strange' payments; like those to Phillip Morris for large quantities of cigarettes. I explained that the traders on the ground in Russia sold American cigarettes for cash and that they would turn over the rouble cash to us to use in tolling. In exchange we would order cigarettes for them directly from the manufacturer.

I was having a conversation in late 1993 with one of the investigators from the Moscow Prosecutor's office when he asked me the same question. I had to tell him I really didn't know. He said that the investigators were sure that some of this money being sent offshore via Menatep was being delivered to accounts operated by the political and security elite of Russia. I couldn't possibly say if that were true but it would not have surprised me a lot. Logically, if it wasn't somehow questionable then it would not have been so secret. Later on, when we were persuaded to establish credit cards for some of these gentlemen and ladies in Switzerland (which came out in a trial there) their names on the cards rather gave the game away.

It was not only Menatep and Alfa which were being formed as major banks. To a lesser extent the KGB itself dabbled in banking. In September 1990, KGB active duty officer Major Chukhlantsev together with a young free-wheeler Alexander Konanykhin established a private company named Rosinformbank. Prior to that, 24-year-old Konanykhin had been involved in an unremarkable construction cooperative. He did not graduate from any college but was energetic and apparently liked publicity. According to the KGB standards, he was a good candidate for a role of a KGB front. In other words, Rosinformbank was a joint venture between Konanykhin and the KGB. Later, Rosinformbank gave birth to a number of other businesses and then vanished without a trace. When asked by US prosecutors the Russian military prosecutor's office was unable (or unwilling) to find a single document pertaining to the establishment of Rosinformbank.

In December 1990, Konanykhin and his wife established a company named Fininvestservice. In January 1991, Rosinformbank (the KGB bank) together with Fininvestservice established a company named the All-Russia Exchange Centre (AREC). In doing so, Rosinformbank provided 100 percent of the initial capitalization of AREC, but gave away 80 percent of the shares to Fininvestservice (Konanykhin.) This may not make sense from a business point of view, but it makes good sense from the KGB perspective: It made Konanykhin a front for AREC. The fact that this also turned Konanykhin into an official stockowner of AREC entitled to 80 percent of the profits did not matter. The KGB had a large arsenal of tools and methods to solve these minor technical issues much to their advantage.

The KGB Major Chukhlantsev was appointed "technical director" of AREC. He also controlled AREC's finances. Other KGB officers — Boldyrev, Chukhlantsev and Sumskoy — were appointed to the board of directors of AREC. Konanykhin officially served as the chairman of the board and unofficially — as a front for the KGB-run AREC. Later, the All-Russia Exchange Centre established the All-Russia Real Estate Exchange, the Secondary Resources Exchange and finally created the All-Russia Exchange Bank (AREB). The KGB controlled all those businesses through its officers placed in key positions. Usually, they would take the top positions, or positions of deputy boss, and always filled in positions that controlled company's finances.

The All-Russia Exchange Bank was established on 24 April 1991 by the All-Russia Exchange Centre (controlled by the KGB), Investtrade (Director — KGB officer Boldyrev), Souzinformatizatsia (General Director Ryzkhov — KGB) and the All-Russia Real Estate Exchange (created under KGB control.) All key decision-making authority for the establishment of the All-Russia Exchange Bank was the responsibility of the All-Russia Exchange Centre, established and controlled by the KGB. In other words, the KGB had full control over all those businesses from the very start.

Konanykhin fronted the KGB in the All-Russia Exchange Bank as its president. Among the Bank's employees there were about 200 KGB officers, including several Generals. Shortly after the aborted coup d'etat of August 1991, Konanykhin employed General Leonid Shebarshin, former KGB Chairman and the right-hand man of Vladimir Kryuchkov, leader of the aborted coup d'etat.

After the August 1991 failed coup and the unprecedented public outrage against the KGB, most Russian government institutions, which traditionally had served as KGB fronts, declared after the aborted coup d'etat that they would close their KGB positions. Despite the change from KGB to FSB the KGB men, who had penetrated businesses and banks, continued to operate there as 'individuals'. On 21 October 1991, the All-Russia Exchange Bank received a license from the Central Bank of the Russian Federation that authorized the All-Russia Exchange Bank to execute transactions with hard currency. The license actually granted the All-Russian Exchange Bank a monopoly on banking transactions between Russian businesses and organizations and foreign institutions. Also, it authorized the Bank to buy and sell hard currency. The rouble was in a free fall. Trading it was a bonanza.

In 1993 Khodorkovsky was used as a "front" for a major Russian intelligence operation aimed at establishing a Russian bank in the US. When this plan failed, the SVR attempted to use US territory to establish a bank in Uruguay. According to the plan, the bank, with an initial capitalization of $1 billion, was to receive a large amount of cash from Russia. The other part of the plan was to obtain foreign (preferably diplomatic) passports for approximately one hundred Russian citizens, each of whom was purportedly worth at least $100 million. These citizens were supposed to become the first customers of the Uruguayan bank, and they needed foreign passports to flee Russia in case of major social upheaval.

Some of his information is derived from the September 1999 Congressional testimony before a House Banking and Financial Services Committee hearing on Russian corruption and money laundering. This testimony states that in 1993 Khodorkovsky and his Menatep lieutenant, Alexander Konanykhin, (the man mentioned above as the founder of the All-Russian Exchange Bank) allegedly operated "a KGB money-laundering operation with stolen funds that were passed through Khodorkovsky of Menatep Bank as a KGB-controlled front firm." [xxxv] According to the testimony, Konanykhin ran the US side of the operation out of the Willard Hotel in Washington. The hearing witness, who had acted as an unpaid intelligence asset in investigating the operation, testified to the CIA's, FBI's and Department of Justice's interest in Khodorkovsky and Konanykhin at that time. The witness went on to state that the investigation of the operation was compromised by convicted spy Aldrich Ames and was never reported to Congress.

According to Russian investigators, this entire operation was coordinated by SVR headquarters in Moscow and was personally supported by Aleksandra Korzhakov, former President Boris Yeltsin's personal bodyguard. Khodorkovsky reportedly financed the operation though funds sent through Menatep.

By the end of 1992 tolling was underway in most of the Russian metal smelters and several key banks had been set up to move the cash around the world. A massive amount of cash was being accumulated outside of Russia controlled by the security and political elite and managed by Russia's new bankers, the nascent oligarchs.

During this same period another group of 'biznizmen' were forming international ties. In the early years of the Yeltsin government organised crime began to establish itself as an important economic player in Russian business. There is a great deal of misunderstanding in the analyses of the development of organised crime in Russia because the analysts do not differentiate between ordinary crime and international financial manipulation. Every country in the world has organised criminals and has done since time immemorial. I have met and dealt with scores of them in Africa, Asia, Latin America, Europe and, especially, North America. The traditional businesses of these criminals are the protection rackets, gambling, labour racketeering, prostitution, stealing, money lending and drugs. These are non-intellectual businesses and require more brawn than brains. The criminals may take over some businesses or control them, but their aim is shaking-down money not achieving the possibilities inherent in the company's business plan.

There is one distinctive feature of this type of organised crime. Their goal is money. It is what defines and circumscribes their activity. The button man who has several thousand dollars 'on the street' shylocking has the goal of collecting his 'vigorish' every week. Wise guys who have women working the street have, as their aim, the acquisition of cash. The guys who act as runners in the 'policy racket' ('la bolita') between local shops and the bookies which allows punters to bet on the "mutual" number(the last dollar digit of the daily total handle of the Win, Place and Show bets at a local race track, read from top to bottom) do it for money. The chaps who run illegal gambling establishments in which they act as the 'house' do it for money. The pushers sell drugs or stolen goods for money. This is true across cultural and political boundaries. It was stated most succinctly at his trial when Willy (The Actor) Sutton was asked by the judge "Mr. Sutton, would you please tell the court why you rob banks." Sutton replied "Because, your honour, that is where the money is".

These criminals are very rarely political people or political actors. To a large extent they are anti-communist because communist states have generally frowned on criminal activity conducted by non-communists. This is why it was so useful to the Allies to use the deported anti-communist mafia leadership in Italy, Vito Genovese and Charlie Lucky Luciano, to prepare for the Allied invasion of Italy in the Second World War. Mussolini had declared war on the Mafia so the Mafia declared war back by joining the Allies. Organised criminal gangs played an important role in the Cold War as well. The Allies used anti-communist gangsters from the Union Corse (Pierre Ferri-Pisani in particular) and some of the French mafia to attack the communist unions who sought to stop the entrance of Marshall Plan aid to Europe. These same Union Corse leaders were later used against the Viet Cong in Indochina, a process which helped create the initial drug routes from the Shan states in addition to fighting communism.

I have never been to a port, a railroad hub, a trucking depot or an airport anywhere in the world where organised crime had not 'organised' things. Usually this is an irrelevant problem because it is only a matter of cost to deal with them, not principle. In fact, the better organised the crime environment, the less aggravation there is for the people who have to deal with them.

For example, I was contacted by a Greek ship-owner, Dimitrios Manios, who was interested in putting a floating cement silo in Philadelphia to deliver cement for the refurbishment of the port area in a giant urban renewal program. I had already installed a floating silo in New York. I travelled to Philadelphia and was shown a number of potential sites and they looked promising. My host took me aside and asked if I were interested. I said that, as a general rule, it looked interesting but I needed to know more. He told me we should fly that night to Miami and I could meet the main people. That made me very nervous; I had just emerged from a conflict between two Families in NY over my cement business there and didn't want to go back into that milieu; one contract on my life was enough. I called some friends in NY and asked them about Philadelphia. They laughed hysterically and told me I should get out of Philadelphia on the next train. Apparently there was a war going on in Philadelphia. Angie Bruno, the head of the Scarfo family had been shot down by Tony (Bananas) Caponigro who was, himself assassinated a week later. All in all by the time I had arrived there were already fourteen guys accounted for. I excused myself politely and went home.

However, when it is properly organised it works much better. Some Nigerian partners of mine wanted to set up some businesses in the US and asked me to help them. We bought three black stretch limousines and used them to ferry people from NY hotels to Atlantic City which had just opened as a gambling resort. It was a good business. The drivers paid us $150 a week to drive the cars because they made so much on the tips. I had to get the cars insured. My sister found that there were three car insurance firms in NY who specialised in stretch limos. The lowest rates were offered by a company on Lower Park Avenue so I walked down to their office. I met with one of the salesmen who told me about the policy and the rules. It was at a very attractive rate and we agreed to insure all three cars. I was given a printout of the policy and a sticker for the bumpers which attested to my sponsorship of the Police Benevolent Association and another sticker with the name of the insurance company, Joseph P. Bonnano Insurance. In my innocence I enquired why their rates were so good as compared to GEICO. He explained that they had experienced very few claims over the years and that they could pass on these savings to their customers. In fact, he said proudly, "No one screws with our cars". He was right. At the arrival of our limos at the casinos the drivers were allowed priority and the police never gave them a ticket.

One could find organisation everywhere. I was delivering cement to Lagos, Nigeria (Tin Can Island) where there had been a rash of piracy. The captain of the "Lindinger Ivory" had just been attacked and killed. We were advised to hire "bowmen"; that is a bunch of people with bows and arrows (since firearms aren't allowed on ships) to patrol the decks to prevent pirates from boarding. I paid $150 a day for ten men to walk up and down the decks keeping pirates at bay. I had a chat with the head bowman and asked him if it wasn't a fairly precarious living waiting for ships to guard. He smiled. I asked him what he did when he wasn't a bowman. He said "Sah, when I am not a bowman, I am a pirate".

It was the same when I travelled around Russia. I used local contacts to tell me who was in charge; who controlled which ports; who controlled the railroads; who ran the stevedores and who controlled the fuel supplies. By the mid-1990s most of the conflicts and in-fighting had been settled in Siberia and things were becoming organised. Moscow was still in flux. As in the emergence of leading figures in the political establishment and the Chekists, there were some leading figures emerging in the criminal world. These gentlemen were able to move beyond the narrow confines of a city or region and were able to expand their reach overseas. In doing so they established working relationships with the Mafia, the Camorra, the 'Ndrangheta, the Colombian cartels and others and became world-class criminal organisations.

There are several very interesting studies on the development of the Russian Mafia and lists of who was important in which region and replete with tales of murder, mayhem and crimes.[xxxvi] There are hundreds of similar articles in journals and newspapers. These are all very interesting and intriguing and give a good picture of how criminal activities spread across the world. They are all mainly deficient in one important element. They do not elucidate the fact that organised crime exists in a symbiotic relationship with an organised state. The close relationship and modalities of interaction between organised crime and the functions of the state are universal but have reached their apogee in Russia. That is really its importance.

In my experience there is a close working relationship between government and organised crime on virtually every level. Starting at the bottom the policemen on the beat know of the criminals in their area. When I was young I had a part-time job in an Italian-American club on Mott Street in New York. I was a 'gofer'; I went and brought things for people; I brushed the pavement; I poured out the little glasses of 'anizett'; I carried out the little black "tuscana" cigars for the bocce players. Downstairs was a full-time gambling club where people played poker and briscola for modest sums. Gambling was illegal. Every Thursday afternoon I had to prepare a little white envelope, "la bustarella", for the police sergeant who would come in to collect his fee for not closing the club for illegal gambling. The police liked Thursdays so they could divide things up for the weekend. The mob guys came on Friday for their cut but I didn't deal with them.

As a graduate student in London I lived in Soho. This was right after the Wolfenden Report which stopped street prostitution. The girls all had to work indoors. At that time British (at least London) criminal behaviour was well organised. Every month there was a quota of people who were arrested and sent to jail, often for three months, for pornography, pimping, gambling, etc. They would go to jail and receive full wages while inside and have their jobs protected for them when they were released. The police were happy as they got their convictions and villains were happy to do their stretch knowing their futures were secure. I was able, through a friend, to get a part-time job moving from place to place filling-in for the guys in jail. I worked at the Mandrake Club in Meard Street (right next to the Gargoyle). The punters would come into the club and they would be encouraged to spend a lot of money on drinks for their companions. Then the girls would tell them that nothing untoward could go on in the club but that they'd meet them outside. The men would go downstairs to wait but the girls wouldn't come. I and my friends had to persuade the men not to go in again. It wasn't difficult as there was a policeman twenty feet away by the phone box. If I raised my hand the policeman would come and speak to the disappointed punter and that would be it. London was well-organised until they allowed gambling in Soho and things degenerated.

This type of low-level interaction is institutionalised. If you walk down the streets of the garment district in New York you can see hundreds of trucks parked with their doors open delivering fabrics and taking racks of finished goods away to the stores it is a hubbub of activity. You will see lots of policemen; old policemen and young policemen. You will also see signs on most lampposts which say "No Parking". Every week (on Thursdays) the police will collect 'on the spot fines' in white envelopes from the garment factory owners for their illegal parking as well as small fines from the truck drivers. The reason that the police are very young or very old is that young policemen struggle to live on rookie policeman's wages and the old guys are preparing for retirement so they are each given two years to work in the garment district.

In most cities of the world there is a political machine in some form which controls a borough, a district, a neighbourhood. This political machine is invariably aware and co-operative with the criminal element which controls the same area. They need to prevent crime becoming a political issue and seek to gain a source of income for allowing these criminals to take over the waste disposal business, the street cleaning jobs, the construction jobs there. Their gambling clubs are left alone and their clubs are un-raided. As a reward the politicians earn money for the political party and the criminals assist in getting the votes out when the elections take place. In many cities election night is known as "The night the dead men walk". Electors are immortal. When they die their names stay on the electoral roll. A substitute voter casts the dead man's vote. Sometimes it can be too obvious. The story goes that the last 512 voters in Cook County (Chicago) voted for Jack Kennedy in alphabetical order.

While most governments are capable of generating and pursuing their own corruption without the necessity of partnering with organised crime, sometimes the governments act in such a way as to foster an immense amount of activity in the criminal world. This was true in both the US and Russia when the state introduced Prohibition. In the US the prohibition of the legal sale of alcohol created a giant smuggling and bootlegging industry that put millions into the coffers of organised crime. In Russia, Gorbachev launched the anti-alcohol campaign in 1985 by closing down most liquor stores and limiting per person vodka consumption to two bottles a month. As in the US the campaign turned out to be a failure, creating huge bootleg liquor industry and pouring money into the "obshak" (mob treasury) of the various criminal organisations.

The financial rewards from the responses to prohibition had a more far-reaching consequence. In both cases organised crime was faced with having to deal with cash mountains from the illegal sale of alcohol. In Russia it was worse. The banning of alcohol took place at the same time as quantities of opium and heroin were arriving in Russia from the failing Afghan War. The Russian organised criminal fraternity had the revenues from bootleg alcohol as well as its substitute, heroin. They were unprepared to deal with such a large cash flow.

In the US the Mob tried to handle this money on its own. Al Capone's money man, Jake "Greasy Thumb" Guzik handled the Chicago's Mob money but was more honest than adventurous. It wasn't until Meyer Lansky (born Meyer Suchomlanski – in Grdno, Russia) and his protégé Benjamin "Bugsy" Siegel took over the financial reserves of organised crime in the US that the true financial potential of organised crime was achieved. Meyer Lansky and Bugsy Siegel saw that this vast influx of cash to the criminal world had to be handled properly. There was no point putting it into banks in the late

1930s because many of the banks had failed and were boarded up. After October 1929 the stock market was no place to keep the money. Meyer and Bugsy used the cash to buy and build hotels, especially in Miami. They set up nationwide gambling centres in the US, Canada and the Caribbean. They put their money behind a number of Hollywood studios. They bought controlling interest in several surviving banks and banks overseas. They helped finance Fulgencio Batista's Cuba. Most successfully, Bugsy went to a little desert town in Nevada and built the giant gambling resort of Las Vegas. The cash for this came from the New York families, from Chicago, Boston and Philadelphia. The various mob clans used Meyer as a bank. In return he gave them a legitimate cash flow from hotels, Las Vegas and Hollywood films. Meyer and Bugsy turned normal criminal cash generated by the protection rackets, thieving, shakedowns, prostitution, etc. into 'legitimate' cash.

There were parallels to Meyer and Bugsy in Yeltsin's Russia. In the early 1990s the Russian state collapsed. Many of the former *vory* had maintained their organisations intact and were doing their usual crimes across Russia. But this sudden opportunity of prohibition and heroin attracted a new group of younger, less traditional criminals into 'the life'. They were aided by the fact that the traditional *vory* concerned themselves primarily with crime and didn't see the opportunity of turning their newly acquired cash into political power. Perhaps the best example of this rise to power was Sergei Anatoliavic Mikhailov ('Mihas'). In 1984 Mihas was sent to the Gulag for a short spell. He learned many skills there and made useful contacts. On his return to Moscow he, and some colleagues, set up their own criminal family. He named it after the zone in which he operated and the gang became known as the Solsnetskaya Organization. In the beginning Mihas concentrated on the normal criminal activities: extortion, counterfeiting, drug trafficking and blackmail. The existing criminal organisations fought the Soltsnevo gang for turf, but Mihas' people won and their gang expanded. He could now expand into more lucrative businesses like arms dealing, money laundering and drugs. He walked free from an arrest in 1989 when the witness disappeared. In Russia, as in parts of Latin America, the verb "to disappear" is a transitive verb; it is grammatical to say "I'll disappear you".

With the collapse of the Soviet system and the rise of Yeltsin new horizons beckoned for the new group of criminals like Mihas. Crises are opportunities to the criminal fraternities. These young criminal groups took advantage of the confusion and moved to join up allies in the political establishment left without a power base. Using these political connections they soon owned banks, casinos, car dealerships, hotels, restaurants and real estate. Mihas even acquired control of Vnukovo Airport.

Mihas was not alone in setting up a powerful 'krysha' which blended criminal activity with political power. Another successful leader was the late Anton "Antoha" Malevsky who was the head of the Izmailovo group (until his unfortunate parachute dive in which his chute didn't open). The most successful entrepreneur was Semion Yudkovich Mogilevich , the Russian equivalent of Meyer Lansky. While vory like Antoha and Mihas headed their own gangs Mogilevich turned his skills to the financial opportunities which were opening. In 1994 he took control of Inkombank; one of Russia's biggest new banks. He used cash of his own and cash of others to invest in a wide range of legal businesses (especially in the gas industry) and the worldwide spread of criminal enterprises. He was the banker for the Russian mobs. Grigory Luchansky was the Bugsy Siegel of Russia, using his company, Nordex, to open up new frontiers across the globe for Russian criminal activity.

Through all of this criminal renaissance the symbiotic relationship with the Chekists continued and thrived. "Former and present officers of the KGB secretly supported leaders of the criminal world, especially those who grew out of the hooligan groupings of the early 80s rather than from the traditional criminal environment. Those groupings were able to "launder" the racket money they received through structures and banks connected with the KGB. The secret services supported organized crime, manipulated it, turned against opponents, and turned itself into organized crime."[xxxvii]

This development of a well-funded international criminal superstructure, combined with a close working relationship of the mobs with the Chekists and the parallel emergence of Russian banks like Menatep created the conditions for the "perfect storm" of the 1993 Yeltsin election and the 'loans for shares' privatisation measures. Russia would never be the same.

CHAPTER ELEVEN

After Yeltsin took effective control of the government after the August 1991 putsch he had a very clear idea of what he opposed, since for many years he was a party hack in Ekaterinburg (Sverdlov), but he was unclear about what he supported. The Russian people entrusted him with ridding the state of the burden of a Communist Party and putting in its place organisational steps towards building a parliamentary democracy. The fundamental problem was that parliamentary democracy was never Russia's strong point and Russia lacked many of the institutions which keep parliamentary democracy going – a politically neutral civil service; effective communications throughout the nation; and a will towards the sharing of power towards a mutual goal.

If one likened the governance of Russia to a large, sophisticated computer program the inherent impediments would soon manifest themselves. Russia has a program of governance that looks complete from the top level. However, many of the subroutines are 'stubs; they are part of the program but have no information in them. They only return you to the main program when you try to address them. So if you look for "democracy" it is there but has no information or structure; "free elections" are there too as well as an "industrial policy". These are empty and no one has bothered to work out or agree on what the stubs should contain. It's a lot like the Soviet Constitution; freedom and justice for all but not for any person in particular.

The other major impediment was that the people in the lands east of the Urals wanted nothing to do with Moscow or St. Petersburg. Early in Yeltsin's time in office, the election of regional governors was introduced for the first time in Russian history. Power legally shifted from Moscow to the eighty-nine regional capitals of Russia. The question of "states rights" became an operative problem, especially among the ethnically based constituent republics of the Russian Federation. Wherever I travelled in Siberia or the Far East or the Arctic I never met anyone who felt that what was going on in the Moscow and St. Petersburg fishbowls had much relevance to their lives. As the governor of Krasanoyarsky Krai, Viktor Ishayev, said to us in a meeting "Don't bother yourselves with what is happening in Moscow. It has nothing to do with us. Moscow is politicians and monuments. We have the resources, the industry and our future is in the East." He was right. Except for some small-scale industries in the Western Urals and the foodstuffs from Krasnodar most of Russia's wealth was produced in Siberia, the Far East, Yakutia (Sakha Republic) and the northern Kola Peninsula. That's where the oil, gas, ferrous and non-ferrous metals, gold, diamonds and timber were produced. Moscow produced trouble, taxes. interference and orthodoxy.

Not only was this true for industry it was also true for government services. When I had to arrange for the transport of alumina and coke to the smelters and the transport of the aluminium from the smelters to the ports I had to deal with the Russian Ministry of Transport and the Ministry of Railroads. I was told that the Ministry of Rail in Moscow would be the people to whom we should address our queries about providing rail cars. Iskander Makhmudov told us that Mischa Chernoy had made the arrangements in Moscow with the Ministry and it would cost $US 8.00 per metric ton to move the alumina to the smelters. The Russian Rail Ministry had its own contracting company "RITM" which would sign the contract with us. That sounded reasonable until we met with Mr. Ivan Leonov, the head of the BAM in Komsomolsk-na-Amur. He had come to Vanino at the invitation of Valentina Tsareva to meet with us to discuss the practicalities. We explained what we needed and told him that RITM was charging us $8.00 per metric ton. At that Leonov went ballistic. After explaining the details of his intentions relative to the mothers of the staff of RITM and the Railways Minister, he said that Moscow was intending to pay the BAM Far East $2.00 of the $8.00 and to pocket the $6.00 for themselves for doing nothing. He said that the entire operation would be conducted in his territory using his rolling stock. He suggested that the proportions of the payment be reversed. He should get $6.00 and RITM $2.00. We said we had no objection as we were cost-neutral in the transaction. He said he would work on it and that we should visit him in a week to see what had been arranged,

We waited for a week and then Niksa called Leonov. Leonov said that he had had a long discussion with RITM and the Ministry and told them that they were his railcars and that he would not do the work and get paid very little. He said the Ministry had agreed his terms and were sending a copy of the contract to him. He waited two weeks but the contract didn't arrive. It finally came, by rail, and they had not adjusted the price. Leonov said he would use it to wipe his bottom and gave us his own contract for the full amount payable to the BAM Far East. That was good enough for me. How they divided it was not my worry although Sergei, Mischa's lawyer, said it might be a problem later on. In many of our dealings with the regional government agencies they showed little regard for Moscow or Moscow policy. They were no longer afraid of Moscow or concerned at what Moscow might want.

Moscow was an island to itself. Wherever we went in the regions it was clear that power resided with the governor, his bureaucracy, the Red Generals of the local industries and the regional security services which took their orders from their regional offices. This was equally true of the organised criminal gangs. There was nothing Moscow could do or offer the regional and city-wide gangs who worked in a symbiotic relationship with the regional and city power structures. The police and the military also asserted their own authority. When we had to fly out a lot of equipment from Norway to Vanino we had trouble finding an airport capable of handling the giant Ruslan (Antonov 124) aircraft. A colonel in the air force put me in touch with the head of the airbase at Mongokhta (the base which was responsible for shooting down the Korean airliner KAL003) not far from Vanino. We contracted with him to land the plane there and the soldiers unloaded the plane and a military convoy took the gear to Vanino. I enquired if we needed clearance for this and he said he would arrange it as they were 'his' air traffic controllers and 'his' base. He said if he asked Moscow they would demand payment so we should leave it with him. The same thing happened at Kronstadt when I had to make a quick pickup of aluminium wire rod in coil. St. Petersburg Port was trying to get more money from us for letting the shipment through so my naval friends took me to Kronstadt and the navy and its sailors handled the shipment for us. We paid the counter admiral in cash. It gave us both a good laugh to reflect that, unlike 1921, this time Trotsky wouldn't send in troops to suppress our Kronstadt Rebellion.

With the beginnings of privatisation the increased levels of regional autonomy grew. The governors had their own budgets which were gleaned by imposing local taxes and duties, instituting a wide range of taxes and fees for government services which they often made up on the spot. The police and criminals established a good symbiotic working relationship in which the protection racket thrived and the cash sales of vodka and cigarettes saw a piece of each transaction find its way into the regional and municipal coffers. The government agencies sold licenses and permits and the criminals shook everyone down and sold everything *na leva* (outside the normal channels). Moscow had no money to pay the regions nor harboured any great intention to do so. Traditionally, Moscow took; it didn't pay.

It was in the early 1990s that <u>*blat*</u> became moneterised. The exchange of favours and mutual protection was no longer done exclusively for mutual assistance. By 1990 everything had a price. As the use of cash spread out across the regions it became the means of achieving commerce and trade, although barter was often used as well. In Moscow and St. Petersburg it was unusual for large businesses to accept roubles at all. We had an account at the Moscow Olympic Hotel. Everything was priced in Deutschmarks. Roubles would do you no good. Later they gave up on Deutschmarks and went to dollars. It was bizarre. The national telephone system worked on a jeton or a 15-kopeck piece. These were hard to get so one had to pay 5 roubles for 15-kopeck piece to make a call.

The most obvious aspect of the monetarisaton of <u>*blat*</u> was the concomitant development of "kryshas" ('roofs') which served to provide a parallel economic and legal structure to the post-Soviet system which had suffered a stunted growth. For Russian businessmen there was no security that contracts could be enforced; no way in which supplies or materials could be guaranteed; no security measure that would allow finished goods to reach the customer. There was no guarantee that the cash reserves which were building in the banks could be secured. Bankers were an endangered species. From 1992 to 1996 the Association of Russian Banks tallied one hundred and twenty attempts on the lives of Russian bankers and their workers, or one every few weeks. Eighty or so were successful and the assassinations completed. Less than eight percent of these killers were ever apprehended and brought to trial. Willy Sutton's epigram translated well into Russian.

In every town, village, city, region and oblast there were kryshas formed out of the existing symbiotic relationships between local government and local criminals. Sometimes they were competing and sometimes they were co-operative. They took their 'bite' from every transaction. In the same way the post-Soviet bureaucracy at every level took their 'bite' for every piece of paper, permit, license or governmental form that was issued. By 1995 there were more than double the numbers of bureaucrats in Russia than in 1989; almost every one of whom had to improve their poverty-line wages by extorting fees from the public they served.

The penalties of falling foul of the kryshas were severe and, quite often, terminal. I was sitting in a Korean restaurant in Khabarovsk one evening with some gentlemen in leather jackets, short hair and gold teeth. They were offering me two truckloads of aluminium ingots they had happened to find at some company's yard and would deliver these to Vanino for us to sell overseas. After our negotiations they had a drink and were chatting about beating up a bunch of Japanese businessmen that afternoon who had tried to deliver some televisions from the railroad station without making provision for the financial improvement of the krysha. I asked them why they were so violent. A Japanese was seriously wounded in the affray. They said that these foreigners and many of the new Russian businessmen were unaccustomed to the traditional practices so they were obliged to set an example. They assured me that, after a while, they would only have to threaten violence and that would suffice. I asked how they knew that the Japanese would be importing these televisions. They told me that the railroad administration gave them lists of everything that was coming into Khabarovsk and the city offices gave them lists of everyone who sought and obtained a permit. These sources would, of course, get a reward.

I reflected on how basic and primitive Russian criminal practices were. I remembered being at Elizabeth, New Jersey docks on summer's day waiting for the arrival of a MGB I had bought in England. It was coming by sea and I had been in contact with the longshoremen's union to see that all would be well. I was put in touch with the Solomon brothers who controlled the car docks at Elizabeth and was given a time to visit to pick up my car. I sat in the union office and watched as the cars were being discharged from the ship. Most of the cars were brand-new Jaguar XJ6s from England. As they were being discharged, a young man walked in and spoke to the chief saying that he had chosen the yellow car just delivered. The chief said it was all right and made a note on a pad. The young man walked over to the yellow Jaguar and drove it into a wall, damaging the front of the car. I asked what that was all about and was told that the union had negotiated a 5% 'breakage' allowance with the port and the damaged

Jaguar would be one of the cars listed as 'breakage'. The young man, whose turn it was, would buy the car for $600 (the scrap value) and would have it repaired. When he sold it or kept it he would pay the office $7,500 which would go to the 'pot'. They had had to negotiate the breakage allowance instead of just stealing 5% of the shipment because containerisation had come in and it was too difficult to steal a whole container so a flat 5% was agreed. No one cared because the insurance company had allowed for a 5% breakage and adjusted its premiums accordingly. The Russians had a long way to go with their criminal enterprises to catch up with the Jersey docks.

One characteristic of the development of kryshas in Russia was the simultaneous development of "Red" kryshas. These Red kryshas were policemen, _spetznaz_ soldiers, and other uniformed guardians of the public peace who the state organisations rented out to businessmen to act as their 'protectors'. This was a lucrative business but not too remunerative to the people with 'boots on the floor'. The big money for the Red kryshas most often went to their officers and the politicians. Sometimes one Red krysha ended up fighting with another Red krysha. It was not a well-run endeavour. There were several more successful 'security firms' set up by the Red kyshas. Many were tied in directly with the governor's or mayor's office (for example in Chelyabinsk and Vladivostok).

These could be hired out to occupy business premises and factories. A friend was building large residential Russian Business Centre near Sheremetyevo Airport. When it was completed and just open for business the OMON (Otryad Militsii Osobogo Naznacheniya, Special Purpose Police Unit) visited and told him he had violated a building code. In the argument he was cut down by a machine gun and someone else opened the business centre for visitors instead of him.

Inexorably these criminal activities and the endemic massive state corruption complimented each other and criminals got involved in politics and politicians got involved in crime. Regional and municipal politics was a mixture of bribery and corruption mixed with criminal activities sheltered under a roof of criminal violence and state-run violence. It was not a voluntary system; there was no 'opt out'. To be fair, however, it didn't really affect us very much. As a foreign 'toller' we were the geese who were laying aluminium eggs. They left us well alone. We were everyone's allies. If this governmental-political nexus tried to threaten us anywhere we would have many powerful friends throughout Russia who would stomp on any adverse or hostile activity. The local enterprises and governments were dealing in millions; for us that was chump change. The Russian elite did not want to endanger their long-term prosperity. However, it was dangerous for Russians.

This exodus of power from Moscow to the regions and the loss of the national power of the communist party in general had a dramatic effect on Russian politics and on Boris Nikolayevich Yeltsin in particular. His initial assertions of power were supported by the last Supreme Soviet and the other emerging leaders of the Duma (the national parliament). Having banned the communist party and taken over its assets the Supreme Soviet and the Duma further agreed to give Yeltsin a free hand for one year. On 1 November 1991 they agreed that Yeltsin could appoint ministers and issue decrees to accelerate the transition to a market economy without consulting the Supreme Soviet. In addition, the elections for provincial heads of administration were postponed. Four days later, Yeltsin assumed the post of Prime Minister. On 8 November, Gennady Burbulis, Yegor Gaidar and Aleksandr Shokhin were appointed Deputy Prime Ministers of what on 15 November was declared a 'government of reforms'[xxxviii]

This government was anxious, in addition to promoting economic reforms, to work to introduce parliamentary democracy in the Duma, including the development of political parties with some degree of representation and with a greater recognition of the problems of Russia outside Moscow. Together they worked to end the rule of the Soviet Union and, on 8 December 1991, agreed the Belovezha Accords which abolished the Soviet Union.

The problem which gradually appeared was that Yeltsin did not trust the reform leaders of the Duma, especially those who represented the Moscow power concentrations. Yeltsin had a long experience of confrontation with the Moscow power brokers when he was First Secretary of the Sverdlovsk party and didn't trust them even though they were now 'democrats'. This was particularly true of his suspicions of Ruslan Kasbulatov the former head of the Supreme Soviet. Yeltsin reverted to the old Russian practice of working through a group of 'home-town boys' brought into Moscow and given high posts in the government and the civil administration. Just as Yuri Andropov had ruled through the "Saratov Mafia", Yeltsin ruled through the Sverdlovsk Mafia.

The Sverdlovsk Mafia included Gennady Burbulis State Secretary of the Russian Federation and First Deputy Prime Minister and Yury Petrov, the first head of the Presidential Administration. These gathered around them a group of like-minded supporters (Oleg Lobov, Viktor Iliushin and others) along with their 'youth section of Gaidar and Chubais who were in charge of the 'shock therapy'. Foremost among these loyalists was Alexander Korsakov, who had been Yeltsin's personal bodyguard since 1985. Korzhakov was a General in the KGB 9th Department (mainly thugs and bodyguards) and became head of Presidential Security under Yeltsin. This Sverdlovsk Mafia gradually emerged as the "Family" when key Yeltsin family members, mainly his daughter Tatiana Dyachenko, joined the cabal.

This Family was concerned, perhaps obsessed, with who was in control of the security apparatus. Throughout Yeltsin's terms in office the Family sought to keep the security people under their control. A variety of schemes to create security ministries were tried but they all had problems getting through the Duma and the courts. In January 1992 Yeltsin issued a decree creating an amalgamated Ministry of Security and Internal Affairs but it was rebuffed by the court on the grounds that it violated the principle of the separation of powers. The President complied with the court ruling. The combined ministry reverted to a separate Ministry of Security under Viktor Barannikov and a Ministry of Internal Affairs (MVD) under Viktor Yerin. In reality these were little more than Soviet institutions transformed into Russian ones. Their organization and the bulk of their personnel remained the same. [xxxix]

On 2 January 1992 Gaidar's price liberalisation went into effect. State controls were lifted on 80 per cent of wholesale prices and 90 per cent of retail prices. The consequences were catastrophic. Living standards plummeted over night, as did production, especially of consumer goods. Prices rose astronomically in the first month. According to official Russian statistics, which probably underestimated the situation, in January consumer prices and the cost of services increased 3.5 times. The price of foodstuffs increased four-fold, while non-foodstuffs rose 2.5 times. Consumption contracted abruptly, as demand switched to essential items such as food. Nevertheless, demand for staple commodities, such as milk fell to 24 per cent and meat and meat products to 14 per cent of that in December 1991. Half the budget of the average family was spent on food. Production contracted sharply, especially in consumer goods, ferrous metals and oil extraction. The total volume of production for the first two months of 1992 was 85 per cent of that for the corresponding period in 1991. Meanwhile, mutual indebtedness between banks and enterprises accelerated from 39 billion roubles at the beginning of January to 650 billion at the end of March. Hundreds of enterprises and tens of banks were teetering on the edge of bankruptcy[xl]

Price liberalization, instead of encouraging production as intended, produced an abrupt contraction of the economy. Imposed by Gaidar on a still highly monopolised economy, the [xli]producers reacted by limiting production and raising prices. An already crippled economy now found itself in free fall. Inflation was rampant in 1992. Consumer prices rose by 2,500 per cent. Inflation slowed over the next three years, but was still running at an annual 63 per cent at the end of 1995. By that time consumer prices had risen by a factor of 1,411". Inward investment dried up. The unions, especially the coal miners, held periodic strikes because they had some leverage. People noticed when coal was scarce. There were precious few other commodities or services which could be restricted by labour action and have an effect as they were usually in decline, too expensive, and out of the reach of the normal consumers. If workers had not been paid their wages for three or four months it was not terribly attractive for them to go on strike for any reason. The population was fast giving up on this new 'democracy' as an expensive folly. Their savings were wiped out; their pensions trivialised, and their goods and services out of reach. This was 'shock therapy' indeed.

There was widespread opposition to the effects of the 'shock therapy', not only in Kasbulatov's Duma but among the business community. The Red Generals and their supporters were organised by their ex-KGB backers under Arkady Volsky (Andropov's man) into an industrialists' group, the Union of Industrialists and Entrepreneurs formed in 1991 and which also formed its own political bloc inside the Duma, the Civic Union, in June 1992. The disenchanted Russian Vice President Alexander Vladimirovich Rutskoy railed against the work of Gaidar and Chubais. Rutskoy was vice president of Russia from July 10, 1991 to October 4, 1993.

The collapse of the economy and the rising poverty of the broad masses of the new Russia was accompanied by a dramatic falloff of Yeltsin's popularity and support. Although disappointment in him was widespread there was the typical Russian view applied to the situation "a good Czar misled by unscrupulous advisers", long a tradition in Russian analysis (a lot like the Gulag inmates bemoaning that "if only Comrade Stalin knew..."). A number of face-saving programs were mooted but the growing hostility towards Yeltsin and the Family within the Duma and the business community blocked any of these programs from having their expected effect.

Yeltsin tried to head off a confrontation by announcing a cabinet reshuffle. In June 1992 three new Deputy Prime Ministers were appointed: Viktor Chernomyrdin, the Gazprom director (with special responsibilities for the energy sector); Vladimir Filippovich Shumeiko erstwhile president of the Confederation of Associations of Entrepreneurs, was appointed first deputy prime minister responsible for industrial administration; and Georgy Khizha, the former vice-mayor of St. Petersburg and a key player in the military-industrial complex. Yeltsin had gambled that if he put in the old _nomenklatura_ he would be safe. This would enable him to establish better ties with the Duma.

This didn't happen. Although Yeltsin had moved closer to the centrists he still kept Gaidar and Chubais busy with their disastrous economic policies. As tensions rose, the clock was ticking, Yeltsin was due to have his plenary powers end in December. There was to be a new Constitution and the various committees were working on new drafts. Yeltsin was determined to take control of the Duma or to prorogue it to maintain his position. In late October Yeltsin removed the control of the 5,000 man Duma's security force and put them under the control of the MVD. The Saratov Mafia leaders, Burbulis and Mikhail Poltoranin (Deputy Prime Minister for Information) demanded that Yeltsin confront the Duma and Kasbulatov. They drafted a speech which Yeltsin delivered in early December which stated that the conservative forces of the Duma were making it difficult to govern and demanded a referendum on just who should be in charge, the President or the Duma.

The same day (December 10, 1992) the tensions were reduced when Valery Zorkin, the head of the Constitutional Court, announced that the Court would, if the parties could not agree, hold a referendum on the new Constitution in April 1993 to settle the matter. It was clear that this was a situation that could only get worse.

Complicating this struggle in Moscow was the escalating battle for control of Chechnya. Regional and local autonomy were two major themes of Yeltsin's 1990 campaign and, following the December 1991 dissolution of the Soviet Union there was a high degree of uncertainty about the status and powers of Russia's autonomous regions. There was an urgent need for legislation to clearly define the powers of each federal region. Such a law was passed on March 31, 1992, when Yeltsin and Ruslan Khasbulatov, then chairman of the Russian Supreme Soviet and an ethnic Chechen himself, signed the Federation Treaty bilaterally with 86 out of 88 federal subdivisions. In almost all cases, demands for greater autonomy or independence were satisfied by concessions of regional autonomy and tax privileges. The treaty outlined three basic types of federal regions or subdivisions and the powers which were reserved for the local and federal governments. The only regions not to sign were Chechnya and Tatarstan.

This was not unexpected. On September 6, 1991, militants of the All-National Congress of the Chechen People (NCChP) party, under the leadership of former Soviet Air Force general Dzhokhar Dudayev, invaded a meeting of the Chechen-Ingush ASSR Supreme Soviet in Grozny with the aim of asserting independence. By the end of the year Dudayev won an overwhelming popular initiative and was made president and declared Chechen independence from the USSR. While this was happening Yeltsin had sent in some troops in November 1991 to restore order but these were ambushed at the airport in Grozny and sent home. Fighting erupted in Chechnya and Ingushetia as their civil war continued. Throughout early 1992 and 1993 the civil war raged with Dudayev finally coming out on top. Dudayev consolidated his power.

Yeltsin was determined to resist this independence movement and consulted with his military leaders. The military wanted no part of any war against the Chechens. As General Eduard Vorobyov stated as he handed in his resignation it was "a crime" to "send the army against its own people." [xlii] Although the actual full-scale war against the Chechens didn't start in earnest until 11 December 1994 there were numerous skirmishes and actions which ramped up the situation. This preparation for a war in Chechnya did not have the support of the Russian military. Yeltsin's adviser on nationality affairs, Emil Pain, and Russia's Deputy Minister of Defence, Boris Gromov, also resigned in protest of the invasion, as did Gen. Boris Poliakov. More than 800 professional soldiers and officers refused to take part in the operation; of these, 83 were convicted by military courts and the rest were discharged. Later Gen. Lev Rokhlin also refused to be decorated as a Hero of Russia for his part in the war. This is why the war in Chechnya was fought almost entirely by the military forces of the MVD, not the Army.

To a large extent the Chechen adventures broadened the gulf between the Russian military and the Yeltsin Family. One problem was that the military had very little money to do anything and had overcrowded barracks and dissatisfied officers and conscripts. Niksa and I had arranged to fly to the ports of Zarubina and Posyet, south of Vladivostok and near the Chinese/North Korean border. We hired a helicopter in Khabarovsk and set out for Zarubina. Normally this would be a three and a half or four hour flight. It took us almost nine hours. There was nothing wrong with the helicopter but we had very little fuel because supplies were limited. We flew from one small air base to another on the route south, having to negotiate to buy enough fuel to take us to the next base. We disembarked at each base and haggled over the fuel. We were shocked to see the conditions in which the soldiers lived. It was very primitive and unkempt. In each common room there was a big pan full of *kasha* (buckwheat groats) sitting on a low heat and a small bowl of some kind of brown sauce which had a skin on it. That was the rations for the people at the airport. As they got hungry they went in and got some food which was washed down with weak tea from a samovar. They told me that was all they had for over a week. They offered us a Kalashnikov and a Strela (Grail – RPG7) for cash. I declined the offer. It was very sad to see how they lived. This was true of all the bases we visited.

It wasn't much better at higher levels. I was with some of the U.S. military (in Operation Jeremiah) when they came over for some meetings with their counterparts at Kubinka. The Soviet Navy were sending ships to South Africa for some naval display but needed the help of the US Navy to get sufficient fuel to get their vessels home. The US Navy was happy to assist. Even years later, in 1997 when the Russian Air Force was celebrating the 60th anniversary of Valery Pavlovich Chkalov's s 63-hour non-stop flight from Moscow to Vancouver, Washington, via the North Pole on a Tupolev ANT-25, the Russian Government barely supported the celebration. We had to raise money in the US so that the Russian Air Force could fly over and perform aerial displays and celebrate this seminal flight in aviation history.

The Russian armed services were kept poor, underfunded, crowded and without much to do since Yeltsin took office. There were no jobs for all the returning officers and most of the ranks lived in squalor. Additionally the recruitment or conscription of new soldiers was most effective among many of the minorities. I was visiting the Northern Fleet when the admiral in charge of the large submarine fleet in Severomorsk told me that he was having nothing but trouble with many of the recruits he was being sent. He told me that they didn't speak Russian very well (mainly Uzbeks, Tajiks, etc.) He said they couldn't read the dials on the control displays on the nuclear subs so they had to put on stickers in their own languages to be sure they knew what they were doing. He said that if the tapes and the glue became dislodged then God only knows what button they would push. One of the main objects of the Jeremiah program was the hopes by the Russian military to get assistance from the US in containing the spread of these nuclear weapons, the stopping of the sales of these purloined radioactive materials, and the dismantling of the nuclear fleet which the Russians were not equipped to handle.

There was a growing co-operation between the US and Russian armed forces. Despite the hangovers of Cold War rhetoric what they were building was an important program to protect both countries from rogue elements stealing dangerous substances from Russian arsenals and labs as well as sophisticated weapons. What was at risk was not just stolen nuclear materials like mini-bombs and plutonium. There were cases of people stealing osmium, cesium and similar substances to make 'dirty bombs.' Frequently these were stolen from laboratories in areas in which the Russian writ was written small. Abkhazia, for example, was an area where the sale of cesium-137 was frequent. There were eight cesium-137 containers stolen in Volgagrad in one week alone. One man flew into the Czech Republic with a small vial of cesium in his breast pocket. It made a black hole in his chest and he died in great pain in two days after arrival. There was stealing of nuclear and related materials throughout Russia. The US, indeed all of NATO, was concerned as was the Russian military.

When the Soviet Union dissolved, its submarines which remained in active service faced two dangerous challenges. First, when the newly independent states of the former Soviet Union declared independence from Moscow, many of these vessels lost their home ports and other related facilities in the Black and the Baltic Seas. The remaining naval bases within Russia could not handle such a large number of operational vessels, particularly when combined with additional Soviet-era diesel submarines and surface ships moved, *en masse*, to the Russian bases. Second, and more ominously, the Russian defence budget could no longer afford to keep many of the nuclear-powered submarines adequately and safely maintained—much less in active service. Without the capacity to dismantle these vessels, decommissioned submarines began to pile up around Russia's naval bases; especially around Severomorsk in the North and Sovetskaya Gavan and Bolshoi Kamen in the Far East, The Strategic Offensive Arms Elimination Implementing Agreement, signed in August 1993 by the US and Russia, provided a framework for the US to aid in the dismantlement of several Russian strategic submarines. It was followed by similar European initiatives and the CTR (Comprehensive Threat Reduction) programs. [xliii] Companies like the Hughes Corporation were given contracts to dismantle nuclear subs and to assist in the destruction or protection of the rescued fissile material. The Russian Government was of little help in this as they repeatedly said that they had no money for their participation. The Russian military, with the exception of a few hothead Cold Warriors, seemed much more able to relate to the US negotiators than to their Russian political bosses. They did not trust Yeltsin or his colleagues as they felt they really had no grasp of the parlous state of the Russian armed services. At the end of one of the planning meetings in 1992 one of the key interpreters, Borisov, told me that is was like a fairy story seeing the two enemies gathered together amicably to discuss programs of mutual benefit. It was all highly classified; not because it was very secret, but the Russians didn't want to be embarrassed by seeming weak, and the US Department of Defence didn't want to risk a large chunk of its budget created to fight an enemy that barely existed reduced to fit the real threat. Secrecy benefitted all.

It was also interesting in dealing with the military leaders to see how little effect the collapse of the Warsaw Pact had on the collaboration and communication by the Russians with the militaries of the former Soviet republics and the new states of Eastern Europe. In the rush to independence and self-assertion of the re-emerged independent states of East Germany, Czechoslovakia, Poland, Hungary the Ukraine and Yugoslavia there were deep and comprehensive purges of the communist parties and the national intelligence organs (Stasi, AVO, etc.) but there was very little turnover in the military and military intelligence organisations. When one considers that most of these officers and intelligence people there were trained by the Russian Army and the GRU it makes sense. This gave the Russian military a unique perspective on the political developments in Eastern Europe and not a little envy of how they were being funded and encouraged by their own governments while the needs of the Russian military were ignored and they were allowed to decay.

Although General Grachev had agreed to put the weight of the Russian military behind Yeltsin in the assault on the White House, Yeltsin and his advisers were very wary about relying on the military. The Family and the Sverdlovsk Mafia sought to protect themselves by gathering in the forces of the security apparatus around them. Yeltsin issued a decree issued on 21 December 1993 that disbanded the Ministry of Security, putting the coercive apparatuses of the state in his hands alone. He already controlled ministries of defence and internal affairs and now added a direct control of the security and intelligence agencies. He took over direct control of the Foreign Intelligence Service (SVR), the Federal Border Service (FPS) as well as the Federal Counter-intelligence Service (FSK, the successor to the Ministry of Security). He put his own loyalists in the Foreign Intelligence Service (SVR). In an effort to control the national media he took under his wing the Federal Agency for Government Communications and Information (FAPSI) and then set up system of direct communications with the commanders of all the army formations. Yeltsin controlled the Organs of the state once again.

The KGB had disappeared but in its place was the 76,000 strong FSK, which became the Federal Security Service (FSB) in April 1995 The KGB was reborn under a new name, but was staffed by many of the former officers from the 9th Department; the thug wing, This was not unconnected with the powerful role of the Presidential Security Service (PSB), under the command of Yeltsin's friend and chief bodyguard, Alexander Korsakov, also of the 9th. Barsukov's 40,000 strong Main Security Directorate (GUO) expanded by assimilating the special forces units into the GUO, including the Alpha and Vympel squads, together with a special tank regiment. In March 1994, Barsukov was appointed to the cabinet. In November 1991 he had

DR. GARY K. BUSCH

become commandant of the Kremlin due to the good offices of Korzhakov. With the patronage of Petrov, Barsukov simultaneously became chief of the Main Security Directorate (GUO), which had been formed out of the old Ninth Directorate of the KGB by secret presidential decree. Barsukov was rumoured to be the eyes and ears of the President in the Kremlin. These praetorian figures were reputedly members of the so-called 'party of war' which advocated military intervention in Chechnya. They were disliked and distrusted by the regular military commanders.

This search for ever-greater control by Yeltsin did not mean that the corner was turned on the economy. Despite putting Chernomyrdin in as Prime Minister the 'reforms; continued to destroy what was left of the economy. Chernomyrdin formed a new government with Boris Fedorov, an economic reformer, as deputy prime minister and finance minister. In January 1993, Fedorov announced a so-called anticrisis program to control inflation through tight monetary and fiscal policies. Budget deficits were to be brought under control by limiting wage increases for state enterprises, by establishing quarterly budget deficit targets, and by providing a more efficient social safety net for the unemployed and pensioners.

This didn't stop them from just printing more money although it eased slightly in mid-1993.The printing of money and domestic credit expansion moderated somewhat in 1993. Fedorov's anticrisis program had some effect. In the first three quarters of 1993, the Central Bank held money expansion to a monthly rate of 19 percent. The 1993 annual inflation rate was around 1,000 percent, a sharp improvement over 1992, but still very high. In June 1994, Chernomyrdin presented a set of moderate adjustments but stabilization was undermined by the Central Bank which issued credits to enterprises at subsidized rates, and by strong pressure from industrial and agricultural lobbies seeking additional credits.

By October 1994, inflation, which had been reduced by tighter fiscal and monetary policies early in 1994, began to soar once again to frightening levels. On October 11, a day that became known as "Black Tuesday", the value of the rouble on interbank exchange markets plunged by 27 percent. The ecoonomic policies of Yeltsin were a disaster. These pale into insignificance, however, when compared with the even greater disaster Yeltsin was about to bring upon the Russian people.

In 1992 and 1993 the independence of Chechnya declared by Dudayev had been repeatedly challenged by local resistances funded by Russia. After staging another coup attempt in December 1993, the opposition organized themselves into the Provisional Council of the Chechen Republic as a potential alternative government for Chechnya, calling on to Moscow for assistance. In August 1994, the coalition of the opposition factions based in north Chechnya launched a large-scale armed campaign to remove Dudayev's government. Moscow clandestinely supplied rebel forces with financial support, military equipment and mercenaries. Russia also suspended all civilian flights to Grozny while the aviation and border troops set up a military blockade of the republic and eventually unmarked Russian aircraft began combat operations over Chechnya. The opposition forces, who were joined by Russian troops, launched a clandestine but badly organized assault on Grozny in mid-October 1994, followed by the second, larger attack on November 26–27, 1994.[xliv]

On December 11, 1994, Russian forces launched a three-pronged ground attack towards Grozny. This attack and the aerial bombardments virtually destroyed the Chechen capital, Grozny. Official figures admit that about 27,000 civilians died in the first five weeks of fighting alone. Russian historian and general Dmitri Volkogonov said the Russian military's bombardment of Grozny killed around 35,000 civilians, including 5,000 children, and that the vast majority of those killed were ethnic Russians. While military casualties are not known, the Russian side admitted to having lost nearly 2,000 soldiers killed or missing.[xlv]

According to the General Staff of the Russian Armed Forces, 3,826 troops were killed, 17,892 were wounded, and 1,906 were missing in action. According to NVO, the authoritative Russian independent military weekly, at least 5,362 Russian soldiers died during the war, 52,000 got wounded or sick, and some 3,000 more remained missing by 2005. The estimate of the Committee of Soldiers' Mothers of Russia, however, put the number of the Russian military dead at 14,000, based on information from wounded troops and soldiers' relatives. Chechen casualties are estimated at up to 100,000 dead or more, of which most were civilians. This was an unnecessary and self-inflicted disaster for Russia and for Yeltsin in particular.

This was reflected in the results of the December 1995 election to the Duma. Despite all his centralisation of power the Russian people turned sharply against Yeltsin. The Communists had won over a quarter of all the seats; more than double what Yeltsin's party had won. With their allies in the Agrarian Party the Communists could command a majority in the Duma. This would mean disaster for Yeltsin in the Presidential elections due to take place soon if the same result was achieved by his enemies. He resolved to do everything in his power to fight the Communists and their allies in the election. Some of his advisors (Korsakov, Soskovets and Barsukov) told Yeltsin to postpone the election. This couldn't really be done because the Army couldn't guarantee its support if that were to happen. Yeltsin had to go ahead with the election.

At the same time, at the economic summit meeting in Davos, two media moguls sat down with Yeltsin's Family and decided that they would use their vast financial resources to assist Yeltsin. Boris Berezovsky, head of a vast conglomerate of car dealerships (Logovaz), media outlets (Russian Public Television, the journal Ogonyok and the newspaper Nezavisimaya Gazeta) and several banks, teamed up with an arch rival Vladimir Gusinsky, head of Most Bank and owner of NTV public television. These 'politicized capitalists' were the core of a group of businessmen who threw their vast financial and media resources behind Yeltsin. They agreed to support Yeltsin, along with a number of other successful businessmen. Their price was the introduction of a new type of economic 'reform', the 'loans for shares' program.

This was originally a proposal developed by Vladimir Potanin who was deputy Prime Minister under Chernomyrdin. One of the reasons why Russia was so poor and the state had so little cash at its disposal was that few of the new industrialists were paying their taxes and thus the state could then not pay its bills. Many of these new industrialists who had been selling their wares abroad had accumulated large sums of hard currency overseas. Some still had access to the KGB funds and the revenues from the sale of state assets, like gold, which had been stashed abroad in places like Cyprus. Potanin suggested that these banks would offer cash as a loan to the Russian Central Bank in exchange for shares in the companies controlled by the State, principally the oil industry shares. If the government could not pay back the loans on the collateral of these shares the banks would, with the assistance of the State, take complete ownership of these shares. The people behind the banks would own the shares of the largest, as yet unprivatised, state assets and the government would have cash to fight the election and pay its bills.

The government agreed and an avalanche of state privatisations took place, often at very generous terms. Since, in most cases, the bank that won the tender for the shares was the bank that was controlling the tender there were many bargains to be had. Having run the largest money laundering operation in the history of the world, the Russians were now arranging for the largest drying operation of the laundered cash. It went far better than planned and a new breed of Russian entrepreneur was born; the oligarch.

CHAPTER TWELVE

By the end of 1995 Boris Yeltsin was in a difficult position. His polarisation of the political process to centralise power in the Presidency (and the Family) had shattered the relationship with the parliament. The elections of 1995 confirmed this with the Communist Party making its resurgence to become the largest party in the Duma. Yeltsin was worried and in desperate need of cash. He was not collecting sufficient tax revenue to pay the state bills. His war in Chechnya was a heavy drain on the state purse. His economic policies had damaged the national economy and impoverished many of the poorest in the country and destroyed their savings. Worst of all, he had no idea of what to do to get himself out of the hole he had dug.

Equally as important as Yeltsin's impotence was the fact that Russian business had emerged from its stunted state at the passing from power from Gorbachev. There were very rich Russians. There were powerful businessmen, and these had emerged despite the actions of the state, rather than because of these actions and policies. In the immediate post-Gorbachev period there were three emerging types of Russian entrepreneurs.[xlvi]

The first group were the Soviet-era factory directors of small and middle-size factories who continued to operate in the vacuum of governmental control with the passing of the Soviet Union. They just kept control of their factories in a *de facto* privatisation, often making deals with the local criminal gangs who helped them with raw materials and distribution. An important part of this relationship was access by these factory directors to the liquidity provided by these criminal organisations, their banks and their close working relationships with the local and regional civil services and elected leaders. They acquired their shares in their companies by buying them from their employees or extorting the shares from them in a bargain for job security. These were the "New Russians" who were famous for flaunting their new wealth in a feast of *nouveau riche* excess.

The second type of entrepreneurs were the people like Chernomyrdin; members of the Soviet *nomenklatura* (the elite) who had become the owners of major national businesses; e.g. Gazprom. Many of these were the Red Generals who had co-operated with the KGB organisers in the schemes developed by Andropov to prepare for the collapse of the Soviet system and who moved the state assets out of the country; the program initially supervised by Arkady Volsky. These evolved into the Union of Industrialists and Entrepreneurs. These were not just large Russian companies with major businesses to run. They became international businesses as the *nomenklatura* capitalists set up overseas facilities to hide their shares and influence and to diminish their reliance on solely Russian capital... No company was as blatant as Gazprom. One of the first was Mikhail Rakhimkulov, an official in the Soviet Ministry of the Gas Industry who created a corporation called Interprocom. Although initially it was partially owned by the state, in a short time it became wholly private and Rakhimkulov and his deputy Oleg Vaynerov ended up with majority control.[xlvii] On October 15, 1997, Interprocom was turned over as a gift to Khorhat, a company created in Moscow in 1991, which was owned at the time by Rakhimkulov's wife Galina and Irina Kravtsova, a woman living with Vaynerov. A year later on November 2, 1998, 90 percent of Khorhat stock was transferred equally to five individuals. They included Chernomyrdin's son Vitaly, Vyakhirev's daughter Tatyana Dedikova, Rakhimkulov's son Ruslan, and Vyacheslav Sheremet's daughter Yelena Dmitriyeva.[xlviii]

This wasn't the end of the overseas movement of Gazprom shares and ownership. In 1992 they formed the group ITERA in Jacksonville, Florida. Two years later it broadened its mandate to handle natural gas and it began trading with Gazprom. Igor Makarov, a former Olympic cyclist, became the Chief Executive Officer of the entire ITERA Group of Companies. The other shareholders were hidden but most investigators believe that they were Gazprom officials or their children, as well as Semyon Mogilevich and Dimitry Firtash of the Ukarine. Makorov's ties to Gazprom are intriguing. He sits on the board of numerous Caribbean tax-haven companies which act for Itera on Gazprom business. In 2005 Massimo Ciancimino, the don of the Sicilian Cosa Nostra, informed Italian courts that he had met with Makarov in Cortina d'Ampezzo to discuss the possibility of using mob money to set up a gas distribution network through which he could "broaden his business interests"[xlix] Makarov gained instant fame in the United States when news broke that he was funding Representative Curt Weldon and his daughter Karen in exchange for having the congressman lobby on Itera's behalf for an $868,000 loan from the U.S. Trade and Development Agency.

Makarov, however, is an important, if often overlooked, part of Vladimir Putin's team. He is a member of "Putin's komanda," which is his protection from prosecution. Makarov is a member of the Energy Council of the Government of the Russian Federation, the Presidium of the Russian Chamber of Commerce, and the powerful and highly influential Russian Gas Society. As a prominent member of Russia's energy elite, Makarov frequently accompanies Russian Prime Minister Vladimir Putin on trips abroad.[1]

Another of these nomenklatura capitalists is Vagit Alekperov, whose business trajectory is similar to Chernomyrdin's and Vyakirev's. He managed to get appointed general director of Kogalymneftegaz in 1984 which he managed until 1990. He then moved to Moscow, where he became Deputy and then First Deputy Minister of Fuel and Energy and finally, in August 1991 after the coup attempt, Acting Minister of Fuel and Energy. He was now ready to supervise the breakup and privatization of the Soviet petroleum industry. Among those which were privatised was the largest, LUKoil, which Alekporov kept for his own. Although the state held a majority share at the outset, its holdings were gradually whittled down to twenty-one percent.

Perhaps the most entrepreneurial of these nomenklatura capitalists was Vladimir Olegovich Potanin. Potanin was less of a true nomenklatura capitalist as he lived for many years outside the Soviet Union where his father served as a foreign trade representative and was viewed as an 'outsider' by many of the Red Generals. On the other hand Potanin had talent and international connections. He was a successful student and member of the Komsomol. He was picked to attend the prestigious Moscow State Institute of International Relations from which he graduated in 1983 with a specialisation in International Economy. Throughout his youth he lived well as one of the nomenklatura and was becoming a Party member through his Pioneer and Komsomol activities. It should be noted that the Moscow Institute of International Relations was essentially a KGB training school

When Potanin left university he took up a position in the Ministry of Foreign Trade. By 1985-1986 he benefitted from the recruitment program of Silayev and Ligachev to find talented young men whose skills could be turned to protecting the state's interests after the upcoming changes (similar to the recruiting of Khodorkovsky, Aven, Fridman and others). As a result of his work in the Ministry and his connections with the new Russian leaders Potanin was made head of INTERROS which was a new Foreign Trade Organisation which supplanted the former State Trading Companies which had disappeared virtually overnight. And, like the others, he was given a bank. He became vice-president of the Joint Stock Commercial Bank (International Company for Finance and Investments) MFK and, in 1993 President of the United Export Import Bank (ONEXIM BANK). The assets of the Soviet Vneshcombank (the Foreign Trade Bank) were made available to him for the success of ONEXIM. In this role he helped supervise the transfer of Soviet assets outside the country to be brought back as private banking funds.

Among the most successful of these 'loans for shares schemes' was the takeover by Menatep of the Yukos Oil Company. In June 1996, Yukos, Russia's second-largest oil company, confirmed it had virtually been taken over by Menatep Bank, electing a new board headed by Menatep President Mikhail Khodorkovsky. The move completed a complicated strategic alliance between the two firms and followed logically from the appointment a few weeks earlier of Yukos President Sergei Muravlenko as chairman of Rosprom, Menatep's industrial holding company.

Menatep was easily able to secure its control over the Yukos board, having acquired 85.1 percent of Yukos stock in a series of controversial privatisation sales over the preceding six months. The advantages were not only economic. There were other political reasons behind the speedy alliance between Yukos and Menatep By joining together they made it as difficult as possible to reverse the earlier "loans for shares" auctions. Menatep had taken a 45 percent stake in Yukos from the state as part of the controversial "loans-for-shares" privatisation auction after the government, on questionable technical grounds, threw out a rival bid. Menatep paid the government for the shares, but the government retained the option to buy the shares back. Menatep picked up another 33 percent of Yukos from the government in an investment tender held on the same day, and a further 7.1 percent at a second cash privatisation auction. With the purchase of the Yukos shares directly, the government's option was effectively vacated.

This acquisition was, in the minds of most observers, the swallowing of a whale by a minnow. Yukos, with annual sales of over US$5 billion was acquired by Menatep whose assets were less than

US$1.6 billion and a majority stake in Rosprom with sales of less than US$1 billion.

Throughout Russian industry, Russians with money (usually overseas) offered loans to the State and took shares in return. This was in marked difference to the earlier voucher privatisation scheme. The failed voucher privatisation earlier had attracted some non-Russian players as well. The naive economic planners brought in by Gorbachev and Yeltsin for it had no real experience. They were academics from Saint Petersburg who were determined to remove communist structures. With the attempt to promote the voucher system new people were installed. People like Yegor Gaidar and Anatoly Chubais were hired in October of 1992 to help implement voucher privatization. As part of the scheme they had distributed 144 million vouchers to the people which could be exchanged for stock. However, they had no effective plan for using these vouchers to take over the companies or promote their growth. They decided to bring in foreign advisors along with some more Russians. The enabling legislation was developed by a team of Harvard specialists, led by Jeffrey Sachs. These were mainly lawyers, not businessmen or investment bankers. They knew they needed someone more familiar with markets so they added to their team two investment bankers working in Russia for Credit Suisse, Boris Jordan and Stephen Jennings, to show them how to market and manage these assets.

The first company to be privatised was the Bolshevik Biscuit Company on December 8, 1992. It was a success in that the shares were sold at the auction but the price realised was terribly low. There had also been a Bolshevik Biscuit Factory in Poland that Credit-Suisse First Boston had sold a year earlier to Pepsi-Cola for approximately US$ 80 million. The Russian biscuit factory, at a price based on the voucher auction process, traded at US$ 684,000, opening up an incredible arbitrage opportunity because of the lack of interest in voucher privatization. Jordan and Jennings saw the opportunities and founded a Russian-based investment bank, Renaissance Capital, and began to take advantage of the opportunities which presented themselves. Eventually the Harvard people were sued by the US government for their poor advice and an out-of-court settlement was reached (US $35 million). Renaissance went from strength to strength as did its competitor firm, Troika Dialog, founded in 1991 by Reuben

Vardanian, U.S. bankers Peter Derby and Bernie Sucher. Others, like Leonid Rozhetskin, joined their ranks.

There have been an immense amount of studies and analyses of the effects of the 'loans-for-shares' business. These have concentrated primarily on the economic effects of the process on the Russian economy and how it allowed Yeltsin to snatch a Presidential victory in the 1965 election. These may all be important but for those of us engaged in the day-to day business of Russian transformation there were far more important consequences. The results of the privatisation of the Russian companies through the share auctions had several very important effects.

The first effect was that the new Russian capitalists suddenly had to deal with internal Russian industrial problems. As these budding oligarchs took over factories, refineries and smelters across the ten time zones of Russia they soon realised that they had very little management control of their scattered operations. Taking over the shares and ownership of a company, especially one which was moving from a state-owned structure to a private structure left, at best, a management vacuum at the factory, refinery or smelter. The ownership of these new assets required installing an effective management structure among them to make them work and which could establish a working relationship with the regional and municipal authorities. This would be a management structure that would have to deal with resource allocations, finances, transport and 'human relations'. None of these new enterprises were ready or staffed for this.

In many areas there was an immediate conflict with the former managers of the plants. Local mayors resisted change; governors fought against the changes in traditional practices and the labour force was unprepared to face a distant management in Moscow or St. Petersburg whom they didn't know or trust. However, there were local organisations who were organised, in place, and who would be of immediate use to these new oligarchs. These were the groups of organised criminals who controlled the on-the-scene structures and who had worked out a symbiotic pact with the local politicians. These smaller gangs, after a flurry of violence and conflict, were quickly incorporated into national criminal enterprises and an initial dividing of the turf took place in key sectors. The Solnestvo Gang led by 'Mihas' moved quickly to take over the oil and gas industries. The Ismailovo.

under Malefsky, took over the aluminium industry. The Uralmash fought its rivals in a bloody battle for the Urals copper industry. This was mirrored in every region, factory, port and rail centre across Russia. There was no way for these oligarchs to manage the vast and unco-ordinated sprawl of Russian industry on their own and the Russian government was of no use at all. Despite the active investigations by the Prosecutor's office and an extensive monitoring plan run through Interpol, the criminal authorities were unable to have much of an effect on policing this.

The takeover of Yukos by Khordokovsky was initially of particular interest to the security agencies. Just as the gas industry was linked to Itera and Semyon Mogilevich, Yukos was believed to be closely linked to the Solnestvo Gang. The Prosecutor's office investigated several 'leaks' from their 'stukachi' that there was a "special relationship" between Khodorkovsky, his Yukos Oil concern and the Solntsevskaya Organization of Moscow. One of the attractions was that these new private enterprises provided a giant international money laundry for the criminals. They had reported that Sergei Mikhailov ('Mihas') had invested large sums of his money into Yukos Oil projects. One such project was identified by the source as Mikhailov and the Solntsevskaya Organization's financing of the adaptation by Yukos Oil of new drilling technology from Canada. This activity began in early 2000. One of the individuals who was reportedly involved in this activity was Aleksandr Sedov, a.k.a. "Moskovsky," a central Moscow "brigade leader" of the Solntsevskaya Organization. It was thoroughly in Mikhailov's interest to be a "partner" in the development of foreign technology such as the Canadian drilling equipment. By investing his and his criminal organization's funds in the Yukos Oil project, Mikhailov, in effect, "laundered" vast sums of money into the legitimate operations of a major Russian petroleum company. The co-ordinator of this relationship was said to be Arnold Arnoldovich Tamm.

Equally as important the internal oil refining structure was structured to allow participation by local kryshas. Yukos Oil did not have distributors or "intermediaries." Instead, it had its own personnel serving as the company's representatives in marketing its products. Yukos Oil had a rather large structure consisting of between twenty and fifty refineries located throughout the Russian Federation. Petroleum was pumped into each of these refineries or processing facilities, or "MPZs," and at these refineries the material was turned into residual oil, gasoline and diesel fuel.

In Yukos, as in other big petroleum companies in Russia , each MPZ facility was controlled by a particular criminal group. According to the investigators, the control exercised at the MPZ by the various criminal groups provided discipline out of chaos. The communities surrounding each MPZ saw the facility as a source of money in a country where such resources were otherwise scarce. The criminal organization, therefore, was able to impose a sense of order by prioritising who could get access to this large source of funding and its products. The controlling criminal group got exclusivity to provide services to each MPZ, including such areas as distribution of products and protection from extortionate demands. In return, the major oil companies, such as Yukos, got "control" over the anarchy, particularly in the more remote areas of the Russian Federation.

At that time, the three largest Yukos MPZ facilities in Russia and their controlling organizations were Kemerovo, Omsk and Uha. Kemerovo and Omsk were controlled by the Kemerovo, a Russian criminal organization, which was headed by an individual identified as "Kostya Schram" (a.k.a "Kostya the Scarface"). "Kostya Schram" was further described as a close associate of Solntsevskaya Organization leader Sergei Anatolyevich Mikhailov. A different branch of the Solntsevskaya group controlled Uha, in Bashkortistan. As part of Yukos' and other companies' arrangements with the criminal structure at each MPZ, the organized crime leaders controlling the facility had the option and the right to set up "independent deals" for large-scale clients. The expansion of organised crime into the oil, gas and metals industries was an important element of their stability and the culmination of several years of attempts at symbiotic relationships.

In addition to the share takeover of these far-flung plants the work environment deteriorated as the changeover to private ownership was often accompanied by violence and death. In 1995, when the Yukos company passed into the control of Menatep, the Mayor of Nefteyugansk, Vladimir Petukhov, soon started to complain that Yukos was not paying its taxes; was laying off workers by the dozens, and getting behind in paying the workers. In addition he complained that Yukos was trying to write off a debt from the comany to the city of 450 billion rubles. He started a campaign against Yukos; even writing an open letter to Yeltsin and Kiriyenko about

Yukos' failings and testifying to that effect at the Duma. Soon after, he was shot to death. His successor did not raise the issues again. This was not unique. In 2005 Alexei Pichugin, Yukos' security chief, was convicted of the murders of Yevgeny Rybin, Sergei Kolesov, Olga Kostina and Sergei and Olga Gorin. Also charged was Leonid Nevzlin, Khordokovsky's partner.[li]

There was frequent violence in 1995 and 1996 as the mafias fought for turf; the companies sought to avoid paying taxes to local authorities; and the political structures wavered over competing pressures seeking control at national and regional levels. As Russian entrepreneurs took over Russian companies they followed the traditional Russian path of management. In most cases violence or the threat of violence was a powerful motivator and the easiest solution.

When Potanin took over Norilsk Nickel he had to battle the existing organisation in the plant and at Dudinka (the port). For many year Norilsk, the city and the plant, were the domain of Anatoly Filatov, the last red director of Norilsk Nickel. Filatov was more than just a plant director, he was supported by the workforce and the region in that he was able, after 1989, to preserve the viability of the plant and the region in the face of the austerity cuts which threatened to close it down. . Due to his efforts in 1989 a state concern for the production of non-ferrous and precious metals Norilsk Nickel Combine came into being. It comprised Norilsk Nickel, the Krasnoyarsk Plant of Nonferrous Metals, the St. Petersburg Gipronickel and enterprises of the Kola Peninsula: the combines Severonickel and Pechenganickel and also the Olenegorsk mechanical plant. Through Filatov's connections with the Council of Ministers he saved much of the industrial production the Kola Peninsula and in Norilsk.

Filatov used his influence to get the workers in these plants to take up the privatisation opportunities. Almost 300,000 local workers became shareholders in RAO Norilsk Nickel and around 230,000 more from the region acquired a stake. New housing was undertaken and pensioners were given preferred treatment. I visited Norilsk and Dudinka to explore delivering fresh food to the region on the invitation of Filatov and the Northern Governors. It was a nightmare of a place. It had been one of the worst forced labour camps in the Gulag and had only recently become free of the harsh rules which governed such camps. It had massive supplies of copper, nickel and palladium. It was freezing cold, as befits an Arctic location, and social amenities were limited. Working conditions were marginally better than under the Gulag but there was a desperate need for infrastructural investment. This is what Filatov was trying to achieve. Business started to boom but, with the economic depression which accompanied the dissolution of the Soviet Empire the metals business reduced dramatically.

The state concern, Norilsk Nickel, struggled to stay afloat and to pay its way. It struggled to raise credits from merchant banks and borrowed heavily from the Ministry of Finance to cover their export deals. They were successful in selling and exporting the metals and were able to survive, but not thrive. Then, the Russian government suddenly imposed a range of new taxes and announced that they were unable to fund the export credits. The company was on the edge of financial collapse. It was just then that the shares-for-loans auction of Norilsk Nickel was held in November 1995. At that point the Norilsk loans from the merchant banks were called and the Ministry of Finance cancelled all export credits.. Unicombank (the main bank, which had performed banking services for RAO Norilsk Nickel enterprises) was totally blocked on the market for inter-bank credits. The cupboard was bare. They couldn't pay wages or their bills.

Potanin and Onexim Bank took over the Norilsk Nickel company. Early in 1996 the Russian Government opened a criminal prosecution against the former managers of Norilsk Nickel, accusing them of misappropriating money from earlier loans. In April, Oneximbank scored a victory over Norilsk Nickel's management on the corruption issue. A government order dismissed Norilsk Nickel president Anatoly Filatov. Vsevolod Generalov, the deputy chairman of the Russian Metallurgical Commission, was appointed to replace him. Norilsk Nickel's board of directors were replaced soon after. Later that same month Generalov quit Norilsk and was replaced by Alexander Khloponin, who stayed at the company until 2001, when he became governor of the region.

Potanin replaced the old directors and installed his new ones. A massive purge took place. Eventually Potanin was able to install his people as company directors, mayors of the towns and governor of the region. For the most part the shareholders who had acquired shares in the earlier privatisation, were left with nothing. Potanin had a natural advantage. From August 1996 to March 1997 he was First Deputy Prime Minister of the Russian Federation Government, responsible for economic issues. Through his company, Interros, he acquired control over twenty formerly state owned enterprises. Potanin's industrial enterprises encompassed Norilsk Nickel, the world's largest producer of nickel and palladium; Svyazinvest, a telecommunications company; Sidanko oil and number of other privatisedl firms, including Perm Motors, Northwest Shipping, Magnitogorsk, the Gaz automobile plant, and various other metallurgical plants. There were also a host of newspapers including Izvestia, Komsomolskaya Pravda and the magazine Expert. He managed to get George Soros to invest in Svyazinvest with him.

He and his partner in Interros and Onexim Bank, Mikhail Prokorov, prospered but life was very hard for the remaining workers at Norilsk and the Kola Peninsula. While visiting Norilsk to look at shipping the metals from the port of Dudinka for Filatov I was also engaged to explore the creation of a short rail link (using the wider Russian gauge) from the Russian Kola stations to the nearby northern Norway port of Kirkenes. Kirkenes was the point where the Gulf Stream ended and it remains largely ice-free in the winter. The Norwegian iron-ore plant at Sydvaranger south of Kirkenes was closing down and it had an excellent port facility and a connection to Kirkenes. The Northern Russian industrial centres at Nikel, Apatity, Olenogorsk and others could have a warm-water outlet to the world market. My colleague, David Rees, from our office at Stavanger, travelled to Kirkenes on several occasions for this and we both met with the Norwegian authorities in Oslo. I travelled around the settled areas of the Northern Arctic area on my own and was appalled to see scores of broken oil pipes dripping oil in puddles, almost ponds, on the white snow. I was warned to wear my lead underwear as the radiation count from discarded nuclear waste and subassemblies was very high. They used to tell me that if I could see the local Inuit (Eskimo) populations glowing in the dark at night it was too dangerous to stay.

The idea of a Northern exit for Russian products died as the Russians, especially the military at Boris Gleb and Zapadnaya Litsa. became nervous that there would be insufficient control of the business from Moscow. The Norwegians were even less happy, so it died. Marc Rich eventually set up an alumina import facility in Murmansk but this only helped the aluminium industry. The opportunities for progressing development in the North put forward by the Northern governors disappeared as they lost power to the new industrialists. It was frustrating but I did get to see several beautiful evenings filled with the magical display of the Northern Lights.

The admixture of new private ownership had dramatic impact on many regions. In some regions the alliance between the new capitalists, organised criminal gangs and the regional administrations shaped both the political as well as the economic scene. This reflected a major battle for power in Moscow as well. From 1994 to 1996 Chubais and Soskevets had a major falling out over industrial policy. Chubais wanted a broad privatisation of the state's share in most companies under state ownership. Soskovets was determined that it was in the Russian interest, and especially in the interest of the defence-industrial complex for whim he spoke, that the state would unite all the non-privatized shares in the metals sector into one large state holding.

Chubais asked the banks to draw up a list of the state-owned companies in which they had an interest to invest in the loans-for shares scheme. On that list were several important metal companies, primarily in the iron and steel business, including Magnitogorsk, Novoliptesk Steel, Mechel, Severstal, Zapsib, NTMK and Oskolsk electrometallurgical plant (OEMK). The directors of these balked at the plans for privatisation and wrote Soskovets to object.Soskovets raised their objections

Despite Soskovets' objections, these firms found themselves on the privatisation list. Soskovets flew down to Sochi to meet with Yeltsin who signed a decree creating Rossiiskaya Metallurgia (a holding company which grouped all these firms into one basket). Despite this, Soskovets was unable to keep the companies intact. He had the political advantage but Chubais and the banks had the economic advantage. These metal companies were heavily in debt to the banks who wished to take over their shares. The banks called in the loans outstanding and sucked out the capital from these companies before the privatisation auctions. They were effectively bankrupted by the very banks who wanted to buy them. Sometimes these debts were real; sometimes they were notional. There was nothing the companies could do as they needed cash immediately to keep going. By the time of the major privatisation auctions in 1996 these metal and allied companies were trading while insolvent and ripe for a raid on their shares.

New Russian banking and mega-corporations sprung up to take over the plants which they had acquired. In most cases they had to physically take over the plants by locking out the existing management, removing them bodily from their desks and occasionally using violence or the threat to violence to assert their control. In several cases, especially in regions governed by accommodating governors, the local political forces assisted. One of the most famous cases was the MIKOM (the Zhvilo brothers) takeover of KMK in Kemerovo Oblast They sent in its general director, Nikolai Fomin to occupy the administration building and to oust the head of the concern, Evgeny Braunshtein. Braunstein was kidnapped and held as a hostage but soon escaped and brought back his own men to oust Fomin. This was achieved by getting the support of Governor Mikhail Kislyuk, However, MIKOM then issued new stock warrants for the increase of the share capital by 1,000% and the exiting directors could not find enough money to avoid their dilution to minor players. They were out. In this the Zhvilo were assisted by Aman Tuleev who later became governor. Tuleev joined forces with the Zhvilo brothers and took over control of the Oblast. However, after a falling out, the Zhvilo brothers hired Victor Tikhonov to assassinate Tuleev. He was sentenced to four years imprisonment in 2000. The Zhvilos were later charged with trying to poison the governor.

Similar takeovers and occupations took place in the copper industry, involving both Governors Tuleev and Eduard Rossel. In that area the primary player was Iskander Makhmudov. Iskander was trained in the Faculty of Oriental Studies at the University of Tashkent and became an excellent linguist in Arabic and English. He went to work for the Ministry of Defence and Rosvooruzhenie soon after graduation and became a valuable part of the Soviet effort to promote the sales of weapons and weapon systems around the world (Iraq and Libya in particular). He spent some time in "Uzbekintorg" and then moved to Moscow to become part of the Trans World Group. He worked very closely with Mischa Chernoy and handled a substantial sector of his business. Iskander is a very bright and sophisticated gentleman and was extremely capable. He was a friend and was very helpful in explaining to me many of my ignorant questions about Russian business. I saw him quite often in London and occasionally in New York at Sam Kislin's office on 6th Avenue. I remember trying out my new 'bug detector' in his office and finding four different bugs planted there. Someone was interested in the business being conducted there. We concluded that this must have been four different people as there was no need for redundancy.

Iskander told me a story which I have never been able to forget. He was in Libya installing some very sophisticated radar gear for the Libyans at the very time that the US was attacking the Gulf of Sirte. Ghaddafi was flying around in a rage ordering the Russians to turn on the radar and the missile defence system attached to it. Iskander was the man who had to tell Ghaddafi that the installation wasn't complete and they couldn't turn it on. They had had an urgent message from Moscow telling them not to turn it on. The Russians wanted to be free of any association with shooting down US planes. The system actually was working but it fell to Iskander to make them believe that it wasn't yet ready to engage.

Iskander was one of two people with whom we worked in Russia who had the education, language skills, sophistication and intellect to be a success in any country in which he chose to work. The other was Vladimir Lisin. The other young men, like Oleg Deripaska or Roman Ambramovich, were mainly focussed on Russia and Russian values. They were competent but had nothing of the spark or drive of Iskander or Lisin. The latter were international and experienced outside of Russia. They made up a formidable management base inside Russia for carrying on business while all the machinations, intrigue and in-fighting took place in the metals industries.

The loans for shares interlude had very little effect on the aluminium business directly as these dealt mainly with external capital coming in to do tolling.. On the other hand it did spur on those Russians with interests in the smelters to set up their own banks and stockbroking operation to take advantage of the opportunities and to use their new cash mountains. On a visit to our Moscow office I was introduced to Jeff Millikan, a US banking specialist, who had been engaged to develop a bank or banks for the Trans World Group, as well as to seek a license to buy and sell shares. Eventually the Trans World Group created the Zalog Bank and other financial companies which they used to acquire shares in the aluminium smelters and related businesses.

The privatisation of the Russian aluminium industry was marked by controversy and accusations of all manner of crimes. Lt. Col. S.A. Glushenkov of the Special Investigation Committee amassed a mountain of evidence and allegations against almost everyone in the aluminium business as part of his famous Case 009. They ranged from false credit notes, theft, tax avoidance, beatings, murder and similar capital crimes. As far as I know, these accusations against TransWorld, the Chernoys, the Reubens and the others in the organisation were never proved. There are many studies, reports and exposes in circulation about the 'Aluminium Wars' and several major lawsuits in the US on the basis of RICO complaints. Some are attached as appendices.[lii] They make interesting reading. I don't know if any of them are true as I never witnessed any violence or killings during my years in the Russian aluminium business. I heard rumours and allegations but these were not in my area of responsibility so I was not curious to discover the veracity of the allegations. I lack a morbid curiosity.

There were fifty-eight separate cases brought by the officials of First Deputy Minister of Interior Affairs, Vladimir Kolesnikov against Trans World and Lev Chernoy concerning, *inter alia*, the affairs of Krasnoyarsk and Trans World's main Krasnoyarsk partner Anatoly Bykov. None came to any conclusion. Bykov finally skipped the country but later returned with no consequence or any findings of guilt.

One of the problems I discovered about the willingness of the population to believe the worst about the Chernoys in particular was their association with people who were viewed as criminals. Some of this was chance. One of the famous Russian underworld figures, Alimzhan Tokhtakhunov (better known as 'Taiwanchik), the man who fixed the Winter Olympics, was a schoolmate of Mischa Chernoy in Tashkent. Another schoolmate was Sharmil Tarpichev, the coach and trainer of the Russian Tennis Federation. There was no good reason that they shouldn't associate with each other when they all reached Moscow.

Soon. many of the cowboys were forced out of the aluminium smelters. Sensible professionals like Leonid Blavatnik of SUAL, Access and Renova brought their international expertise to Russia and turned many of the northern smelters into viable concerns. He was an early émigré to the U.S. and had become a U.S. citizen. That has given him a lot more strength in his Russian dealings (like Boris Jordan, Simon Kukes, Leonid Rozhetskin and others) because he was, in part, out of the Russian system of mutual blackmail. These émigrés gained in power by being U.S. nationals in that it was harder for the Russians to 'muscle them' as there was the fear of international publicity and the possibility that these émigrés could be compelled to testify in U.S. courts. On the other hand, because they were U.S. nationals, a subpoena from a U.S. court or a query from the FBI had a greater meaning for them than for Russian oligarchs.

The efforts to build an aluminium business were fraught with problems. SUAL had several smelters in which they had a major share of the interest (Irkutsk and Sayansk). Their main rivals, the TransWorld Group, were determined to squeeze them out. TransWorld tried to cut off their energy supplies and restrict their transport opportunities. SUAL fought back and sued TransWorld in court in Moscow over the Irkutsk smelter and won.

This victory also inspired the management of Achinsk (virtually the only domestic supplier of alumina at that time) to fight back. The privatization had left them victims to 'private capital' of the organized crime variety. These new owners bankrupt the company and the bankruptcy court placed Achinsk under "external management," in which an outside official appointed by an arbitration court was charged with returning the plant to solvency. The first appointed manager was Nail Nasyrov of Trans World. This virtually free acquisition of Achinsk by TransWorld was resisted by the new governor of the Krasnoyarsk region, Alexander Lebed, who, with funds from Berezovsky (and it is widely believed SUAL), took back Achinsk and kept it separate from the TransWorld holdings which later became RUSAL.

This illustrated the second phase of the struggle for dominance in the aluminium plants. It had become clear that in doing tolling it was crucial to deliver as many of the inputs as possible. After alumina the next biggest input was electricity. Except for the great hydroelectric dams the major source of electricity was coal. The battle for control of the coal mines was crucial for aluminium, copper and ferrous metals. When Chubais took over UES (the main energy supplier) he entered directly into the war with the metal barons. That fight continues.

This struggle for supremacy in the aluminium business was largely irrelevant to what I was doing. There was not sufficient alumina to go around, Many of the smelters still relied on imported bauxite. The SUAL Kola bauxite was a long way off from becoming commercial. Many companies were having real difficulties in moving in the raw materials and difficulty in exporting the finished aluminium from the

East. Bratsk had started constructing its own alumina import facility in Rajjin, North Korea using the Vigan system. It was very inefficient and relied on the rail link to the Trans-Siberian railroad which had to change its carriages on to new, wider, bogies to travel on Russian rail lines. I was sure that my work at Vanino was crucial for the industry. I was wrong.

CHAPTER THIRTEEN

While all these changes in the ownership structure of the Russian aluminium industry were taking place the success of TransWorld in grasping almost 70% of the industry placed greater pressure on our transport and logistics business, Sunil and I were chartering and operating on time charter over forty vessels. Most of this was handled by Sunil and our team in London. At its peak we were moving around seven million tons of cargo each year of supplies and finished metals. The logistics of getting these into the ports and to and from the smelters was a very complicated business and always fraught with unexpected events and demands. The documentation alone was a major endeavour. Victor spent a lot of time making sure that the goods moved freely and were properly documented. He spent a lot of time in Vanino on this. Hugo kept everything in order, documented and accounted for. This was a special kind of responsibility because we were also building the import facility at Vanino for alumina with the hopper and the Pneuma-grab.

In addition we were constructing the slab and the ring beam for the inflatable building which would be used as an onshore storage. Gordon Calder sent out two Scottish engineers from Morrison's to supervise the laying of the slab and the creation of the ring beam. They also supervised the installation of the giant hopper which had been constructed at Sovetskaya Gavan. When we finally arranged the shipment of the Pneuma-Grab and the fittings for the hopper from a centralised point in Norway we had to negotiate the landing rights at Mongokhta Airbase with the military. Niksa and I travelled frequently to Vanino to supervise and to bring money for the work.

We had some support from our erstwhile Russian employees at the port but not a great deal. I finally realised that my expectations for them were too high. I remembered a lecture I had attended at university on cultural anthropology. What I was expecting to be a workplace devoted to achievement was actually the head temple in a local cargo cult. A cargo cult is a group of people whose religious set of beliefs are developed to deal with their response to their sudden interaction with technological change of an advanced culture. The cults are focused on obtaining the material wealth, technology and appurtenances of the more advanced societies through prayers, magical thinking and rituals. They are sure that their ancestors and their shamans had promised them these goods and if certain rituals were conducted and prayers sent the material wealth would be theirs.

Victor and I sat in the office one day and watched what was going on with two new women who had come to work for us. They were specialists in accounting. All day long they wrote notes on small pieces of paper and passed them to each other. Nothing more was done with these notes and, at the end of the day, these notes would disappear. We had no idea of why this was happening as we had an excellent accounting system on the computer. We finally asked them what they were writing, but they couldn't tell us. It kept them very busy but we had no idea what it meant. It was a powerful ritual that engaged them every day.

Our port installation was the object of the cargo cult and we reinforced this by actually bringing real cargo to their shores. Their rituals and magical thinking did not often involve work or responsibility. While being fairly ecumenical in my outlook a less magical response from them might have been useful. The foundations and the laying of the concrete slab for the air-supported building had to be redone twice because there was no one there full-time to do the supervising at the site. We finally sent down the two Morrison engineers to supervise. There was no one from the port to supervise the erection of the hopper at the site so we brought in the Swedes. It was perplexing.

However, I soon learned from a neighbour at the port who was building a giant storage and refuelling depot on the other side of the port for Trans-Bunker that he had hired a crew of Chinese labourers from nearby Harbin to do the manual labour. They worked very hard and efficiently and managed themselves. They were paid about 65% of the wage of a Russian worker but produced around 200% of the Russian output. I was told by the Russians at the port that the Chinese had to work harder because their country was poorer than Russia and that they were still communists. They were sure that, somewhere, they had been taught that democrats worked less hard than communists.

I tried to explain that personal responsibility was also a feature of democratic economic models but this was rejected. When it came to performing actual labour it was no longer a theoretical argument. They told me the story of Stalin's speech to the workers. He stood up and announced that after the Bolshevik victory the communists would take away the lands of the aristocrats and share them with all. There was a great cheer. They would remove the big cars, dachas and yachts of the boyars and share them with all. There were great cheers. Finally he said that the communists would remove the extra bicycles and carts and share them with all. There was no cheer. Stalin asked what was wrong. Why did they cheer when he said they would take the lands, cars, yachts and dachas of the rich and share them; but they refused to cheer when he announced that he would share the bicycles and carts? An official told him "Because Comrade Stalin we have bicycles and carts."

There was a great deal of disillusionment with the new democracy. The people had lost their savings; currency was unstable; they were not suddenly politically empowered. The old system of *blat* no longer really functioned and the old communists had suddenly morphed into new democrats and were still in charge of the towns and villages. Even worse, the criminal gangs now flourished with impunity and violence. There was no justice to be had.

Niksa and I were flying to Vanino from Moscow. Niksa started to speak with two young women returning to the Far East on the same plane. They were weeping and disconsolate. When we left the plane at Khabarovsk Niksa invited the girls to have dinner with him later that day. They turned up at the hotel and over dinner they told us their story. They had been modestly successful in bringing into Khabarovsk leather jackets and overcoats bought from Moscow traders. They had accumulated some cash and decided that they would fly to Moscow and buy up a stock of jackets wholesale which they would sell themselves. They got their money together, along with some funds from their friends, and set off to Moscow. They visited Izmailova Market that Sunday and were able to buy some jackets at a reasonable price. They took the jackets to their hotel. There was not enough stock available at the market so they had arranged with the trader to meet him at his warehouse on Tuesday to pick out some more and complete their order. They visited the warehouse on Tuesday and were shown the jackets. They agreed a price. The girls went to pay the trader and suddenly several men appeared. They took back the jackets, took all the money, abused the girls and threw them out on the street. The girls went to the police who told them that they could do nothing. They had no proof and, anyway, it happened all the time and they weren't interested. The girls were able to sell the jackets they had bought and left at the hotel so that they could buy a ticket home. They were devastated. They had lost their savings; they owed money to their friends; and their business as traders was over.

This nightmare story was repeated to me over and over in different variants during my stay in Russia and there was nothing to be done; unfairness was the rule. There is an old Russian saying which was repeated frequently to me. "Chelovek cheloveku volk!" (A man is a wolf towards other men.)

Sometimes disillusionment with the New Order was more mundane. I was working with the stevedores on the deck of a vessel making sure about the stowage of a mixed cargo of T-bars and ingots for Japan. A stevedore turned to me and said, "You know what is going on. Can you answer for me a question my 9-year old daughter asked me this morning?" I said I'd try. He said "She said to me. You go to work every day and work long hours. Mommy goes to work every day and works long hours Uncle Boris goes to work every day and works long hours. Why is there no sugar at the table for our tea?" I was unable to answer him.

Some others regretted the change in government for other reasons. An older woman I was speaking to at the market in Khabarovsk told me she was sad about the changeover from the 'old system'. She told me she had a daughter with Down's syndrome and was worried sick about what would happen to her daughter if the mother died or was incapacitated. She said that in the old days she knew that, whatever happened to her, the system would look after her daughter. It wouldn't have been nice or luxurious but there would be some kind of social institution which would care for her. Now there was no such institution. She didn't know what to do.

Wherever I travelled in Siberia and the Far East I met with people who had no faith in their government or politicians. The ravages to the economy by Gaidar's reforms; their loss of savings and pensions; the disgust at the breakdown of law and order; the televised antics of Yeltsin dancing; the unthinkable prices charged in the shops were proof that the system wasn't working. This was later capped by the 1998 bank collapse which took away even the last vestiges of capital in this bereft society. It was better in Moscow and St. Petersburg because the locals could read about and see what was happening. Knowledge improved hope. In Siberia and the Far East there was total apathy as it was clear that they were powerless and without any influence on events.

The brave hopes and aspirations of 1992-1993 died and were replaced by cynicism and despair by 1994-1995. Perhaps that accounts for the lack of ambition among our employees at Vanino?

This despair was in sharp contrast to my optimism. The TransWorld accountants had told me that our operation in London had saved the company $6.5 million in shipping the first year. The export of aluminium from Vanino accounted for almost 85% of all production at the two largest smelters and our transport design had shaved six days off the transit time to the port. I had travelled to Japan to make arrangements for the import of coking coal and other minerals needed in the production of aluminium and helped arrange a delivery chain for alloy wheel blanks and billets for the Japanese auto industry from KRAMZ

We had designed and constructed the first alumina import facility for the Russian Far East. The hopper was up and in place. The Pneuma-Grab was installed and working. The two Atlas Copco compressors which powered the Pneuma-Grab and the hopper were installed and operational. The slab and ring beam for the inflatable storage building was completed and the air structure was ready for shipment in New York. The Neuro machine and the temporary hopper were erected and functioning as a backup.

Sunil and I had negotiated the purchase of a ship, the "Dynamic Future" from some Greek owners. It was to be our 'silo ship' at the port until the land storage was completed and tested. We signed the Norwegian Short Form for the purchase of the ship in the name of International Bulk Trade (my company) and we insured it and put it on our P&I club register. We sent out the inspectors and she was approved as seaworthy and operational. We completed the purchase and she was renamed the "River K". We put our own crew and officers on her, led by Captain Ralph Coutinho. It was an all-Indian crew and officers supplied by Captain Barve in Mumbai. I had had Indian crews on some of the other vessels I owned or bare-boat chartered. They didn't fight as much as Russian, Ukrainian or Philippine crewmen and the food in the galley was very good indeed.

I had the ship, the "Al Jabalaine", permanently moored in the Medway near London delivering cement into the local market and to the Channel Tunnel. It was a relatively large vessel (34,000 deadweight tons) so we had a twenty-man crew. The cooks on board were Indians. Their food was so good that the UK Customs officers visited us twice a week for a free meal and a free carton of cigarettes and a bottle of scotch whiskey from our bond. There was nothing we could do. The port officials came on the weekend. We later moved the ship to Cardiff Docks and the Customs officers arrived, telling us that their colleagues in Sheerness had told them of the good meals to be had so we didn't escape by moving there.

I reported to David and Lev that we were ready to start the import of alumina at Vanino. By this time Mischa Chernoy was out of TransWorld. They had paid him US$400 million and he left. David seemed very happy that we were about to take this step forward and quizzed me about whether the system would work. I told him that all was tested and that we had redundant systems in place. I learned from Hugo that Victor had been telling David that the system was too complicated and that it wouldn't work. I wasn't happy. I told Victor to return from Vanino immediately and go find a job somewhere else. David agreed to put him on the TransWorld books. I had the River K ready to come into Vanino to be permanently moored there. It had been fitted with grabs in case anything happened to the Pneuma-Grab. The connection to the hopper was installed and tested. I brought the local Greens to the port so that they could watch us operate the test with some cement. They were very happy. There was no dust.

I asked David to please transfer the last payment to New York for the air structure as this would take several days to process and about a week to get to Vanino. Then it would take at least a week to install. He agreed. I then went to Moscow. Niksa and I visited Lev in his office. I gave him a full report on everything we had done and said our first delivery was imminent. Lev, who walks with the aid of a cast metal cane weighing around forty pounds as a result of childhood polio, stood up and smashed his cane on the table, shouting "No, no!" "Do not actually deliver any aluminium to Vanino!" I was dumbfounded. He explained that he had taken over Achinsk which supplied alumina to the smelters. He was able to do this by threatening to import alumina into Vanino. If we actually did import alumina it would diminish the value of Achinsk and his stranglehold over the smelters. Lev's ties with Meshin in the Nikolayev alumina plant was the last piece of the puzzle I was told to look as if I could import alumina but I should not actually do so. I could not understand what he wanted me to do or if David was witting to this plan.

I flew back to London before going out to Vanino and had a meeting with David. I told him what Lev had told me and that I had been reliably informed by several knowledgeable figures in the prosecutor's office and the GRU that Lev had been to visit with Yeltsin's daughter and Berezovsky at Berezovky's villa in the South of France and that an arrangement had been made with the Yeltsin Family to increase their role in the aluminium industry. I advised David that if he didn't insist on controlling the supply of alumina into the Far East himself he would soon lose control of his part of the business. I suggested that TransWorld would be squeezed out of the business within three years as they would have no leverage. The Russians had made lots of money and were well integrated into the world market. They didn't need TransWorld any longer. I suggested that the Russians would take back control of the aluminium industry and David would be paid off and ousted.

David was outraged. He was furious with me that I could suggest such a thing. His partner would never treat him like that. There must be a misunderstanding. I suggested that smashing his cane down on the table and shouting "No" was not very ambiguous. I was told to leave this and to go to Vanino to make sure everything was ready. TransWorld had ordered 26,000 tons of alumina from Australia on the ship the "Spar Seven" and it would be loading soon for Vanino.

I flew out to Vanino and tested out the equipment again; examined the receiving hopper and checked the rail line to our berth. All seemed to be in order. All I needed was to be sure that our vessel, the River K would arrive earlier in Vanino so that we could discharge the Spar Seven with ordinary grabs as quickly as possible into the River K and the Spar Seven could leave without demurrage. The Pneuma-Grab would load the hopper from the River K so that if there were any hiccups we would have time to deal with it since the River K was going to be permanently moored at the berth anyway. All seemed to be in order. Four days before the Spar Seven arrived at Vanino I was told that TransWorld had stopped the River K off North Korea. I was confused. Why would they do something like that? The ship actually belonged to my company. How could they order it to stop or do anything else?

I sent an urgent telex to Sunil in London asking why he had given such an order. He told me that David had spoken to Moscow and that the TransWorld partners had decided to stop the ship. He was powerless to fight their orders. That would mean that there would be no intermediate storage in the port and we would have to load directly from the Spar Seven into the hopper. That was not impossible but it might be slower. I checked out the equipment again and it was working perfectly. I awaited the arrival of the Spar Seven.

Just after noon on the Thursday I was scheduled to leave, the Spar Seven arrived. It was a Norwegian vessel but crewed by Indians. I greeted them and went on board to meet with the captain and officers. I explained what I would like to happen in the discharging and introduced them to Niksa and the Vanino team. I supervised the loading of the equipment onto the deck of the Spar Seven (the compressors and the Pneuma-Grab) and I left to go back to London. Niksa stayed on to supervise.

One of the reasons I had to go back was that my sister-in-law was getting remarried in Colorado and I was scheduled to accompany my wife and children to the US. I arrived back in London and got ready for my trip. The very morning, as we were getting ready to go to the airport, I got an urgent call from David. He said that everything had broken down in Vanino, the compressors were broken and the Pneuma-Grab wasn't functioning. They couldn't discharge. I had to go back immediately to Vanino. My wife and children were furious but I really had no choice. I took them to the airport, made sure they were all set and left them to fly to the US. I took the next plane to Moscow and then connected to Khabarovsk and Sovetskaya Gavan.

When I arrived at the port there was mass confusion. I went to the equipment and looked at the compressors. They were perfectly fine but someone had sabotaged the fuel. The filters were clogged with dirt and sticks so they wouldn't work. Niksa, who was leaving, said he had bought some fuel but it turned out to be full of dirt and sticks. To this day I don't know if this was deliberate or accidental but it couldn't have happened at a worse time. I sent a message to Gordon Calder who immediately sent me two engineers on the next planes. I was able to clean out one of the compressors myself with tools that I borrowed from the port's Technical Director and started up the Pneuma-Grab. It worked fine.

I stayed on the Spar Seven and operated the Pneuma-Grab myself all night. It was around minus 35° C so I needed regular supplies of warm drinks. I had removed about 450 tons from the vessel into the hopper by the morning. The hopper had enough in it to start loading hopper rail cars. I supervised the loading of the four hopper rail cars under the discharge hopper. I averaged about one rail car every three minutes. I figured that this would be fine and, after the engineers arrived to fix up the other compressor we wouldn't be too delayed. I waited for the loaded hopper cars to be moved away down the track and replaced by empty cars. There was no locomotive to move them. I was furious and tried to contact the dispatcher in the rail station. She wouldn't talk to me and avoided me when I went over to her office. I then decided that drastic action was required. I stood on the rail line in front of a locomotive and refused to move until the dispatcher would talk to me. The train couldn't go forward without running me over so the dispatcher said she would see me.

I went to see the dispatcher and she apologised for avoiding me earlier. She said she had no locomotives available to move my alumina cars and, more importantly, there were no more empty cars nearby which I could load. There were 45 on their way but they hadn't arrived. I explained that I needed 472 rail cars not 45. She said there was nothing she could do. I then got calls from London. David was angry at the delay and said that I had designed a flawed system. Victor had told him that the system would never work. Niksa agreed that it was incorrect. I explained that it worked perfectly and that I had discharged 450 tons overnight but needed railcars. The only problem was dirt in the compressors which was easily mended. I explained that they had refused to allow the River K to arrive so I had no intermediate storage. David informed me that he had suspended all payments on the air-supported building so I shouldn't rely on that either. I asked when they would send the railcars.

David said he and Lev had arranged to have 2,000 tons worth of railcars sent to the port. When I had taken 2,000 tons off the Spar Seven she could leave Vanino and travel to Rajjin, at the Bratsk facility, and she would discharge there. There would be no storage in Vanino. The partners had decided to rip apart the top of my hopper and to load the alumina into it with grabs using a shore crane. It was an environmental disaster and grossly inefficient. I couldn't stay to watch.

I discharged the 2,000 tons myself and then flew back to London. I had had enough of betrayal and sabotage. I went to the TransWorld office and packed up my papers and computer disks and went home. I went back the next day to formally end my relationship with TransWorld. David came up to my office and told me that he had set up his own shipping company, Universal Bulk Trade, which would do all the TransWorld shipping instead of using my International Bulk Trade. He announced that he had hired all my staff to work in that company. He then informed me that he owned my company International Bulk Trade. I asked how that had happened as he never paid me for it nor had I signed any transfers of ownership. He said that his business had built it up so, in fairness, if I were leaving he should own it. I suggested that was not the way company law worked. He said he had transferred the ownership of the River K to Universal Bulk Trade and that all the vessels on charter were also transferred. He also had taken over my P&I Club for the new company.

He also informed me that my share of the Vanino operation, which we had agreed was 15% of its value, had been sold to Alcoa. I asked where the money for the sale was and was told, "Don't worry; we'll do something else". This was a fairly typical way that David operated. He promised equity but it never happened. Lisin took Novolipetsk despite David and had to fight for it. David had promised him the equity but couldn't face actually delivering it. This was a regular occurrence. David suggested that it might be a good time to leave and I told him I had every intention of doing so and had already cleaned out my things. I had only come in to quit. I went downstairs and said goodbye to all. I have never spoken a word to David since that day.

I was owed quite a bit of money by TransWorld for the address commissions paid by the owners to International Bulk Trade as charterers. I made up a list of vessels and the address commissions and asked to be paid. I was told that this was not appropriate as David had never agreed to the 1.5% address commission in writing. Unfortunately for him, TransWorld owed International Bulk Trade the freight for a number of ships. They were obliged to pay us. I received around $804,000 in outstanding freight. I contacted Alan Bekhor, the official head of TransWorld and asked him to figure out the amount of address commission we were owed. He did so and sent me the total. I deducted that sum and sent the other money back to TransWorld. In my eyes we were even. David wouldn't accept that and kept grousing to Alan and everyone else. He said he might give me something but that I shouldn't just take it. I ignored this.

Most of my friends in London and Moscow advised me to keep all the money and sue. That would have been wrong. David knew I wouldn't sue him or make a fuss about my treatment. He knew my son was still employed there and knew I wouldn't do anything which might impede his career. I just walked away and got on with my normal business without TransWorld.

I was right about TransWorld's future in Russia. Within three and a half years the Reubens had been ousted from Russia. Their place was taken by Russians, exactly as I had warned. The Reubens got a nice payoff of $500 million, but they were no longer the aluminium kings. I have never met anyone who expressed any sorrow at their passing from the aluminium scene; certainly not the Russians.

For the next couple of years I carried on shipping metals from the Russian ports for Glencore, ASI, Sual and others. We started the North Pacific Lines at Vanino with some group from Vancouver, Canada. However, there was no adventure in it. I was having lunch with some friends at the Russian Main Air force building in Moscow in 1997. They said they had a proposition for me. They knew of my expertise, experience and contacts in Africa. They asked if I would work with them introducing Russian aircraft to the African commercial market and in building a sophisticated repair base in Africa for Russian military aircraft. That sounded more challenging. I agreed and went to Africa to spread the market for Antonovs, Ilyushins and Russian pilots and crews. I became a tourist in six African wars. It was very interesting and a lot safer than the Russian aluminium industry. My Russian aluminium adventure was over.

Later, as I reflected on my experiences in Russia I noticed that my experiences in Russia had essentially the same trajectory as the experiences of the Russian population. Initially I was excited about the possibilities which had opened in the changeover from the Soviet to the Russian system. There was growing, if cautious, optimism as the communists left power. There was great confusion about the new rules and the new system but there was faith that things would work out despite the lawlessness. People began to travel. They no longer were restricted to their home areas. Young people, in particular, felt liberated and optimistic about their new opportunities. The older people were surprised that their financial situation hadn't improved but felt that the future would bring positive change, especially as they began to acquire new goods formerly unavailable to them.

Soon the Gaidar reforms had priced almost everything but the basics out of the reach of the average Russian. They went back to their traditional diet. As my grandfather used to tell me "Shi da kasha, pisha nasha" (cabbage soup and kasha are our food). Although the shops were full of designer clothes and unimaginable luxuries in Moscow and St. Petersburg, the Russians I knew in Siberia and the Far East were not buying them. As the state was no longer responsible or capable of supplying food to the factories scattered across Russia they closed in remote areas. Leaving Tynda and Chita on the BAM towards Vanino would take the traveller past scores of ghost towns whose inhabitants had fled to urban areas. To most of the Russians I met the naked greed, avarice and anomie of the new society was appalling. Almost all of those I met, except for the very young, had had a Soviet education. Their teachers, even if they had private doubts, taught the students that they were part of a worldwide movement which sought the universal improvement of mankind and social justice. Most people could adjust their thinking to fit their political and economic realities to this but they didn't put away their notion of 'decency'. The constant complaint that was registered against the changes which were sweeping Russia after 1992 was that these changes enshrined bad men in power and that the breakdown of law and order was not 'decent'.

I remember having tea at the Intourist Hotel in Khabarovsk with some Russians who had gathered there in the summer along the banks of the Amur River. Most were young and discussing their plans. They wanted to travel to Moscow and to travel abroad. The young sister of one of these students was there. She was around twelve years old. One of the girls asked her what she wanted to do with her life. She said that she thought she was very pretty and hoped to be a prostitute for rich foreigners and make a lot of money. An older woman sitting nearby started to weep. She turned to me and said "Look what they have made of us."

I was as appalled as they. Most of the military and intelligence professionals I met in Russia were more appalled than I. They felt that there were certainly gains in opening up Russia to become a modern state but the lack of social discipline, the triumph of the criminal elements and the loss of real world-class power was probably too high a price to pay. The bank collapse of 1998 was the final blow. The depression and despair that I met whenever I travelled in Siberia and the Far East was too difficult to deal with.

My disappointment at being forced out of everything I had worked hard for in the aluminium business was trivial compared to the fate of my Russian friends. I could leave. I was ready for new horizons. The Russians were ready for Putin.

CHAPTER FOURTEEN

With the forced departure of Yeltsin from the chaos which followed the 1998 bank collapse the powers of the state were passed to a new generation of leaders, under the control of Vladimir Vladimirovich Putin. Putin was a different character than Yeltsin. Putin was briefly in counter-intelligence (Second Department) before moving on to the Fifth Directorate where he monitored Soviet dissent. He transferred to the First Department when he was offered a post in East Germany where he spent five years essentially looking into the opinions and actions of fellow Soviet officers and officials. When the Soviet Union collapsed he was transferred to Leningrad where he spied on student movements and dissidents. Putin joined forces with Anatoly Sobchak, the mayor of Leningrad as Sobchak's international adviser. He became head of the Leningrad committee to promote investments and foreign commerce. This is where we first met Putin. He was the man to whom we had to speak to get export licenses to use the port of Leningrad/St. Petersburg for the export of non-ferrous metals. Within one year of his appointment, a local commission investigated Putin for understating the prices paid for permits for the export of non-ferrous metals and the missing food aid that never reached the city (a total of US$93 million). No case was ever proved against Putin and he remained in his job. [liii] He survived and prospered in his posts even as Sobchak and his assistants suffered terminal heart attacks almost simultaneously.

On 25 July 1998 Yeltsin appointed Vladimir Putin head of the FSB, the successor agency to the KGB and, in August 1999 he was named a Deputy Vice President of Russia. Later that same month he was elected Prime Minister of Russia. On New Year's Eve 1999, Yeltsin resigned his post as President which left Putin as Acting President. Putin's first decree as Acting President was to issue a "Get Out of Jail Free" card to the Yeltsin 'Family'. [liv] This decree said that corruption charges against the outgoing President and his relatives would not be pursued. This was convenient as there were outstanding charges against the Yeltsin Family in Russia and Switzerland for money laundering, etc. The broker for this generous act by Putin is widely believed to be Boris Berezovsky who met with Putin at least five times during this period. Putin alignment with the Yeltsin Family assisted him in his election as President and Putin won the post on the first ballot on 26 March 2000. Vladimir Putin was inaugurated president on 7 May 2000.

Within days of his attaining the Presidency Putin began his campaign to create his "Power Vertical"; that is a concentration of political and economic power from the top down. Putin started by removing his protection from the oligarchs who had developed and thrived under Yeltsin. starting with Berezovsky and continuing to Mikhail Khordokovsky. Putin felt that the system should be directed more towards empowering the 'oligarchs in epaulets'; the former Chekists who wanted their piece of the action.

The changes which have occurred in the Russian political system as a result of the replacement of Boris Yeltsin by Vladimir Putin have yet to be fully assessed. The most important and fundamental change, however, has been the emergence of a new class of powerful, largely unelected, people who have been put in charge of virtually all the levers and agencies of power in the state as well as in charge of the vast private enterprises which emerged from the privatisation schemes of the Yeltsin period.

Despite the notion that Communism died with the fall of the Soviet Union, the state, its agencies and its companies are populated by the Undead; the unreconstructed nomenklatura of the failed communist system. In his book, Capital, Marx wrote that 'capital is dead labour which, vampire-like, lives only by sucking living labour' He coined the term 'Vampire Capitalism"; of corporations whose exploitations 'only slightly quenches the vampire thirst for the living blood of labour', and that 'the vampire will not let go while there remains a single muscle, sinew or drop of blood to be exploited'. What Putin has created is a society of Vampire Communism where the Undead suck the life blood from private corporations and government agencies; leaving drained and powerless structures behind them.

The new and powerful people ('siloviki') have been almost exclusively drawn from the ranks of the 'Chekists'.. Under Putin, these new 'siloviki' have been firmly installed in the corridors of power.

Under Putin, the Chekists, primarily the St. Petersburg flavour of Chekist, openly took power as ministers, government advisors, governors, bankers and politicians. There may be as many as six thousand of these Chekists in powerful positions in the Russian state. There is no mystery about who they might be; Nikolai Patrushev, FSB director; Igor Sechin, Yuriy Zaostrovtsev, FSB deputy director (and a director of Sovkomflot and first deputy chairman of the board of directors of Vneshekonombank); Viktor Ivanov, deputy chief of the Kremlin administration (who succeeded Nikolai Patrushev as the Head of the Internal Security Department of Russia's FSB and a director of the Antey Corporation and Almaz Scientific Industrial Corporation, developing and producing air defence systems and the Chairman of the Board of Directors of Aeroflot); Boris Gryzlov Minister of the Interior (chief of police); Sergei Ivanov, Foreign Minister; former Prosecutor General, Vladimir Ustinov; Sergei Stepashin, chief of the Audit Chamber; Sergei Pugachov, president of Mezhprombank Bank; Nikolai Negodov, deputy transportation minister; Vladimir Yakunin, first deputy president of the Russian Railways Co.; Konstantin Romodanovsky, chief of internal security at the Ministry of the Interior; Viktor Cherkesov, formerly head of the Tax Police (Deputy Director of FSB under Vladimir Putin and Nikolay Patrushev and now the Chairman of the State Committee for the Control of the Circulation of Narcotic and Psychotropic Substances of the Russian Federation); to name but a few. To this list must be added the names of Viktor Alekseyevich Zubkov, the former Prime Minister (having served with Putin in Sobchak's St. Petersburg) succeeding Fradkov who was named the new head of Russia's Foreign Intelligence Service. Perhaps the most important of the new siloviki is Rosboronexport CEO Sergei Chemezov. Chemezov has a long, personal history with Vladimir Putin, dating back to their KGB days in Dresden.

Well, one may well ask, where's the harm in concentrating power in the hands of the siloviki? The unelected 'vlasti' have always lived like parasites on the backs of the Russian people, from the days of serfdom, to the boyars to the political commissars to today's oligarchs. Well, the answer is that today it is Western investors and economies which are suffering along with the Russian people. Western energy security is at risk. This is a different type of stew. While it is interesting to see the continuity of the 'siloviki' in historical context, it is their present activities which cause concern. There is little unity in the 'siloviki' position. There is no one united plan that they follow. These 'siloviki' are in competition with each other and form cliques, alliances and temporary groupings to further their aims. In doing so, they often attack other members of the clan and do serious damage to Russia. There are more factions of siloviki than there are factions of

Trotskyites. The Medvedev succession changed almost nothing. These factions are engaged in an ever-spiralling war with each other.

The siloviki have established a pattern of behaviour which they have followed to expand their economic strength. The best example was the case of Yukos, but it didn't start there. One of the first battles, a kind of test case, was the effort to prise the railways from the grasp of Nikolay Asenenko, the Railways Minister. Asenenko was a long-serving Minister, associated with the Yeltsin Family, who was active in instituting reforms in the aging and poorly maintained Russian railroad system. After a long period of resistance the railway system agreed to be reformed. After long debate, the government agreed to Asenenko's plan to split the railway into two entities, a managerial state-run system and a private operating railway business. As soon as this was agreed the 'siloviki' moved in to prevent Asenenko from carrying on the reforms and putting himself at the head of the railway monopoly. The then Prosecutor General, Vladimir Ustinov (himself once a Yeltsin man) began to find 'tax errors' and underpayments by the Railways. He purported to find almost seventy million roubles in unpaid taxes. Asonenko prepared his resignation and Putin fired him (3 January 2002). The new people who were moved into the railways were 'siloviki', led by Vladimir Yakunin. Aksonenko was ousted by a temporary alliance between his old enemy, Stepashin, and his new enemy Ustinov. Since then, reforms have been blocked in the railways.

These alliances have had a devastating effect on Russian banking as well, especially the alliance between Ustinov and Ivan Sechin against Alfa Bank. It was Sechin's faction of the 'siloviki' which has been credited with creating and exploiting the banking crisis of June-July 2004. In mid-May, the Central Bank revoked the license of SodbiznesBank. This was strange as SodbiznesBank was one of the largest known contributors to President Vladimir Putin's re-election campaign. The Central Bank revoked its license for what it said was money laundering activities. This was followed by the closure of other, larger banks. The method was simple; the 'siloviki' promoted a general lack of confidence in Russian banking through the circulation of 'blacklists' of banks purportedly in danger. Most bankers were certain the crisis was provoked by the Kremlin, by Sechin and Ustinov in particular. Since Sechin's daughter is married to Ustinov's son they could plot this over dinner. The real target was Mikhail Fridman's Alfa Bank.

The question of why they wanted to attack the Alfa Bank reveals even more about the 'siloviki'. The origin of the problem was the efforts by Leonid Reiman, the Minister of Communications, to keep control of the mobile telecommunications in his own hands and that of the 'Petersburg Group'. Reiman, although he had no security background, had a better trump card. When he was working in St. Petersburg in the private sector in a company he formed, Telecominvest, one of his employees and co-workers was Ludmilla Putina, soon to be the first lady. He helped form the third largest mobile phone company, MegaFon in conjunction with a major Swedish player. The biggest state-owned (except for a large stake owned by Alfa Bank) telephone company, Svyazinvest, was scheduled for privatisation and Reiman wanted to prevent Alfa Bank from taking it over, and to take it over himself. Alfa owns Vimpelcom, the second largest mobile phone provider as well. The Bermuda registered investment company, IPOC, was in negotiations with MegaFon, the third largest mobile phone company. It thought it had an option to buy a 25.1% stake in MegaFon from LVF (the owners of the minority stake – Leonid Rozhetskin). Before the option could be brought to fruition, LVF was merged into Alfa-Eko, the Alfa Bank telecommunications arm. Since then, IPOC has been suing Alfa Bank in every forum it could find and undertook arbitration with LVF in Sweden and Switzerland. Until recently, no one knew who the owner of IPOC was; it was assumed to be Reiman himself. However, it was alleged in court that the true owner was a Danish lawyer, Jeffrey Galmond. When faced with the high Danish taxes which went with it, Galmond soon admitted the beneficial owner was Reiman.

This dispute is important in that this conflict was generalised into an attack on Alfa Bank per se. Alfa is one of Russia's leading banks and has a positive reputation for adopting the best western practices and transparency in its operations. Attacking Alfa has damaged the international faith in the Russian banking system. Combined with the well-documented attack on Yukos, the view of Western investors is that Russia has been moving backwards. It is not a safe place to invest because the 'siloviki' have no controls or self-discipline on their activities. This is not democracy, it is "Bonapartism". Marx wrote a popular pamphlet called the "Eighteenth Brumaire of Louis Bonaparte" demonstrating how the class struggle in France created circumstances and relationships that made it possible for a grotesque mediocrity to play a hero's part. Bonapartism has been used to describe a government that forms when a military, police, and state bureaucracy intervenes to establish order. There are parallels to today's siloviki Russia.

The real question is why these 'siloviki' are so determined to move into business and take over control of public companies and take others back into public ownership. The answer is very simple – greed. There are no laws against insider trading in Russia. Putin actively promoted the creation of oligarchs in epaulets. There were phenomenal sums of money being earned in Russia as a consequence of the Yukos case. There is no insider trading law which prevents this. The government knew when it was going to make an announcement about Yukos; an announcement that would send its shares up or down dramatically. It knew when it would announce news about stopping or starting oil flows; an announcement that would send oil prices up or down. There is a principle, known as Occam's Razor to guide us. This is a logical principle attributed to the mediaeval philosopher William of Occam. The principle states that one should not make more assumptions than the minimum needed. There is increasing evidence that foreknowledge of government intentions led to trades in Yukos shares and oil futures, betting on a 'sure thing', by the same groups of people who were making the decisions. They were milking the Yukos cash cow for months. Much of these profits come from foreigners or private investment funds. If Occam is right, there is little need to look further for motivation. When I was a boy my father said to me, "Son, if it looks like a duck; if it quacks like a duck; if it waddles like a duck; it is probably a duck". There was a lot of quacking in the Yukos Case.

In July 2004, Yukos was charged with tax evasion, for an amount of over US$7 billion. The Russian government accused the company of misusing tax havens inside Russia in the 1990s so as to reduce its tax burden; havens were set up by most major oil producers in outlying areas of Russia which had been granted special tax status to assist in their economic development; such "onshore-offshore" were used to evade profit taxes, resulting in Yukos having an effective tax rate of 11%, vs. a statutory rate of 30% at the time. Yukos claims its actions were legal at the time. Yukos subsidiaries also declared the oil they produced to be "oil-containing liquids" to avoid paying full taxes. Moreover, only Yukos was charged with such tax evasion.

In a move to prevent bankruptcy, management made a friendly offer to the government to pay eight billion dollars in a period of three years. A management presentation from December 2004 shows that the government's tax claims put the "total tax burden" for 2000, 2001, 2002, and 2003 at 67%, 105%, 111%, and 83% of the company's declared revenue during those years. As a comparison, the annual tax bill of Gazprom is about $4 billion on 2003 revenues of $28.867 billion.

According to a resolution of the Council of Europe, "Intimidating action by different law-enforcement agencies against Yukos and its business partners and other institutions linked to Mr. Khodorkovsky and his associates and the careful preparation of this action in terms of public relations, taken together, give a picture of a co-ordinated attack by the state." This "raises serious issues pertaining to the principle of nullum crimen, nulla poena sine lege laid down in Article 7 of the ECHR and also to the right to the protection of property laid down in Article 1 of the Additional Protocol to the ECHR."

"The circumstances of the sale by auction of Yuganskneftegaz to "Baikal Finance Group" and the swift takeover of the latter by state-owned Rosneft raises additional issues related to the protection of property[iv]. This concerns both the circumstances of the auction itself, resulting in a price far below the fair market-value, and the way Yukos was forced to sell off its principal asset, by way of trumped-up tax reassessments leading to a total tax burden far exceeding that of Yukos's competitors, and for 2002 even exceeding Yukos' total revenue for that year." In short, the siloviki used its power in the tax office and the Procurator's office to issue grossly inflated tax demands on Yukos and effectively put the company into bankruptcy. Putin's vampires sucked the cash out of Yukos, arrested Khordokovsky, threatened his partner Nevzlin with a trial for attempted murder and stole the company in a fake auction which left the assets with Rosneft (I. Sechin, proprietor). In the meantime, the siloviki were busy milking the Yukos cow through insider trading and depriving any Western investors of their stakes in Yukos shares.

The Yukos model has been followed in other takeovers; especially by Sergei Chemezov. As Mr. Chemezov's influence expanded, the line separating his different roles -- civil servant and entrepreneur -- became increasingly blurred. His alliances with other siloviki (especially the Sechin faction) have given more muscle to the Rosboronexport power inside Kremlin, Inc. Chemezov's proximity to the Kremlin gives the company an overtly political dimension to its decision-making process.

Since the appointment of Chemezov, Rosoboronexport has exhibited very aggressive tactics in regards to competing exporters and in forcing industry acquisitions, with full Kremlin support. This has made his enemies crumble under the pressure. Sergei Tsivilev, the first deputy director general of the privately held Russian Aircraft Corporation MiG, came under the scrutiny of the Procurator General; accused of mass fraud for allegedly attempting to sell counterfeit aircraft parts to Poland (although Polish representatives came forth to his defence and stated clearly that they have no complaint against Tsivilev). Another case of Yukos-like tactics has been Rosoboronexport's ham-handed takeover of the AvtoVAZ, the manufacturer of the Lada. In December of 2005, Mr. Chemezov, whose company had no experience in cars, was accompanied by 300 heavily armed men to forcefully seize control AvtoVAZ, in what some have called a "creeping nationalization." In order to force out the old management and install Kremlin loyalists, the government had to assist Rosboronexport with force.

A similar "creeping nationalization" occurred with the takeover of 66% VSMPO-Avisma, the company responsible for manufacturing almost one-third of the country's titanium (a vital component of air frames and missile systems) To win control of this already troubled company the siloviki muscled the two major shareholders of the company with threats of ruinous tax penalties (2.45 billion roubles) and personal incarceration. They sold their shares to Rosboronexport at greatly reduced prices (and which has never been fully paid).

Rosboronexport announced that it was considering selling a 25%-plus-one-share blocking stake in the carmaker, AvtoVAZ, to either a major European or US carmaker. Sergei Chemezov, Rosboronexport's general director, explained that AvtoVAZ was currently holding strategic partnership talks with car-making majors Fiat (Italy) and Renault (France) and hoped to offer a blocking stake in the company by end-year. He added that the company was holding talks with Severstal, Russia's largest steel maker, and Metalloninvest, a leading mining and metallurgy group, concerning the sale of up to a 10% stake in AvtoVAZ, explaining that the carmaker needed to secure high-quality steel supplies for car production and that joint share-owning would lock their interest together.

Following the Yukos model, Putin's vampires have sucked the blood out of many of what they call the 'strategic industries' of Russia, returning these industries to effective state control, but with profits going to the private sector of siloviki; the very model of Vampire Communism.

The effect of this Vampire Communism is best known in the energy sphere where countries like the Ukraine are pushed and shoved by the siloviki. Lithuania has lost its supply of oil to its main refinery. The port of Tallinn, having just constructed a major new coal terminal, has just found the Russian export coal shifted to Riga instead. The battles to bring in Sakhalin II on time have foundered on spurious environmental claims. As Putin's term ended these fanciful exercises increased as factional fighting amongst the siloviki grew

Despite their power, the siloviki have had to form alliances of a sort in order to cement their power. They have allied with the huge class of government bureaucrats in the form of the so-called party of power, Unified Russia. In order to maintain their domination of the bureaucracy, the siloviki use the tried-and-true method of selective repression and intimidation. In just a few months, governors, mayors, and other high-ranking regional officials in no fewer than 49 regions have found themselves under arrest or investigation. Such probes occasionally reach federal officials as well.

Finally, the siloviki paradoxically benefit from criminal activity. By some estimates, up to 30 percent of the economy is controlled by organized crime, and Russian crime bosses spend much of their illegal capital on bribes to law-enforcement officials for legal, tactical, and administrative support. Even Putin confessed, in 2006, "Our law-enforcement organs are completely corrupt." With the aid of these alliances and by manipulating the other forces within modern Russia, Putin's siloviki have managed to gain control of the country and even achieve a measure of popular support. They have been assisted in this by the enormous wealth coming in because of high global energy prices, wealth that has enabled them to implement populist measures and raise living standards.

Over the last decade, the siloviki waged a "quiet cultural counterrevolution" with tremendous effect. They worked to systematically devalue and compromise liberal values, standards, and institutions -- values that had massive public support in the early 1990s. This was coupled with repression, and murder, of journalists and commentators hostile to their views. They have indoctrinated the new youth of Russia, who remember little of the Soviet Union, that the siloviki control access to jobs, careers and good fortune in business, government and the civil service.

It was no less of an observer than Mr. Ulyanov (a.k.a. Lenin) who said "The Capitalists will sell us the rope with which we will hang them." Well, the market for imported ropes has been drying up but the market for imported cash has never been higher in Russia. The reconstruction of the Russian economy into a perverse form of state capitalism, led by oligarchs in epaulets, is not a market structure that would have been familiar to Lenin or his successors. The current structure is a kleptocracy without ideology which manages to combine most of the failings of the former Soviet system with rhetoric of a free market. This has been made possible by the triumph of optimism over experience among Western investors who don't seem to recognise that their cash is the new rope for their own necks.

The Russian economy, until the collapse in energy prices, was booming, Raw material prices for metals, gas, petroleum and ores were very high. The value of Russian production was soaring. Russian billionaires dominated the world's press. However, even then, Russia remained desperate for foreign investment and was cash-poor for domestic investment. The collapse in energy prices made this a sustaining crisis.

Those Russian private companies which still exist are taking their investment portfolios out of Russia as quickly as they can. They are listing themselves on the London and New York stock markets to attract foreign partners; not for the cash but for widening of the shareholder base outside of Russia to make re-nationalisation more difficult when the siloviki decide that it their industry which must be retaken for 'the national security'. Any Russian company of note has succeeded or is in the process of widening its shareholder book to include non-Russians. This has also meant that the cash has stayed outside of Russia as well, as a new 'internationalism' has energised Russian companies. They are now moving into the US, Canadian, Latin American and African markets in search of suppliers, alliances with competitors and safer markets.

These developments have had several major effects in Russia. The first is that these companies have become part of the state system. In Russia, this has always meant that there has never been a direct linkage between company activity, productivity and performance with the resources needed for its survival or expansion. The money pot is held by the state, as owners of the shares, and is made available to the companies at the whim or fortune of the group of competing siloviki who control it in the name of the state. Under the Soviet system, Gosplan, was supposed to regulate the management of this process. There has been nothing to supplant it. Theoretically these state-owned companies are the responsibility of a board of directors and management appointed by the state, but their retained capital and cash-flows are controlled outside of the company structure.

This has proved useful when the state wishes to purchase more shares in companies. The state uses mirrors and smoke and fake transfers to acquire companies like Yukos; pretending that these funds have been made available to Rosneft or Gazprom. There are enormous amounts of funds transferring around the Russian economy for share purchases; but no cash. The state can acquire companies this way, but they cannot make them work. Work requires investment in capital equipment; cash for repairs and maintenance; money for research and development, etc. The re-nationalised companies are all competing for the small cash reserves of the state and are dependent on which group of competing siloviki has the ear of the keepers of the purse string.

One needs go no further than the Komi Republic to see massive oil spills from broken pipes; radioactive Inuit glowing in the Arctic night from nuclear leakages, and a rapid depopulation of the region due to the government's inability to manage or invest in repairs. When the state takes over more and more of the oil and gas industry, where will the cash come for the purchase of pipes; the costs of drilling; the maintenance of the rights of way? Ownership doesn't mean that there will be an end product. If that were true all the poor people with oil, copper and metals concessions in Africa would be immensely wealthy. They are still poor but they have valuable concessions. Modern business requires cash; a massive amount of cash and the Russian government is not making this available. The Stohkman fields are a good example.

Modern business also requires trained and experienced managers. As the Russian state takes over more and more of its industry, good Russian managers are leaving for jobs outside Russia.

The oil industry in Africa is full of good, trained, Russian managers and technicians who do not wish to live under a low-ceilinged Russian management structure. The role of state in these management decisions is often destructive.

For example, a new board of directors at Russian automaker AvtoVAZ was elected and representatives of the state gained a much larger role in the management of the company. The state-owned Vneshtorgbank, with just a 7-percent holding in the company, placed four of its representatives on the board. The key positions on the board went to Rosoboronexport, the state company that oversees Russia's arms exports. The deputy general director of Rosoboronexport, Vladimir Artyakov, was chosen as board chairman and, altogether, state representatives occupy six seats, while representatives of plant management saw their share of seats reduced to three. Management had previously held eight seats. This was done despite the fact that Rosboronexport had not invested one kopeck in the company. Boris Alyoshin, the head of the Federal Industry Agency (Rosprom), said that Rosoboronexport had not actually purchased the stock in AvtoVAZ from its private owners but were acting on behalf of the state to provide "effective management".

This is a bit bizarre as the former chairman of the board of directors, Vladimir Kadannikov, had run the former Soviet car-making giant since 1988 and had been considered one of the most effective managers of the perestroika period. In the mid-1990s, he had even served a term as first deputy prime minister in the Russian government. Kadannikov left the company.

The situation at AvtoVAZ is typical of the Putin reorganisation. In recent years at least three major companies passed into state hands. State-owned oil major Rosneft bought the Yuganskneftegaz production unit, previously the crown jewel at the embattled YUKOS oil major; natural gas monopoly Gazprom purchased Sibneft from Russian billionaire Roman Abramovich; and state-controlled electricity and heating monopoly Unified Energy Systems purchased the machine building consortium Silovye Mashiny from Vladimir Potanin, the owner of the Interros industrial holding group. In each, the state put in its own managers.

The siloviki, unfortunately, are inept, greedy and technically incompetent. Russia is losing a large number of trained managers and technicians who used to work for companies like Yukos. They are not likely to come back as their new wages and working conditions are unmatched in Russian, state-owned, industries.

The Duma issued a draft bill to encourage foreign investors to join, as minority partners, with state-owned Russian companies. The Chairman of the Economic Policy, Enterprise and Tourism Committee, Valery Draganov said the bill would, of course, set the limits on investments in the strategic markets; but he welcomed an appropriate presence of foreign investors in space exploration, aviation, defence and energy machine building.

The only way that this wobbly structure can continue is if foreign investors pour cash into minority interests in these state companies. The Russian state doesn't produce cash; it produces a 'constrained market'. The reason why the Russian auto industry thrives is that the Russian government imposes high duties on foreign cars and restricts foreign manufacturers from opening plants in Russia. It seeks to 'protect' its high diameter steel pipe production by issuing 'safeguard' demands against foreign pipe; despite the fact that Russia cannot produce the quality and quantity of pipe required.

The question is why, and for how long, foreign capitalists will be willing to sell Russia the rope? Surely there are better investments elsewhere; even in Bolivia. Russia's skewed economic development manages to combine much of what is wrong in its history with the sad deficiencies of its present. If history is a guide, Russia is driven by small, greedy men, controlling giant assets and will remain so unless the foreign cash tap runs dry. All in all, it is probably wiser to buy Russian private shares on the Western exchanges than to roll the dice by investing inside Russia.

In the few short years of Putin's rule the chaotic expansion and reconstruction of the Yeltsin years has been altered. The old Chekists who built the oligarchs under Yeltsin have been replaced by the new and younger Chekists, primarily from St. Petersburg. These factions have made a good start in reconstructing the control system of the Soviet Union and restoring the blind patriotism which substituted for good food, housing, health care and free expression which Russians expected in the removal of communism.

They didn't reckon with the Undead and the rise of Vampire Communism and the dedication of what Marx called "that Wallachian boyar", Vlad Dracula, in spreading his cloak over the remaining light in the society.

A Russia without high energy prices is a Russia in decline. The mineral wealth is still being exported as is the gas. However, the development on the technology to extract oil and natural gas from the continuous formations of shale oil in the U.S. may have a dramatic effect on the Russian economy. Within a short period of time the US will be self-sufficient in oil and natural gas. Rather than build the planned LNG receiving trains for the import of gas, the U.S. will begin building liquefaction plants and trains for the export of natural gas to the rest of the world. U.S. energy costs will shrink and remain stable. The use of generating clean energy using gas will greatly improve the emission of carbon dioxide. It will also improve the efficiencies of renewable energy sources as a back-up to solar and wind-power stations which stop or slow down when the wind drops and the sun sets. These developments will have a major effect on world trade and development.

The greatest impact is likely to be on Russia. Russia has moved itself into a dominant position, via Gazprom, in supplying gas to Europe. It has been able to exploit its abundance of supply to bully the Ukraine, Belorussia and others. It has compelled many to accede to its demands for the location of key pipelines. However, it needs a massive capital investment to complete its largest project, the Stohkman fields and to modernise its existing structure. Russia will find it very hard to attract such a capital inflow as its virtual monopoly will be broken. It s business plan envisioned exports of gas to the US. That is very unlikely to happen now. Indeed the US may become its competitor. The energy equations are changing and the political equations will change as well.

The short period of eighteen years has witnessed many changes in the Soviet Union and its emergence into Russia. The most important element in my experience is that the fear has largely disappeared. The centralised control of the state, the endless bribes needed to be paid to make the state and regional bureaucracies function, the power of the criminal gangs over commerce haven't disappeared. The unions are still not powerful or representative, despite prodigious efforts in that direction. The military remains weak and underfunded. The civil strife in the Caucasus continues. To some degree Russia remains the same, but with a more pleasant and positive attitude. There is a new generation which has no memory of the Gulag, the arbitrary arrests and the pain of internal exile.

Above all, the Russians have never lost the art of bluffing. They still pretend to a much greater status in world decisions than their economy and military can possibly justify. They still speak of their role as a nuclear power, as if the ability to destroy is a lever for entry to the world's attention. I remember a conversation with a group of generals as we flew together to Gorky. They were speaking about the West's belief in the principle of 'escalation'. They informed me that this was never the Russian position. They told me that they were sure that if they sent their tanks into Western Europe their soldiers would, when crossing the border, tear off their uniforms and go looking for a job, a beach and a drink. The nuclear option was the only option.

It was an enormous pleasure learning about Russia and experiencing the changes in person. My continuing relations with the Russian military and the use of their planes in Africa was also a learning experience. I hope one day to tell that story.

NOTES

[i] For a good account of the history of the Soviet camps, Anne Applebaum, Gulag, Allen Lane 2003 is one of the best in English. Also see Martin J. Bollinger , Stalin's Slave Ships: Kolyma, the Gulag Fleet, and the Role of the West.: Praeger 2003. .

ii http://www.russiansabroad.com/russian_history_389.html

iiiThere are several good accounts of the American Occupation of Siberia. Among them are:

R.M. Connaughton, The Republic of the Ushakovka: Admiral Kolchak and the Allied Intervention in Siberia, 1918-1920, Routledge; William S. Graves, America's Siberian Adventure, Peter Smith, 1941); and . Betty Miller Unterberger, America's Siberian Expedition, 1918-1920,: Duke University Press

iv Robert Conquest, "Gulag History", The Jamestown Foundation 2001.

v See Applebaum, Anne, Gulag: A History, Broadway Books, 2003,

Bardach, Janusz / Gleeson, Kathleen Man Is Wolf to Man : Surviving the Gulag, University of California , 1998,

Bollinger, Martin J., Stalin's slave ships : Kolyma, the Gulag fleet, and the role of the West, Praeger, 2003,

Getman, Nikolai: The Gulag Collection: Paintings of the Soviet Penal System, Jamestown Foundation, 2001

vi Solzhenitsyn, The Gulag Archipelago, vol. 2, p. 49.

vii Gary K. Busch, "The Political Role of International Trades Unions", Macmillan 1983

viii GB2219784A - 1989-12-20

ix Paragraph 1.1 et sequitur

x A good description is Alena V. Ledeneva , Russia's Economy of Favours: blat, networking, and informal exchange, Cambridge University Press 1998.

xi Christopher Andrew and Oleg Gordievsky, KGB The Inside Story, Hodder & Stoughton, 1990; and Vladimir Kuzichkin, Inside the KGB, Andre Deustch 1990

xii Vladimir Kuzichkin, Inside the KGB, Andre Deutsch, London 1990 p113-114.

xiii Russia and the USSR in wars XX century. Moscow: OLMA-Press, 2001

xiv See Patricia Rawlinson, A Brief History in Phil Williams (ed.) , Russian Organized Crime, Routledge 1988

xv "Crime, Inc. Comes to Moscow", Time 24/06/2001

xvi William A. Clarke, Crime and Punishment in Soviet Officialdom, M.E. Sharpe 1994 xvii Mark Thomas, Mafianomics, How Did Mob Entrepreneurs Infiltrate and Dominate the Russian Economy?.: Journal of Economic Issues. Volume: 32. Issue: 2. Publication Year: 1998.

xviii+ Federico Varese, The Russian Mafia: Private Protection in a New Market Economy., Oxford 2001

xix Alexander Khochinsky, Kompromat.Ru 19/3/00

xx Gary Busch, Air-Supported Structures, Part 1, Bulk Solids Handling, vol. 17 1997 and Part 2.Bulk Storage in Air-supported Strctures, Bulk Solids Handling, vol. 18 1998

xxi Goskomstat Rossii, Rossiiskii Statisticheskii Ezhegodnik (Russian Statistical Report), Moscow: Goskomstat, 2000,

xxii GNP of USSR: Directorate of Intelligence, Central Intelligence Agency, Handbook of Economic Statistics, 1991,

xxiii ibid

xxiv Giuilitta Chiesa, quoted in Roy Medvedev, Post-Soviet Russia: A Journey through the Yeltsin Era. Columbia University Press, NY 2000 p. 60.

xxv Note by the Procurator-General of the USSR N Trubin on Events in Novocherkassk, June 1962 and Alexander Shubin, Make Way for the Working Class, The Russian Workers' Uprising in Novocherkassk, 1962 1992)

xxvi Sue Davis , Trade Unions in Russia and Ukraine, 1985-95. Palgrave, NY 2001l

xxvii Op cit

xxviiiWalter Connor, The Accidental Proletariat; and "The Soviet Working Class: Change and its Political Impact," in Michael Paul Sacks and Jerry G. Pankhurst (eds), Understanding Soviet Society, Allen and Unwin, 1988.

xxix David Bacon, Where Workers Have to Fight for a Paycheck 16/2/98

xxx "The Role of CEMA in the Soviet Economic Offensive", CIA Office of Research and Reports 1/10/1960, declassified

xxxi Marshall Goldman, Oilopoly, Oneworld Books 2008 is a very valuable source of detailed analysis of the developments in the Russian oil and gas business...

xxxii David R. Stone, "Rosvooruzhenie and Russia's Return to the World Arms Market," in Perspectives on Political and Economic Transitions after Communism (New York, 1997),

xxxiii In 2003 I was commissioned by a client to write up a due diligence on Khordorkovsky for a law firm. I never knew the end client but I was told that it was probably for a major Western oil company...

xxxiv Marshall Goldman, op cit.

xxxv U.S. Senate, Russian Organised Crime in the United States, US GPO 1996.

xxxvi Among these are: Federico Varese. The Russian Mafia: Private Protection in a New Market Economy., Oxford University Press 2001; Phil

Williams, Russian Organised Crime: The New Threat, Routledge 1988;Steven Handleman, Comrade Criminal, Yale 1997; U.S. Senate, op cit..

xxxvii Vladimir Ivanidze, Russian Secret Services and the Mafia., Eurasian Politician Issue 4-August 2001

xxxviii Graeme Gill, Roger D. Markwick Russia's Stillborn Democracy? From Gorbachev to Yeltsin. Oxford 2000

xxxix Ibid.

xl Mikhail Zadornov, 'Sostoianie ekonomiki i blizhaishie perspektivy', Savobodnaia mysl', 6 (1992)

xli David M. Kotz with Fred Weir, Revolution from Above: The Demise of the Soviet System, Routledge London and New York 1997,

xlii Gall, Carlotta; Thomas de Waal, Chechnya: Calamity in the Caucasus. New York University Press 1998

xliii One of the best and most comprehensive sources on this, for the northern area, is the Bellona Foundation http://www.bellona.org.

xliv See Anna Politkovskaya, A Small Corner of Hell: Dispatches from Chechnya, Univ. Of Chicago Press 2003

xlv Märta-Lisa Magnusson, "The Battle(s) of Grozny". Baltic Defence Review (2) 1999

xlvi See, in particular, Marshall Goldman, The Piratization of Russia: Russian Reform Goes Awry, Routledge 2003 p. 99 et seq.

xlvii Op cit p.110

xlviii Moscow Times 21/5/01

xlix Bloomberg, 21/11/06

l Jeremy Peterson, Jamestown Eurasia Daily Monitor 13/3/09

li Marshall Goldman, Oilopoly, p. 109

lii The 'Avisma', "Bank of New York", "Mabatex" and the "Rusal" cases all explain in great detail the role of organised crime in the Russian metals business

liii Washington Post Foreign Service, January 30, 2000; Kovalev, Vladimir (2004-07-23) "Uproar At Honor For Putin". The Saint Petersburg Times. Hoffman, David (2000-01-30). "Putin's Career Rooted in Russia's KGB". The Washington Post ; J. Michael Waller (2000-03-17). "Russia Reform Monitor No. 755: U.S. Seen Helping Putin's Presidential Campaign; Documents, Ex-Investigators, Link Putin to Saint Petersburg Corruption". American Foreign Policy Council, Washington, D.C..

liv УКАЗ от 31 декабря 1999 г. № 1763 О ГАРАНТИЯХ ПРЕЗИДЕНТУ РОССИЙСКОЙ ФЕДЕРАЦИИ, ПРЕКРАТИВШЕМУ ИСПОЛНЕНИЕ СВОИХ ПОЛНОМОЧИЙ, И ЧЛЕНАМ ЕГО СЕМЬИ. Rossiyskaya Gazeta

lv ECHR, Additional Protocol, Article 1

WEBSITES

There are several excellent websites which detail thescope of the problems in the Russian aluminium industry and organised crime:

www.stopcrime.ru	Amdrey Kalitin
http://johnhelmer.net	John Helmer
www.kompromat.ru	Various
www.exile.ru	Various

PARTIAL BIBLIOGRAPHY

Andrew, Christopher and Gordievsky, Oleg (1990). KGB The Inside Story. London: Hodder & Stoughton.

Andrew, Christopher and Gordievsky, Oleg (1990). KGB The Inside Story. London: Hodder & Stoughton.

Applebaum, Anne (2003). Gulag. NY: Allen Lane.

Bardach, Janusz and / Gleeson, Kathleen (1998). Man Is Wolf to Man : Surviving the Gulag. Berkely, CA: University of California.

Bollinger,Martin J. (2003). Stalin's Slave Ships: Kolyma, the Gulag Fleet, and the Role of the West. Westport, CT.: Praeger.

Busch, Gary (1983). The Political Role of International Trades Unions. London: Macmillan.

Clarke, William A. (1994). Crime and Punishment in Soviet Officialdom. New York: M.E. Sharpe.

Connaughton, R.BM (1990). The Republic of the Ushakovka: Admiral Kolchak and the Allied Intervention in Siberia 1918-1920. NY: Routledge.

Davis, Sue (2001). Trade Unions in Russia and Ukraine, 1985-95. New York: Palgrave.

Desai, Padma (2006). Conversations on Russia: Reform from Yeltsin to Putin. New York: Oxford University Press.

Ebon, Martin (1984). KGB: Death and Rebirth. Westport, CT: Praeger.

Gall, Carlotta and de Waal, Thomas (1996). <u>Chechnya: Calamity in the Caucasus.</u> New York: New York University Press.

Glenny, Mischa (2008). <u>McMafia: Crime Without Frontiers.</u> London: Bodley Head.

Goldman, Marshall (2003). <u>Piratization of Russia: Russian Reform Goes Awry.</u> New York: Routkedge.

Goldman, Marshall (2008). <u>Oilopoly: Putin, Power and the Rise of the New Russia.</u> Oxford, England: Oneworld.

Graves, William S. (1941). <u>America's Siberian Adventure.</u> New York: Peter Smith.

Handleman, Steven (1997). <u>Comrade Criminal.</u> New Haven, CT: Yale University Press.

Hill, Peter B. (2003). <u>The Japanese Mafia: Yakuza, Law, and the State.</u> Oxford: Oxford University Press.

Johnson, Juliet (2000). <u>A Fistful of Rubles: The Rise and Fall of the Russian Banking System..</u> Ithaca,NY: Cornell University Press.

Katz, David and Weir, Frank (1997). <u>Revolution from Above: The Demise of the Soviet System.</u> London: Routledge.

Knight, Amy (1996). <u>Spies without Cloaks: The KGB's Successors.</u> Princeton, NJ: Princeron Univerity Presa.

Kuzichkin, Vladimir (1990). <u>Inside the KGB.</u> London, UK: Andre Deutsch.

Ledeneva, Alena V (1998). <u>Russia's Economy of Favours: blat, networking, and informal exchange.</u> Cambridge, UK: Cambruidge University Press.

Markwick, Roger D. (2000). <u>Russia's Stillborn Democracy? From Gorbachev to Yeltsin.</u> Oxford: Oxford University Press.

Marwick, Roger D. (2000). <u>Russia's Stillborn Democracy? From Gorbachev to Yeltsin.</u> Oxforrd, UK: Oxford, University Press.

Medvedev, Roy (2000). <u>Post-Soviet Russia: A Journey through the Yeltsin Era.</u> New York: Columbia University Press.

Peck, Anne E, (2004). <u>Economic Development in Kazakhstan: The Role of Large Enterprises and Foreign Investment.</u> London: Routledge.

Politkovskaya, Anna (2003). <u>A Small Corner of Hell: Dispatches from Chechnya.</u> Chicago, IL: University of Chicago Press.

Rutkand, Peter (2001). <u>Business and State in Contemporary Russia.</u> Boulder, CO: Westview Press.

Sacks, Michael Paul and Pankhurst, Jerry G. (eds), (1988). <u>Understanding Soviet Society.</u> London: Allen and Unwin.

Solzhenitsyn, Aleksandr Isaevich (1973). <u>Gulag Archipelago 1918-1956 vol. 1-3.</u> NY: Perennial and Samizdat.

Steen, Anton (2003). <u>Political Elites and the New Russia: The Power Basis of Yeltsin's and Putin's Regimes.</u> New York: Routkedge.

U.S. Senate (1996). <u>Russian Organized Crime in the United States.</u> Washington, D.C.: US GPO.

Unterberger, Betty Miller (1969). <u>America's Siberian Expedition, 1918-1920.</u> Raleigh, NC: Duke University Press.

Varese, Frederico (2001). <u>The Russian Mafia: Private Protection in a New Market Economy.</u> Ocford: Ocford University Press.

Williams. Phil (ed.) (1988). <u>Russian Organised Crime: The New Threat.</u> New York: Routledge.

Lightning Source UK Ltd.
Milton Keynes UK
23 July 2010

157344UK00001B/62/P